Political Media Relations Online as an Elite Phenomenon

Jan Niklas Kocks

Political Media Relations Online as an Elite Phenomenon

Springer VS

Jan Niklas Kocks
Berlin, Germany

Dissertation Freie Universität Berlin, Germany, 2015

This Thesis was created in the context of the DFG-Research Unit 1381 'Political Communication in the Online-World', Subproject 6 'Media Relations Online', which is funded by the German Research Foundation (DFG).

ISBN 978-3-658-13550-8 ISBN 978-3-658-13551-5 (eBook)
DOI 10.1007/978-3-658-13551-5

Library of Congress Control Number: 2016935978

Springer VS

Printed on acid-free paper

This Springer VS imprint is published by Springer Nature
The registered company is Springer Fachmedien Wiesbaden GmbH

Acknowledgements and Dedication

The present thesis is the result of over three years of research in the field of political media relations in the online sphere. At this point, I would like to thank those that have contributed or otherwise supported me in this process.

First and foremost, I would like to thank my supervisor Prof. Dr. Juliana Raupp for her supervision and support, for constructive critique and the provision of the necessary freedom to develop my thoughts and ideas. I would also like to thank my second assessor Prof. Dr. Aeron Davis for his helpful feedback.

The DFG-funded research group 'Political Communication in the Online World' provided me with the opportunity to conduct the research underlying this thesis. I would like to thank all its members for the interesting and helpful discussions and their constructive feedback. In particular, I would like to thank Prof. Dr. Gerhard Vowe, Prof. Dr. Patrick Donges, PD Dr. Marco Dohle, Dr. Uli Bernhard and Paula Nitschke for their reviews, comments and critique.

My colleagues at the Institute for Media and Communication Studies have been helpful and supportive throughout the process. Here I would especially like to thank Kim Murphy, Charlotte Schnöger and Tina Stalf.

Finally I would like to thank my family and especially my wife Angelica Lanzilotti for all their support during these years.

Jan Niklas Kocks
Berlin, December 2015

*Dedicated to my grandfather Werner Kocks (*1923).*

Abstract (English)

Political media relations have long been considered a type of political communication taking place between a few professional communicators. Journalists from leading media outlets provide political coverage and professional spokespersons employed by leading political organisations provide them with the necessary information. So far, the arrangement has been exclusive and mutually beneficial for both sides. However, it has been argued that digitisation could have the potential to alter such structures and interactions. Technological change would thereby foster new and potentially less exclusive arrangements in the field of political media relations.

Against a background focusing on both the debate on digitisation and its implications and on theoretical reflections grounded in sociological elite theory, this thesis enquires into the effects of now almost ubiquitous online media on political media relations and especially on patterns of interaction in this field.

It first analyses the ways in which leading political journalists and spokespersons perceive digitisation in terms of technological, organisational and political change. This step focuses on the perspective of the communicators directly involved and potentially affected by digitisation. To what extent do they consider digitisation an important process and what effects do they see? Do they perceive changes in the structure of communication networks and which role do they attribute to new and formerly marginal actors? The first analysis explores focal political communication professionals' perceptions of digitisation, seeking to answer these questions.

The second analysis then focuses on actual adaptations of digitisation on an individual and an organisational level. This step enquires into the actual nature of political media relations in the online age as a potential elite phenomenon. To what extent have leading political organisations adapted to new technological opportunities? Are communicative exchanges between political spokespersons and journalists digitised and if so to what extent? How has digitisation affected communication networks, especially regarding their in- or exclusiveness?

The thesis employs a combination of content analyses, semi-structured interviews with 16 political spokespersons and 29 political journalists and social network analysis. Findings indicate that digitisation is generally considered to be an important process affecting political organisations and media outlets as well as individual communication professionals. Journalists in particular perceive strong effects of technological change, yet remain ambiguous in predicting future developments. Political spokespersons on the other hand are often less critical about potential implications, considering digitisation to be a process benefiting new and formerly marginal actors.

Analyses of adaptations show that political media relations are in some regards highly digitised. Political organisations show a high degree of activity online, targeting both professional journalists and the general public. However, at the same time their communications are predominantly unidirectional, often replicating established patterns of communication. Actual communicative exchanges on an individual level are hardly digitised and individual communicators opt mostly for established means. This is also replicated on a level of network ties. Communication networks in the field of political media relations largely appear structurally conservative; they are mostly dominated by established political actors and large offline media outlets.

In accordance with theoretical considerations and some preceding studies, empirical analyses draw a picture of political media relations in the online age as an elite phenomenon. Communication networks are still characterised to a large extent here by exclusive arrangements.

Abstract (German)

Politische Media Relations sind lange als eine Form von politischer Kommunikation betrachtet worden, die vornehmlich zwischen einigen wenigen professionellen Kommunikatoren vonstattengeht. Journalisten führender Medien leisten politische Berichterstattung und die professionellen Sprecher leitender politischer Organisationen stellen ihnen die dazu notwendigen Informationen bereit. Bis dato ist das Arrangement exklusiver Natur und für beide Seiten gleichsam vorteilhaft.

Es ist jedoch argumentiert worden, dass der Prozess der Digitalisierung das Potential haben könnte, solche Strukturen und Interaktionen zu verändern. Technologischer Wandel würde dabei neue und potentiell weniger exklusive Arrangements im Bereich der politischen Media Relations befördern.

Die vorliegende Arbeit untersucht die Effekte der beinahe omnipräsenten Online-Medien im Bereich der politischen Media Relations, insbesondere im Hinblick auf die Interaktionsstrukturen in diesem Feld. Sie tut dies vor dem Hintergrund der sozialwissenschaftlichen Debatte um die mögliche Implikationen der Digitalisierung und darüber hinausgehenden elitentheoretischen Reflektionen.

Sie analysiert dabei zunächst die Perzeptionen führender politischer Journalisten und Sprecher im Hinblick auf technologischen, organisationalen und politischen Wandel. Dieser Schritt fokussiert auf die Perspektive der direkt involvierten und potentiell betroffenen Kommunikatoren. Inwieweit sehen sie Digitalisierung als einen bedeutsamen Prozess an und welche Effekte nehmen sie wahr? Sehen sie Veränderungen in den Strukturen kommunikativer Netzwerke und welche Rolle schreiben sie in diesem Zusammenhang neuen und zuvor marginalen Akteuren zu?

In einem zweiten Schritt analysiert sie Adaptionen der Digitalisierung auf individueller und organisationaler Ebene. Dieser Schritt untersucht die Natur politischer Media Relations im Online-Zeitalter als ein potentielles Elitenphänomen. Inwieweit haben politische Organisationen neue technologische Möglichkeiten adaptiert? Sind kommunikative Austauschprozesse zwischen politische Sprechern und Journalisten digitalisiert und wenn ja, dann in welchem Umfang? Wie hat die Digitalisierung kommunikative Netzwerke beeinflusst, insbesondere im Hinblick auf deren In- oder Exklusivität?

Die vorliegende Arbeit basiert auf einer methodologischen Kombination aus Inhaltsanalysen, teilstandardisierten Interviews mit 16 politischen Sprechern und 29 politischen Journalisten und Sozialer Netzwerkanalyse. Die Befunde indizieren, dass Digitalisierung generell als ein bedeutsamer Prozess betrachtet wird, der politische Organisationen und Medien ebenso betrifft wie individuelle politische Kommunikatoren. Insbesondere Journalisten nehmen starke Effekte technologischen Wandels wahr. Sie bleiben dabei jedoch ambivalent in ihren Einschätzungen zukünftiger Entwicklungen. Politische Sprecher sind häufig weniger kritisch was die potentiellen Implikationen der Digitalisierung angeht, sie betrachten den Prozess häufig als förderlich für neue und zuvor marginale Akteure. Analysen von Adaptionen zeigen, dass politische Media Relations in einigen Bereichen hochgradig digitalisiert sind. Politische Organisationen zeigen ein hohes Maß an Online-Aktivität; ihre Kommunikationen zielen dabei sowohl auf professionelle Journalisten wie auch auf die allgemeine Bevölkerung. Zugleich sind diese jedoch zumeist unidirektionaler Natur und replizieren etablierte Kommunikationsmuster. Kommunikative Austausche auf Individualebene sind hier kaum digitalisiert; individuelle Kommunikatoren setzen zumeist auf etablierte Kommunikationskanäle. Dieser Befund repliziert sich auch auf der Ebene der Netzwerk-Kanten. Kommunikative Netzwerke im Bereich der politischen Media Relations erscheinen zumeist strukturkonservativ; sie werden vornehmlich von etablierten politischen Organisationen und großen Offline-Medien dominiert.

In Übereinstimmung mit theoretischen Überlegungen und einigen vorangehenden Studien zeichnen die empirischen Analysen ein Bild politischer Media Relations im Online-Zeitalter als Elitenphänomen. Kommunikative Netzwerke sind dabei noch immer vornehmlich durch exklusive Arrangements geprägt.

Table of Contents

List of Tables

List of Figures

**Visualisations for Fig. 1 and 3 were made by C. Schnöger*

List of Abbreviations

AA	Auswärtiges Amt [Governmental Body; *Foreign Office*]
ARD	Arbeitsgemeinschaft der öffentlich-rechtlichen Rundfunkanstalten der Bundesrepublik Deutschland [Association of Public Service Broadcasters]
BMELV	Bundesministerium für Ernährung, Landwirtschaft und Verbraucherschutz [Governmental Body; *Federal Ministry for Food, Agriculture and Customer Protection*]
BMF	Bundesministerium der Finanzen [Governmental Body; *Federal Ministry of Finance*]
BMFSFJ	Bundesministerium für Familie, Senioren, Frauen und Jugend [Governmental Body; *Federal Ministry of Family Affairs, Senior Citizens, Women and Youth*]
BMG	Bundesministerium der Gesundheit [Governmental Body; *Federal Ministry of Health*]
BMU	Bundesministerium für Umwelt, Naturschutz und Reaktorsicherheit [Governmental Body; *Federal Ministry for the Environment, Nature Conservation and Nuclear Safety*]
BVerfGE	Entscheidungen des Bundesverfassungsgerichtes [Official collection of verdicts by the German Constitutional Court]
BMWi	Bundesministerium für Wirtschaft und Technologie [Governmental Body; *Federal Ministry of Economics and Technology*]
BMZ	Bundesministerium für Wirtschaftliche Zusammenarbeit und Entwicklung [Governmental Body; *Federal Ministry of Economic Cooperation and Development*]
CATI	Computer Assisted Telephone Interview
CDU	Christlich Demokratische Union [Party]
CSU	Christlich Soziale Union [Party]
DLF	Deutschlandfunk [Public Service Broadcaster]
DPA	Deutsche Presse-Agentur [News Agency]
FAZ	Frankfurter Allgemeine Zeitung [Newspaper]
FDP	Freie Demokratische Partei [Party]
FR	Frankfurter Rundschau [Newspaper]
GII	Global Information Infrastructure
GG	Grundgesetz [German constitution; *basic law*]
ICT	Information and Communication Technology [also utilised in plural: ICTs]
KSTA	Kölner Stadtanzeiger [Newspaper]
M	Arithmetic Mean
NRZ	Neue Ruhr Zeitung / Neue Rhein Zeitung [Newspaper; regional branch of WAZ]
NGO	Non-Governmental Organisation
NW	Network
RTL	RTL Television [TV Channel, belonging to Rundfunk Television Luxemburg]
SD	Standard Deviation
SNA	Social Network Analysis
SPD	Sozialdemokratische Partei Deutschlands [Party]

SZ	Süddeutsche Zeitung [Newspaper]
TAZ	Die Tageszeitung [Newspaper]
VoIP	Voice over IP
WAZ	Westdeutsche Allgemeine Zeitung [Newspaper]
ZDF	Zweites Deutsches Fernsehen [Public Service Broadcaster]

1 Introduction

Political media relations, understood here to be the interaction between politics and political journalism, have long been considered a type of political communication taking place between relatively few professional communicators. Journalists working for leading media outlets provide coverage both on current developments and on long term policies, and professional spokespersons, inter alia working for governmental bodies and major political parties, provide them with the necessary information for that coverage.

The involved spokespersons want to generate (favourable) coverage for their organisations and to keep them present in the public debate, in order to ameliorate their position in the democratic competition. So far, the best way to do so has arguably been by engaging in communicative exchange with journalists working for leading media outlets. Professional journalists on the other hand seek to provide quality (political) coverage, thereby ameliorating their medium's competitive position in the media market. Here it can be argued that the best way to do so has been to engage in communicative exchange with political spokespersons working for leading political actors such as governmental bodies or major political parties. The arrangement is an exclusive one and it generally benefits all parties involved.

It has been argued however that processes of technologically induced media change could alter the conditions here. Digitisation, the proliferation of new communicative possibilities, could change structural conditions and patterns of interaction within the field of political communication, thereby fostering new arrangements.

With the online media now almost ubiquitous, the question is in how far political media relations in Germany have been affected by these processes of digitisation. Which role do new communicative possibilities play for the communicators and organisations involved? Through which channels do they engage in communicative exchange and in how far are their communication networks affected by this? Are political media relations still to be understood as predominantly exclusive arrangements – an elite phenomenon for that matter – or have new and formerly marginal actors found access to this field of political communication?

The present thesis seeks to enquire into political media relations in the digital age in Germany and to thereby find answers to these questions. It asks about the perceptions leading political communication professionals have of digitisation in their field and about the ways in which these professionals and their specific organisations actually adapt to digitisation.

Considering leading political communication professionals positional elites in the field of political media relations, the value of communication, communicative adaptations and related communicative strategies is initially reflected and discussed based on a foundation of sociological elite theory.

The thesis then first seeks to enquire into the perceptions political communication professionals have of digitisation. Political spokespersons and communication managers working for federal governmental bodies and leading political parties and political journalists working for major media outlets are questioned regarding the ways in which they perceive changes occurring in political communication due to the process of digitisation. To what extent do they see patterns of interaction affected by the proliferation of new means? Do they see strategic changes within their own sphere or in neighbouring fields? What about new actors entering their communication networks? Are politics as such affected by digitisation and if so to what degree?

Subsequently it seeks to analyse actual adaptations of digitisation by the actors in question and – in the case of political spokespersons and communication managers – also by their specific organisations. How are governmental bodies and leading political parties represented in the online sphere? Which tools do they employ and to what extent do they adopt new communicative possibilities? Through which channels do journalists and spokespeople interact with each other and how are their communication networks constructed under online conditions? Do new and formerly marginal actors play any substantial role in these?

On an organisational level, the present thesis focuses on federal governmental bodies and leading political parties (i.e. those that were represented in parliament in the 2009-2013 legislative period) and on major media outlets. The individual communication professionals either account for the communication of the political actors in question or provide political coverage as high ranking political journalists. As indicated, they can be considered a positional elite. Their perceptions and adaptations of digitisation are the main focus of interest here.

The following subchapters will give some additional information on the concept of the present thesis, provide a brief initial rationale for the perspective taken and also supplement some terminological clarifications as well as provide a description of the underlying research model. The second chapter then focuses on media source relations in political communication, enquires into the ongoing debate on the possible effects and implications of digitisation and briefly discusses the state of research on political media relations in the digital age. It thereby provides background and contextualisation for the following research. The third chapter elaborates on the elites defining political media relations and seeks to draw implications from elite theory. Subsequently, the fourth chapter presents two empirical studies, the first one focusing on perceptions of digitisation. Here individual perspectives on digitisation are measured and analysed. Then actual adaptations of digitisation are taken into account. Adoptions of new communicative possibilities are analysed here, both with regard to organisational presences and individual communicative exchanges. A conclusive fifth chapter then summarises, compares and critically discusses the findings from all preceding analyses.

Conducted in the context of the DFG-funded research project 'Media Relations Online' (2011-2014), the present thesis seeks to enquire into the changes political media relations face under the conditions of digitisation, focusing on those actors that have so far shaped the field. It seeks to clarify the validity of the notion that political media relations online are an elite phenomenon with regard to the situation in contemporary German political communication.

1.1 Concept

Why should political media relations and the potential changes induced by digitisation be approached from a perspective focusing on elites? Where does the rationale for a framework that considers political media relations online as an elite phenomenon lie? The following aims to answer these questions and thereby simultaneously provides a rationale for the perspective employed.

From a strictly normative perspective on political communication, there are two extreme models of communication: one refers to (authoritarian) societies dominated by elites and the other is generally connected to contemporary (egalitarian and pluralistic) democracies. These models are in contraposition and describe opposing poles in the world of political communication (Mills, 1963, p. 355; F. R. Pfetsch, 2012, pp. 458-460).

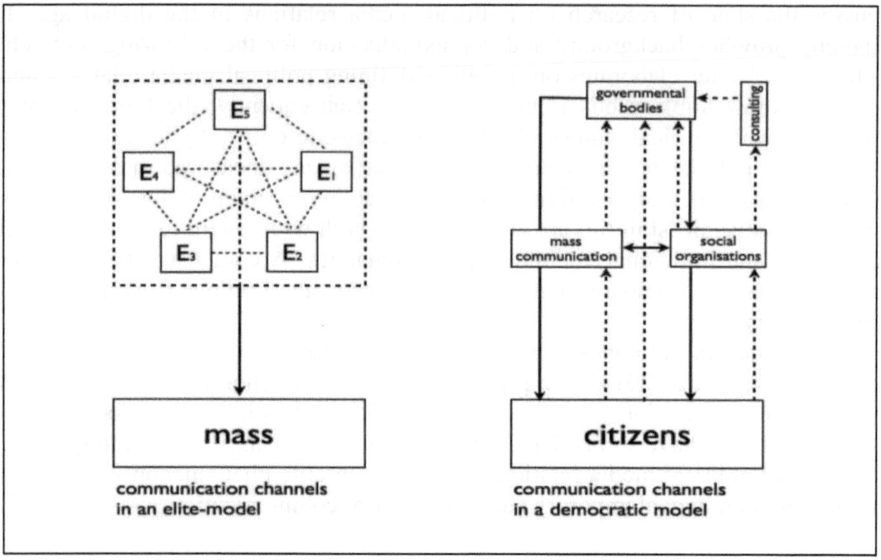

Fig. 1: Political communication in an elite model and in a democratic one; own translation of a model by F. R. Pfetsch (2012, p. 458).

On one side, there are elite groupings communicating with each other. Here one finds constant dialogue and mutual exchange of arguments; issues of political and societal salience are subject to constant and open debate. These groupings basically constitute a sphere of their own, a sphere in which political communication takes place and from which power is exercised. Non-elite actors are excluded from this sphere; visible or invisible boundaries keep them away from political debate and deliberation, from the exercising of power. Whenever communication from the elite-sphere is addressed at them, it is strictly unidirectional and characterised by manipulative and mobilising intentions, aiming at exercising control over them rather than fostering any kind of mutual exchange or participation.

In contraposition to this, there is a pluralistic democratic model. Here public discussion is regarded as a key element. Political institutions, actors that are central to the political field as such, foster communicative exchange with the electorate, with members of the various groupings in society. The formation of political opinion is exercised in constant dialogue; there is mutual exchange between institutions, civil society and interest groups on a regular basis. Boundaries between the sphere of institutionalised politics and its civil counterpart are practically non-existent; people are entitled to have their say in the way in which the entities they inhabit are governed and in the policies that are implemented and exercised.

On the one hand, there is a negative extreme; a model that is extremely far away from every contemporary understanding of how power is to be exercised and communicated. On the other hand, there is a model in which the normative ideals of modern democracy are fulfilled, in which participation and transparency are fostered, in which the people (here to be understood as the democratic sovereign) can have their say and are to be heard.

Of course, these models and their contraposition are more of a normatively coined theoretical conceptualisation than an actual empirically observable reality. The model focusing on elites and inter-elite communication describes the realities in authoritarian states and there is good reason to underline the fact that people were and are deprived of basic democratic and communicative rights in these systems. And yet given both historical facts as well as theoretical implications (inter alia from elite theory), one could doubt the unanimous existence of total communicative segregation in these systems.[1] Far from being entitled to openly have their say, strata of the population are heard by the ruling classes at least on some occasions; some kind of communicative exchange is fostered not least to uphold the current (undemocratic) distribution of power, to keep the authoritarian elites in position. The strictly unidirectional form of communication in which the mass is only subject to manipulation is arguably more of a gloomy scenario than a description of communicative realities.

The opposed model of political communication in democratic systems postulates the absence of (communicative) boundaries between the sphere of the ruling institutions and the electorate. It states that mutual exchange between the various actors in this field is actually existent and executed on a regular basis and therefore negates the notion of a segregated elite in the field of political communication. This scenario comes close to the normative ideals of modern and pluralistic democracy which is to be inclusive and discursive, in which participation and transparency are goods that are to be actively fostered. Again, it is important to underline that it is more of a normatively coined theoretical conceptualisation than an actual empirical observation of the reality of political communication in contemporary democracies.

Early on theorists such as Michels (1949) have described inherent tendencies towards oligarchy, towards a segregation of elites in democratic bodies such as political parties. Critical approaches towards elite theory (e.g. Hartmann, 2004a;

1 In this context see inter alia the reflections on conceptualisations of inclusive political communication in the authoritarian socialist GDR by Kocks and Raupp (2014c).

Krysmanski, 2004; Mills, 1956) have pointed out that one could actually find segregated circles of (political) elites in modern democracies such as the United States or Germany, circles that refrain from mutual exchange with the broader population, thereby excluding larger strata of the electorate from processes of deliberation, collective decision-making and opinion formation. Democracies have, according to this argument, the tendency to yield ruling classes: institutions, organisations and individuals that do exercise the largest share of political power despite constituting a minority. According to this argument, relevant political communication does take place predominantly between members of these ruling groups. They (and their circles of communication) become alienated from the general electorate. With regard to the situation in Germany and its old capital Bonn, such developments have often metaphorically been described with the notion of 'Raumschiff Bonn' ('Spaceship Bonn'), to express the growing distance between the (political) elite 'up there' and the people 'on the ground' (Strobel, 1991).

Even though negativism and the popularity of anti-political resentments in general might have contributed to such considerations, it is clear that there has been a common perception of a gap between those governing and those governed; a feeling of exclusion from processes of political discussion and participation among strata of the general population. Bourdieu (1997, p. 182) once metaphorically described politics and the communications surrounding them as a game of chess conducted between experienced players in front of a purely passive audience and indeed, political communication and political media relations in particular were long understood to be communicative exchanges between small groups of leading communication professionals from politics and the media.

The proliferation of new (digital) means of communication – often subsumed under the notion of digitisation – was then initially regarded as a process that could potentially alter these communicative patterns. Theoretically, the boundaries between (previously) central communicators and the rather more peripheral ranks could be bridged and the inclusion of fringe actors into (political) communication networks – which according to an argument brought forward by Luhmann (1995, pp. 237-264) was indeed one of the decisive resources in contemporary society – could be achieved. Political communication in general and political media relations in particular would cease to be elite phenomena.

Especially early accounts on digitisation – and those brought forward by communication professionals rather than by scholars – were often arguing in such directions (e.g. Morris, 2001; Trippi, 2004). From this perspective digitisation was considered to be a phenomenon that could erode established patterns of power in the fields of politics and political communication (Coleman & Blumler,

2009). Other accounts were more sceptical, stating that patterns of power would – despite all technological changes – remain largely unaltered and that they might replicate in the online sphere (e.g. Margolis & Resnick, 2000; Resnick, 1998). Some went even further, discussing emergent societal distortions and developments such as an actual widening of gaps between elites and non-elites under the conditions of digitisation (e.g. Lanier, 2006; Noam, 2005).

So far the debate on the process of digitisation and its potential implications for politics and political communication has been a polarised one, some even consider it overly polarised (Wright, 2012). There is a trend away from highly enthusiastic accounts towards more empirically balanced and often also more sceptical ones (cf. Chadwick, 2009; Papacharissi, 2009; Raupp, 2011). Yet the questions remain: To what extent does digitisation alter patterns in the field of political communication? How far are political communication in general and political media relations in particular considered to be elite phenomena under online conditions?

These questions are relevant for a variety of reasons. From a normative point of view, the inclusion into networks of political communication is to be regarded an important resource (Luhmann, 1995, pp. 237-264), especially for those actors from the sphere of civil society that do not have any formalised influence within the political system (A. Davis, 2002, p. 17; Emmer & Bräuer, 2010, pp. 322-323). Vice versa, democratic legitimacy is often connected to the inclusiveness of the political system (Young, 2004, p. 53), arguably also to the inclusiveness of the political communication system. If and how political communication and political media relations change under the conditions of digitisation is a question of normative political relevance especially when the in- and exclusion of new and formerly marginal actors in or from elite communication networks is concerned.

However, apart from the normative desirability of non-elite inclusion, there is a further argument for a focus on elite actors and the communications surrounding them. From a positional understanding of elites, these actors are to be regarded as located at the decisive positions within society – here within the field of political communication. How they perceive changing processes and how they actually adapt to these is important in so far as they are arguably the ones shaping the fields they inhabit (Lasswell, Lerner, & Rothwell, 1952). Analysing elite actors and surrounding communications is to be understood as a way of analysing power in the fields of politics and political communication (A. Davis, 2003, pp. 669-670; see also: Savage & Williams, 2008).

Questions surrounding elite actors in the field of political communication and the ways in which these adapt to changing processes such as digitisation are – especially from a normative understanding – of political and societal relevance.

They are furthermore to be regarded as an adequate starting point for empirical analyses of political communication, a fact that has been underlined by a variety of recently published studies focusing on elite actors from this field and on their interactions (e.g. Krüger, 2013; Maurer, 2011; B. Pfetsch & Mayerhöffer, 2011; Schwab Cammarano, Donges, & Jarren, 2010).

Phenomena of digitisation can of course be approached from other theoretical perspectives: they can inter alia be discussed under the notion of mediatisation (Krotz, 2009) or from a neo-institutionalist perspective (cf. Nitschke, Donges, & Schade, 2014). Yet given the political, societal and scientific relevance of an elite perspective, it seems to be justified to employ this type of focus here. Sociological elite theory allows elite interests and the actual communication strategies employed by these actors to be identified (Wasner, 2004, pp. 23-25), it therefore qualifies here as a theoretical heuristic. The second empirical focus regarding actual adaptations then draws on organisational online presences (i.e. one-to-many forms of communication which could however integrate reciprocal elements), communicative exchanges between individual actors and actual communication networks, i.e. all central aspects of political media relations. Elite theory as a theoretical approach concentrating on elite interests and actual communication strategies particularly enables reflections on all of these from a perspective focusing on those that arguably shape the field of political communication.

Despite normative conceptualisations of inclusiveness and reciprocity (cf. F. R. Pfetsch, 2012, p. 459), political communication in general and political media relations in particular often have to be considered elite phenomena so far. However, digitisation has been framed as a process of potentially tremendous consequences for the field of political communication, as a development that could alter patterns of communication and power structures. The present thesis seeks to analyse the ways in which elite actors from the field of political communication perceive the effects of digitisation for their field and the actual adaptations of the process they and their organisations show, not least in terms of inclusiveness and communicative reciprocity. It thereby seeks to assess whether or not political media relations in the online age in Germany could (still) be considered an elite phenomenon.

1.2 Terminology

Terms and notions can be understood as tools of thought. They function as a pair of spectacles determining the way in which we perceive the surrounding world; they are both premises and results of research (Henn, Dohle, & Vowe, 2013, p. 368). Therefore, before the research model underlying the enquiry can be elaborated based on specific research questions, it is first necessary to briefly define some key terms for the present analyses of perceptions and actual adaptations of digitisation by elite actors from the field of political media relations.

In particular, this regards the notion of *digitisation*, employed here to describe the process of the proliferation of ICT. It furthermore also regards *perceptions* and *adaptations*, i.e. the phenomena the following empirical studies try to approach. Subsequently, the understanding of *elites* as employed here is briefly discussed, not to describe the sampling but again to reflect on terminological issues and to arrive at a concise working definition.

Digitisation

The proliferation of ICT is subsumed here under the notion of digitisation. Lexically, this term is defined as "1. The conversion of data from analogue to digital form. 2. The computerization of information. 3. The diffusion of such technologies and techniques" (Chandler & Munday, 2011).

The notion is employed here to grasp the proliferation of digital means in the field of political communication. Such developments have so far been subsumed under the notions of 'digitalisation' (e.g. Heller, 2008; Ludes, 2008), 'digitisation' (e.g. Dellarocas, 2003; Hand, 2009; Watson & Hill, 2006) or in some cases even 'mediatisation' (e.g. Krotz, 2009). The latter notion is however not to be utilised here since it is widely accepted that it grasps wider processes of an encroachment of mass media into various societal areas (Schulz, 2004, p. 98) or, with regard to the political field, the alignment of politics to the regularities of mass media (Donges, 2006, pp. 194-195).[2]

The notions of 'digitisation' and 'digitalisation' are generally utilised synonymously, inter alia by all of the authors previously cited here. There has been an attempt to separate them, either utilising one with regard to technological changes or one with regard to the societal developments induced by them (Dasgupta, 2000), however this did not have any wider impact. Since 'digitalisation' is in fact widely utilised in non-communicative regards (e.g. Haustein, Assmann, & Fiehring, 1980; Kochiadakis et al., 2005; Weiner, Bassan, Jarchovsky, Iusim, & Plavnick, 1983) and sometimes even lexically defined in a medicinal sense (cf. "Collins English Dictionary," 2009), preference is given here to the notion of 'digitisation'.

2 In this context see also Bourdieu's (2010, pp. 291-303) reflections on the encroachment of a (market-driven) journalistic logic into other societal fields, among these also the political one. The processes described go far beyond technological media change and describe the (enforced) adoption of another field's logic by neighbouring ones.

It aims to grasp the proliferation of digital means, the technologically induced change affecting various societal areas, among these the field of political communication and of political media relations in particular. In accordance with the diffusion-related third part of the lexical definition given above (cf. Chandler & Munday, 2011), digitisation is therefore understood here to be the entirety of processes regarding the proliferation of ICTs in various societal areas, in particular as the encroachment of digital technologies into the sphere of political communication.

Perceptions

Perceptions are the first subject of empirical analysis here. A perception is lexically defined as either "the ability to see, hear, or become aware of something through the senses" or as "the way in which something is regarded, understood, or interpreted" ("The Oxford Dictionary of English," 2010). The connected verbum 'to perceive' is defined as "to become aware or conscious of (something); come to realize or understand" or as "to interpret or regard (someone or something) in a particular way" ("The Oxford American Dictionary of Current English," 2002; "The Oxford Dictionary of English," 2010).

Other encyclopaedic definitions distinguish between sensations and perceptions, between the mere grasping of visual stimuli and patterns of cognitive processing and interpretation (e.g. "The New Encyclopaedia Britannica," 2003a; Vol. 9). In this understanding, perceptions are associated with the employment of cognitive processes, with the utilisation of schemes of interpretation in view of entities, phenomena and processes.

Philosophical reflections on the nature of perceptions support this understanding. According to these, sensing entities first stimulates nerves and the subsequent work of the mind then composes the perception (Descartes, 1994, p. 24; II-28; Locke, 1970; II-9, §§3,11,15). Other philosophical accounts introduce further differentiations (Leibniz, Remnant, & Bennett, 1996; I, II) or – from an immaterialist perspective – even postulate that the very existence of entities is only constituted in perceptions of them – *'esse est percipi'* (Berkeley, 1971).

Within psychology the very nature of perceptions is the subject of long-running debate (cf. Mausfeld, 2005). However there is at least a broader consensus regarding a basic textbook understanding of the term. According to this, a perception should be regarded as a process in which the surroundings cause sensations that stimulate the sensing individual, which are then subject to sensory processing, to perceptual organisation and finally to identification and interpretation (Zimbardo, Gerrig, & Graf, 2004, pp. 156-161).

In sum, the process of perceiving is to be understood as one that it about sensing and the work of the mind that follows. It is about processing impressions gained in a sense of organisation and interpretation. Perceptions shall therefore be understood here as the results of processes of the organisation, identification and interpretation of sensually grasped stimuli.

Adaptations

Adaptations are the second subject of analysis here. In a lexical understanding, the term refers to "the action or process of adapting or being adapted", or, in a biological sense to "the process of change by which an organism or species becomes better suited to its environment"; the connected verbum 'to adapt' is defined as to "make (something) suitable for a new use or purpose" or as to "become adjusted to new conditions" ("The Oxford Dictionary of English," 2010). Some encyclopaedic definitions approach the term with regard to a biological understanding ("The New Encyclopaedia Britannica," 2003b; Vol. 1), yet there are others that refer to a variety of contexts such as literature, physiology, psychology, sociology and linguistics ("Brockhaus Enzyklopädie," 2001; Vol. 1). The psychological and sociological contexts refer to the adjustment of attentiveness, thinking, feeling, will and behaviour in response to external conditions.

From a psychological perspective, adaptations can be understood as processes of assimilation and accommodation, of the integration of (new) cognitive elements into existing patterns and of the modification of the latter to allow the improved processing of new information (Zimbardo et al., 2004, pp. 452-453).[3] A (neo-evolutionist) sociological perspective then argues in evolutionary terms, comparing social adaptations to biological processes:

> "Adaptation, the securing and conserving of control over environment, is the orienting process of the specific evolution of both life and culture. And in both the biological and the superorganic realm, the adaptive process has two characteristic aspects: creative and conservative. On the one hand there is the evolution of specialized structures and patterns that enable a culture or a population of organisms to achieve a requisite measure of adjustment to its environmental setting. On the other hand there is a tendency towards stabilization, the conservation of the adaptive structures and modes that have been achieved" (Sahlins, Harding, Kaplan, & Service, 1960, p. 45).

In this understanding, social adaptations connect evolutionary aspects of adaptations (i.e. the achievement of adjustment to an environmental setting) with the tendency of cultures or populations to strive towards a conservation of the structures in which they exist. Structural diversification, achieved through continuous

3 Zimbardo, Gerrig and Graf here make direct reference to the models of epistemology and developmental psychology introduced by Piaget (1926).

adaptations, leads to progress and the development of culture (Sahlins et al., 1960, p. 50).[4]

In sum, adaptations can be understood as processes in which an organism (in a broad sense) becomes suited to its environment. It adjusts its structures and its behaviour to environmental factors and developments, regardless of their nature. Adaptations are a necessity, naturally in biology to avoid evolutionary extinction as well as in sociology to conserve control over one's environment and to allow a continuous existence under changing conditions. Accordingly, adaptations shall be understood here to be the processes by which actors strive to become suited to their environment in order to conserve or even ameliorate their position.

Elites

The group of actors that is of interest for the analyses here consists of political communication professionals that have so far been labelled elite actors. Lexically the term elite is referred to as "a select group that is superior in terms of ability or qualities to the rest of a group or society" or as "a group or class of people seen as having the most power and influence in a society, especially on account of their wealth or privilege" ("The Oxford Dictionary of English," 2010). Elites are defined with regard to some form of superiority; it is underlined that they tend to have power and influence.

The foundation for an elite status can derive from various sources, among these reputation, power in decision making processes and last but not least positioning (Machatzke, 1997, p. 35). Here, the definition of relevant actors from the field of political communication is grounded in a positional understanding of elites, one that defines elite status in terms of the specific position an actor occupies within a given system (Paris, 2003, p. 60).[5] The system of interest is the political communication system, the sphere to which political media relations (i.e. the subject of the analyses here) belong.

Actors of interest occupy work for political organisations and media outlets that – as organisations – occupy focal positions within the communication networks between politics and the media (Raupp, 2010, pp. 211, 217). Here 'focal' is to be understood in a sense of centrality; it describes something "relating to the centre or most important part" ("The Oxford Dictionary of English," 2010). The organisations in question are therefore to be regarded as central inhabitants of the

4 A further example for such processes is inter alia given by Elias (1978), who describes the development of manners in society as the result of adaptive processes.

5 An in depth explanation on the notion of positional elites and its development is – with regard to a different societal context – also given by Mosse (1987, pp. 3-10).

fields of politics and the media. Their belonging to these organisational bodies, mostly also in leading positions, is what constitutes the (positional) elite status of the individual actors here (cf. B. Pfetsch & Mayerhöffer, 2011).

In sum, the elites in question here are to be regarded as individual actors with an authoritative standing in focal organisational inhabitants of the field of political communication in Germany. Their influence and standing in the field are superior to those of non-elite actors.[6]

Summary

The foregoing terminological reflections have provided working definitions for four terms that are of central importance here: digitisation, perceptions, adaptations and elites.[7] The following briefly summarises some key elements:

The beginning of the present subchapter saw the discussion of the underlying phenomenon of **digitisation**. In this context it was defined as *the entirety of processes regarding the proliferation of ICTs in various societal areas, in particular as the encroachment of digital technologies into the sphere of political communication.* Subsequently, two aspects of the analysis, namely perceptions and adaptations, were discussed. **Perceptions** were defined as *results of processes of the organisation, identification and interpretation of sensually grasped stimuli.* **Adaptations** should be regarded as *the processes by which actors strive to become suited to their environment in order to conserve or even ameliorate their position.* The actors in questions were described as elite actors. In this context, **elites** were defined as *individual actors with an authoritative standing in focal organisational inhabitants of the field of political communication in Germany.*

1.3 Research Model and Outline

The present thesis investigates the perceptions leading political communication professionals have of digitisation in their field and about the ways in which these professionals and their specific organisations actually adapt to the process.

---

6 Further reflections on the elite status of these actors and on its foundation are made in the subsequent explanation of the actual sampling employed here; a rationale for the selection of individual actors is given then.

7 These definitions are valid for the subsequent reflections and analyses – however, as working definitions, they do not strive for universal validity out of their context of course.

Digitisation, understood here to be the encroachment of digital technologies into the sphere of political communication, has the potential to affect political communication and politics in various ways:

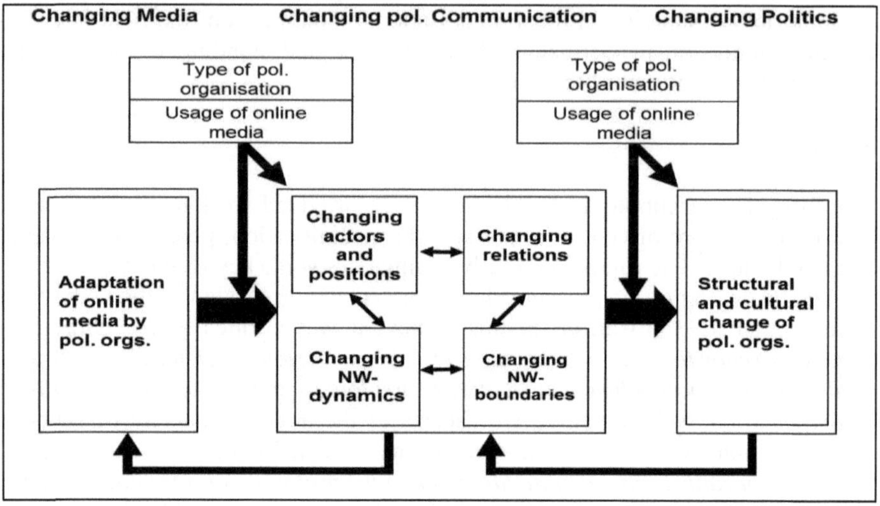

Fig. 2: **Processes of change induced by digitisation;** own translation of the 'Media Relations Online'-research model.

A changing media environment and new communicative possibilities arguably require some form of adaptation by political organisations; here questions revolve around the integration of new means into the communicative portfolios of the actors in question. Subsequently the relations between actors and their actual communication networks could also be affected by digitisation, this might inter alia regard the positions actors occupy within these networks and the actual network boundaries. Last but not least politics might then be affected by these processes of change. A changing media environment, new communicative possibilities and altered patterns of interaction might induce political change, for example in the form of a structural and cultural change of political organisations.[8]

8 The type of political organisation affected and the actual usage of online media can potentially act as intervening variables, influencing the degree of changes in the field of political communication and politics resulting from digitisation (cf. Chadwick, 2007; Nitschke et al., 2014).

Research model

Here, the interest is in the ways in which political communication professionals – elite actors from the field of political communication – perceive these processes of change. How do they perceive changing media environments, changing patterns of interaction in the field of political media relations and also changing politics? Secondly, their (and their organisations') actual adaptations are the subject of interest. How do political organisations integrate new means into their communication portfolio? Through which channels do actors interact? Are network structures and patterns of interaction changing under the conditions of digitisation?

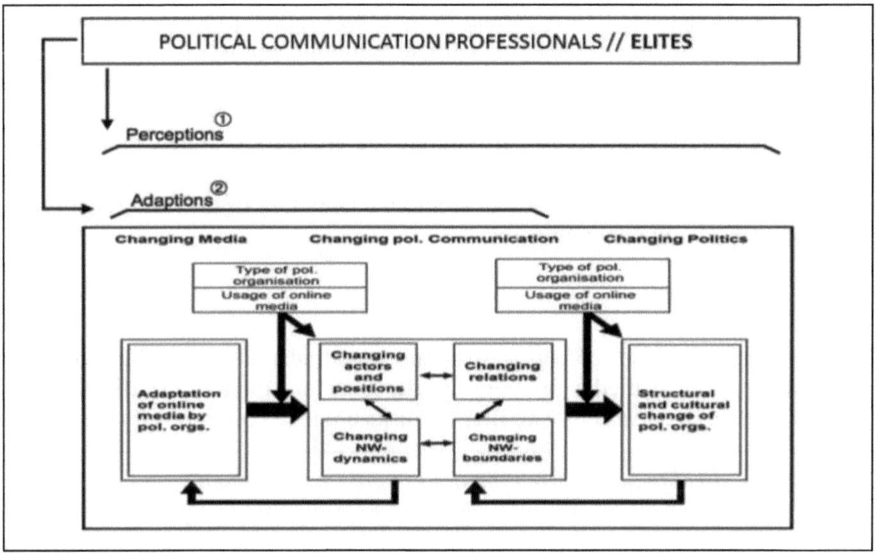

Fig. 3: Research model: Perceptions and adaptations of digitisation; based on an own translation of the 'Media Relations Online'-research model.

The analysis of perceptions (1) focuses on all three areas of potential change: changing media, changing political communication and changing politics. It specifically asks about the ways in which the individual actors in question perceive processes of digitisation and their implications for the fields of politics and political communication. Is the proliferation of ICTs considered important or rather regarded as a phenomenon of only marginal impact? According to those that shape political communication in Germany, which effects might digitisation, have and in how far might it lead to inclusion in or exclusion from communicative patterns and networks in this field?

The subsequent analysis of actual adaptations (2) then focuses on the areas labelled here as changing media and changing political communication.[9] It asks about the ways in which elite actors from the communication network between politics and the media and their specific organisations adopt new means of communication and about how they construct their communication networks under the conditions of digitisation. There are two main questions of interest: To what extent are new means of communication and technological innovations incorporated into the communicative portfolio of the actors in question? In how far do communication networks surrounding these actors reflect processes of potential structural change within the field of political communication?

Both analyses seek to capture the process of digitisation and its implications for the field of political media relations in Germany. As indicated, they do so with special regard to questions surrounding the integration of new and formerly marginal actors into this field and its communication networks. This is to substantiate reflections on the adequacy of an understanding of political media relations online as an elite phenomenon.

Research questions

The subsequent analyses of perceptions and actual adaptations of digitisation in the field of political media relations in Germany are guided specifically by a variety of research questions. The first one asks about perceptions of digitisation:

> *RQ1: How do elite actors from the field of political communication in Germany perceive the process of digitisation and its implications and consequences?*

Since perceptions might regard various areas (e.g. technological and organisational political change, changing patterns of interaction and network integration), the first research question is subdivided into a set of sub questions:

9 Political change is – according to the research model presented which is derived from 'Media Relations Online'– understood here to be partially induced by media change and a change of political communication. As indicated, perceptions of this change are analysed, although actual adaptations (neither on an organisational nor on a systemic level for example) are not the subject of analysis here.

RQ1a: How do elite actors from the field of political communication in Germany perceive technological change under the conditions of digitisation?
RQ1b: How do elite actors from the field of political communication in Germany perceive organisational change under the conditions of digitisation?
RQ1c: How do elite actors from the field of political communication in Germany perceive changing patterns of interaction in their field under the conditions of digitisation?
RQ1d: Which changes do elite actors from the field of political communication in Germany perceive regarding the set of actors present and the patterns of influence prevalent in the field of political media relations?

The second field of analysis regards actual adaptations of digitisation by political communication professionals and their specific organisations. Again the empirical analysis utilises a superordinate research question and a set of sub questions:

RQ2: How do elite actors from the field of political communication in Germany and their specific organisations actually adapt to the process of digitisation?

Here too, adaptations have to be regarded as a multi-level phenomenon; one might find examples on the level of organisational online presences, within communicative exchanges between individual actors and of course also in the actual construction of communication networks within the field of political media relations in Germany.

In particular, the following aspects are of special interest for the analysis of actual adaptations here:

RQ2a: How do organisational political actors construct their online presences? Which communication options do they maintain and in how far do they integrate reciprocal elements?
RQ2b: Through which channels do individual actors from the field of political communication (i.e. political spokespersons and journalists) engage in communicative exchange in the online age?
RQ2c: How are communication networks between politics and the media constructed under the conditions of digitisation?
RQ2d: Which role do new or formerly marginal actors play in political media relations under online conditions?

Outline

The present chapter has provided a rationale on the employed perspective, some terminological clarifications and a brief discussion of the underlying research model. The following second chapter will now take media source relations in political communication into account and then seek to provide an overview of the debate surrounding digitisation and its implication for politics and political communication. It also looks on comparable studies investigating the field of political media relations under online conditions. Both chapters aim to provide initial contextualisation for the research conducted in the subsequent analyses of perceptions and actual adaptations of digitisation.

The third chapter elaborates on the elites arguably defining political media relations and seeks to draw implications from different approaches to sociological elite theory. Subsequently, the fourth chapter presents two empirical studies, the first one focusing on perceptions of digitisation. Data from 45 personal semi-structured interviews is subjected to analysis here. First information regarding the set of interviewees and their professional backgrounds and understanding is analysed for classification and contextualisation. Thereafter perceptions of technologically induced changes in the fields of media, political communication and politics are evaluated. Then actual adaptations of digitisation are taken into account. Adoptions of new communicative possibilities are analysed here, both with regard to organisational presences and individual communicative exchanges. These are measured with regard to the online presences of political organisations, actual communicative exchanges between spokespersons and journalists and also in terms of network construction and network integration. Findings are weighed against assumptions derived from the theoretical framework employed.
The conclusive fifth chapter addresses the findings from all the preceding analyses. Here, the understanding of political media relations online as an elite phenomenon is subjected to critical discussion based on the preceding reflections and analyses. The thesis then concludes by looking at potential directions for further research in the field of political media relations online.

2 Background

The development of political media relations as a specialised sub-field of political communication is often connected to the rise of modern mass media. Since then, the interaction between the parties involved has generally been described as a fairly exclusive arrangement. At times, it might be seen as a complicated relationship of 'uneasy exchange and reliance' (A. Davis, 2009, p. 205; see also: Jones, 1995), one in which patterns of power are often shifting between the parties involved (cf. Bennett, Lawrence, & Livingston, 2007; Reich, 2009; Strömbäck & Nord, 2006; Van Aelst & Vliegenthart, 2014), but nonetheless it generally tends to remain exclusive (Swanson, 1992, p. 399).

In political media relations so far, journalists working for leading media outlets provide political coverage and professional spokespersons working for important political organisations provide them with the necessary information for that coverage. The arrangement generally benefits all parties involved. It allows the involved spokespersons to generate (favourable) coverage for their organisations and to keep them present in the public debate and helps the involved journalists to provide quality political coverage, thereby ameliorating their medium's competitive position in the media market. Journalists rely on quality information for their political coverage – and politicians and political spokespersons rely on political coverage to keep themselves and their respective organisations in the public debate, sometimes even to ensure political legitimacy. At times the exclusive arrangement defining political media relations might be conflictual, yet maintaining it is assumingly beneficial for both sides involved.

It has been argued however that the proliferation of digital means of communication could change the conditions here. Technologically induced media change could alter structural conditions and patterns of interaction within political media relations, potentially fostering new (and less exclusive) arrangements. Such discussions inter alia surround the inclusion of new and formerly marginal actors into networks of political communication (cf. Coleman & Blumler, 2009) or the potential erosion of established gatekeeping functions of professional journalism (cf. Bruns, 2009; Neuberger, 2009).

Now these processes of technological change and their potential to induce effect on politics and political communication have been in the centre of interest of communication and political science for over a decade now. Even looking back to the 1990s – a time when digitisation was still in its earliest stages – one can ascertain a large variety of accounts related to this field.

Political media relations under online conditions and the potentially altered arrangements characterising these have on the other hand not yet been subjected to greater amounts of empirical research. Nonetheless there are some recent studies focusing on interactions between politics and the media in the digital age, some even do so with regard to the situation in Germany or in similar (neighbouring) media systems.

For the present analyses, both the wider debate on the implications of digitisation and recent studies on media relations under online conditions are of elevated interest. This goes inter alia for reasons of contextualisation of the analysed perceptions and actual adaptations of digitisation in the field of political media relations in Germany.

The following subchapters therefore aim to provide an overview of the debate on digitisation and its implications for politics and political communication and to then discuss the still relatively small state of research concerning political media relations in the online age. These steps are carried out to provide the necessary background for subsequent analyses and discussions.

The first subchapter addresses the debate on digitisation and its implications. It first discusses existing systematisations and then takes individual accounts into consideration. The second subchapter addresses recent empirical studies on political media relations under online conditions in Germany or in similar (neighbouring) media systems. A conclusive third subchapter then briefly confronts and summarises the main findings.

2.1 Digitisation and its Implications

In how far does the proliferation of new means of communication affect established communication structures and patterns of power in the fields of politics and political communication? Does technologically induced media change induce changes in political communication and politics in the long run? If so, what is the nature of these changes?

The processes subsumed under the notion of digitisation have long been in the centre of scientific interest, inter alia for political science and media studies. As a matter of fact, there is a sheer endless number of accounts addressing questions revolving around the actual implications of digitisation, especially for the fields of politics and of political communication. Several authors have sought to systematise these accounts and to summarise the debate (e.g. Kies, 2010; Papacharissi, 2009; Ward & Gibson, 2009). The debate as such has often been described as polarised (Schweitzer, 2008), sometimes even as an overly polarised one (Wright, 2012).

This chapter aims to provide an overview of this debate on the implications of digitisation. First existing systematisations are discussed; similarities and differences between them are highlighted. Then individual accounts of visibility within the debate (e.g. those that have been repeatedly cited in existing systematisations) are taken into consideration and analysed for central lines of argument. Discussing the findings of the subsequent analyses of perceptions and actual adaptations of digitisation requires contextualisation and this necessarily implies a comprehensive overview over the state of discussion. The following subchapters aim to account for that.

2.1.1 Systematisations

Several authors – often in the context of their own research – have sought to systematise the scientific debate on possible implications of the digitisation of political communication. Their accounts aim at a description of the often polarised debate on the effects of the proliferation of digital means in this sphere. Yet despite the fact that they all make recourse to a largely similar body of research, there are some differences between their systematisations.

Five distinct systematisations of the debate are discussed here. They represent a variety of approaches towards a description of the different perspectives. There are of course further systematisations, however, these are not discussed in depth here either because they are very similar to those already included in the discussion (e.g. Brants, 2005; Thimm, Einspänner, & Dang-Anh, 2012) or they are set aside for approaching accounts discussing digitisation under largely different aspects (e.g. Reich, 2009). Here the focus is drawn on those systematisations that concentrate on accounts dealing with the potential implications digitisation has for politics and political communication, especially for the relations between the actors involved.

Systematisation:	*Contraposition of:*	*Spectrum of perspectives:*	*Time-factor:*
Kies (2010)	positive outcomes // (very) negative outcomes	structural changes - inclusion - separation	not included
Papacharissi (2009)	utopian accounts // dystopian accounts	structural changes - inclusion - partial changes (unequally distributed) - separation	included
Raupp (2011)	positive outcomes // negative outcomes	structural changes - inclusion - normalisation - separation	included
Ward & Gibson (2009)	structural changes // integration // normalisation	structural changes - inclusion - normalisation	partially included
Wright (2012)	revolutionary changes // normalisation	structural changes - normalisation	partially included
Brants (2009)	*cyberoptimism // cyberpessimism*	*structural changes - normalisation-separation*	*not included*
Thimm et al. (2012)	*cyberoptimism // cyberpessimism*	*structural changes - inclusion - separation*	*not included*

Tab. 1: Overview: Analysed systematisations of the debate concerning implications of digitisation.[10]

Papacharissi (2009) distinguishes between two different directions in the scientific debate surrounding the digitisation of politics and political communication and then labels these as either 'utopian' or 'dystopian'. The former position (e.g. S. Davis, Elin, & Reeher, 2002; Johnson & Kaye, 1998; Negroponte, 1998) places emphasis on the democratic potential of new media while the latter tends to be very cautious in this regard (e.g. Noam, 2005). According to Papacharissi (2009, p. 231), a third group does admit to the democratic potential of new media in principle but at the same time emphasises the vulnerability of this potential (e.g. Blumler & Gurevitch, 2001).

[10] For comparative reasons, the alphabetical order of approaches in this table is not utilised subsequently.

She describes the spectrum of existing perspectives, starting with those that (favourably) discuss the establishment of deliberative democracy through digitisation. Next she makes reference to those accounts that see digital communication as successful in reaching out to certain strata of the population yet in many cases also admit to the absence of such effects with regard to other strata. According to Papacharissi (2009, p. 240) some accounts do discuss democratic potentials of digitisation favourably but at the same time limit these to certain groups; from this perspective, the proliferation of ICT is not benefiting all actors equally.

Papacharissi (2009, p. 243) describes research on political communication in the online sphere as 'frequently rapt in the dualities of determinism, utopian and dystopian' and initially systematises the debate in terms of a dichotomy of accounts. Further enquiry however leads to the description of a spectrum of positions. This ranges from those regarding digital deliberation via those discussing the inclusion of new actors in established patterns, in some cases also with a distinction between profiteers and non-profiteers, through to those that discuss digitisation in terms of a new predominance of inter-elite communication.

It is emphasised that the position of an account within this spectrum of perspectives is often correlating with its year of origin; there is a tendency towards increasing scepticism (Papacharissi, 2009, p. 243). While early accounts had a tendency to be too favourable, more contemporary ones are often considered too sombre (cf. Howard, 2001, p. 949).

In their account, Ward and Gibson (2009) assess an ongoing debate on the state of representative democracy. In this debate, they see two distinct positions. One assumes that representative democracy is in crisis due to declining levels of political interest and participation. It sees representative democracy as failing to promote opportunities for direct input from the public. The other position labels this perception as overly simplistic, postulating that political organisations (i.e. one of the central elements of representative democracy) are rather in flux than in crisis (Ward & Gibson, 2009, p. 26). According to this view, the situation is to be regarded as one of complex transformations. Based on this assumption, the authors indicate that digitisation might have to be regarded as one of the prime movers both for intra- as well as for inter-organisational change.

In an intra-organisational context, new ICTs are discussed with regard to various usages and connected outcomes. Patterns of usage range between the extension of organisational reach ('the Internet as a recruitment tool'), the deepening of supporters' engagement ('the Internet as an activist tool') and the flattening of existing organisational hierarchies ('the Internet as a democratic tool') (Ward & Gibson, 2009, pp. 28-31).

Here, the systematisation of perspectives provided with regard to inter-organisational change is even more important. The authors point out that:

> "(…) commentators have suggested that such technologies may eventually alter the organizational landscape of democracies and that certain types of organizations can more readily adapt the technology and benefit from it. A variety of possibilities have been advanced, from radical deinstitutionalization through a 'politics as usual' scenario" (Ward & Gibson, 2009, p. 32).[11]

Ward and Gibson broadly distinguish between three scenarios. The first one discusses digitisation in terms of disintermediation and an erosion of traditional structures, both in favour of increasingly direct democracy (e.g. Morris, 2001; Rheingold, 1993). The most radical accounts postulate the idea that "the Internet may hasten the demise of traditional representative democracy by producing a process of deinstitutionalization as organizational hierarchies are flattened and displaced by direct input from citizens" (Ward & Gibson, 2009, p. 32). The authors emphasise that this view is prevalent among the early accounts on digitisation (i.e. those from the mid to late 1990s).

The second scenario discusses digitisation in terms of equalisation. From this perspective, ICT diminishes the amount of resources necessary for maintaining a visible presence in the public sphere and allows even small and marginal groups to present themselves in a professional and representative way (e.g. van de Donk, Loader, Nixon, & Rucht, 2004). New technology is said to level differences and integrate new actors into existing structures (Ward & Gibson, 2009, p. 32).

The third scenario in this systematisation is discussed under the notion of 'normalisation'. It postulates a replication of real-world power structures in the digital sphere (e.g. Resnick, 1998). Actors that are already powerful and have a standing in the 'classic' media will, according to this position, come to a state of predominance in the digital world as well. According to Ward and Gibson (2009, p. 34), this normalisation thesis builds on four assumptions: 'commercialisation', 'fragmentation', 'new skills' and 'increasing regulatory control'. These describe the Internet as being dominated by business interests and – due to its nature as a pull medium – as inhabited by fragmented audiences. Contradicting assumptions of the equalisation perspective, the maintenance of a professional web-presence is described as demanding in terms of professional and economic resources. Last but not least, the depiction of the Internet as an uncontrollable medium is described as not sustainable given the attempts to impose measures of control and censorship by authoritarian regimes as well as (to some extent) by Western democracies.

The systematisation by Ward and Gibson states a triad of scenarios connected to the process of digitisation. These are located in a spectrum between the postu-

11 Here and in the following chapters, the spelling within direct citations has always been retained from the original quotes.

lation of fundamental structural changes, of changes regarding the integration of new actors into the existing structures or of no (durable) changes at all.

With regard to debates about the possible constitution of a new public sphere through the Internet, Raupp (2011) suggests a categorisation into two types of accounts. These either stress positive or negative effects of the proliferation of digital means in the field of political communication.

The author admits initially that purely cyber-optimistic points of view are hardly present in the current debate; it is emphasised that a majority of existing empirical studies presents findings supporting the more pessimist approaches (Raupp, 2011, p. 77). She thereby makes a point similar to the argument about correlations between the position of an argument in the systematised spectrum and its year of origin employed by Papacharissi (2009).

Subsequently, the two categories (i.e. positive and negative accounts) are further subdivided. Raupp (2011, p. 77) points out that – from a cyber-optimistic viewpoint – digitisation has so far been discussed with regard to the alteration of established (organisational) structures but also and more importantly with regard to the inclusive potential of new technologies. Here the focus is on their abilities to foster political participation, mobilisation and the accessibility and accountability of political institutions and organisations (e.g. Bimber, 1998). In these accounts, digitisation is attributed with changing potentials both on an organisational and a societal level. Marginal and new actors are described as profiteers of the process of digitisation (e.g. Voss, 2010). It is emphasised that digitisation has been connected with improved access to the mainstream media for individuals, potentially leading to a greater diversity of opinions.

Sceptical accounts are also differentiated into two subcategories (Raupp, 2011, pp. 77-78). One is described as focusing on a replication of real-world structures in the online sphere (normalisation thesis; c.f. Resnick (1998)), the other one as concentrating on negative effects connected to the proliferation of digital means in the field of political communication. The latter perspective argues that digitisation could fragmentise issues and publics and thereby disintegrate society. It could deprive quality media of their agenda-setting function, which again would have negative consequences for societal integration.

The approach by Kies (2010) systematises the debate in the context of a study regarding the deliberative potentials of digital communication. The author distinguishes between optimistic and very pessimistic perspectives of the phenomenon (Kies, 2010, pp. 2-3). On the one hand, he ascertains a variety of accounts describing effects of digitisation leading to processes of decision making that are more participative, inclusive and plural (e.g. Coleman & Gøtze, 2002; Grossman, 1995). This either regards new deliberative structures developing in the online sphere or increases in the inclusiveness of established structures due to the proliferation of digital means.

On the other side of the debate, Kies identifies cyber-pessimistic positions that "see dire consequences for the future of democracy" (Kies, 2010, p. 3). Authors subsumed under this category generally share a view in which computer mediated communication "is conducive to cheap talk on private matters but certainly not to deliberative political debates" (Kies, 2010, p. 3). In this regard, digitisation is discussed as a phenomenon that leads to an ever increasing polarisation of opinions and thereby ultimately also to a Balkanisation of society (e.g. Sunstein, 2001). Existing knowledge gaps are potentially widening under online conditions. further digital divides are emerging (e.g. R. Davis, 2005). Here, the cyber-pessimistic side of the debate is not described in terms of normalisation, but with regard to emerging distortions and (normatively) negative developments induced by digitisation.

Wright (2012) then highlights two major currents in the debate on digitisation and its implications: cyber-optimism and cyber-realism. He states that:

> "The notion that the Internet might have a revolutionary effect on politics, and particularly that it might facilitate the creation of a deliberative virtual public sphere, has sparked an intense and at times acrimonious theoretical debate between the so-called 'revolutionaries' or cyber-optimist school and the so-called 'normalization' or cyber-realist school (…)" (Wright, 2012, p. 245).

In this context, Wright criticises what he perceives as a schism between these positions, arguing that it leads to inappropriate approaches to empirical research in this field (Wright, 2012, p. 244). He describes a division between perspectives that postulate fundamental changes to politics and political communication and others that argue towards a replication of existing power-structures in the digital sphere. This division is often quite confrontational:

> "People who believe in the potential of new technologies to revolutionize politics and society think that there will be wholesale changes to the functioning of the political system. Effectively, technology deterministically generates a democratic state of affairs – however conceived – because the characteristics of new technologies overcome barriers to 'idealized' direct or deliberative democracy. Such 'believers', and it is often presented in such religious terms, are often accused of a blind 'faith' – an almost cult-like obsession, detached from the reality of how technologies are experienced and used in society at large" (Wright, 2012, p. 246).

Wright criticises that an over-emphasis on the 'revolutionary' aspect leads to a state in which every empirical observation that does not clearly indicate revolutionary and fundamental changes is dismissed as a peripheral matter. According to this argument, a majority of studies necessarily has findings indicating a state of normalisation simply because the stakes for the realisation of the other scenario have been set unachievably high (Wright, 2012, pp. 250-253).

The systematisation employed by Wright distinguishes between two opposing currents in the debate: one postulating scenarios of revolution and one postulating scenarios of normalisation (cf. Nitschke et al., 2014, p. 2). The former debates digitisation in terms of improved political accountability and increasingly direct democracy. The latter sees no substantial changes at all, leading to a state in which new means of communication might be available but in which existing structures of power are replicated in the online world.

Wright focuses on highly optimistic accounts and on those discussing digitisation in terms of normalisation, seeking to describe a prevalent dichotomy of perspectives. In so far this systematisation is different from those found in the accounts of Ward and Gibson (2009), Raupp (2011), Papacharissi (2009) and Kies (2010), which all include further subdivisions and distinctions between various forms of cyber-optimism and cyber-pessimism.

Considering the different systematisations of the debate together, four scenarios connected to the digitisation of politics and political communication become apparent. A strong form of cyber-optimism postulates effects that would lead to an alteration of established structures of decision making and political communication. Here, digitisation is discussed in terms of direct democracy, e-deliberation and completely altered forms and patterns of communication. Secondly, another cyber-optimistic current discusses digitisation in terms of inclusion and equalisation. Patterns and structures remain largely unaltered, however new and formerly marginal actors are included; they gain access to what were so far considered to be largely exclusive fields. From a more pessimistic, or according to inter alia Wright (2012, p. 245) realistic point of view, digitisation is then discussed under a notion of normalisation. This position postulates that technological changes might very well occur but that they would not induce any considerable changes to established patterns of decision making and political communication. Despite technological change, politics and political communication would remain unaltered and as 'normal' as they were before. A last cyber-pessimistic position then focuses on possible distortions and widening societal, political and communicative gaps induced by digitisation. From this perspective, the proliferation of digital means would in fact lead to an even higher degree of exclusiveness in the fields of politics and political communication and largely set aside new and marginal actors.

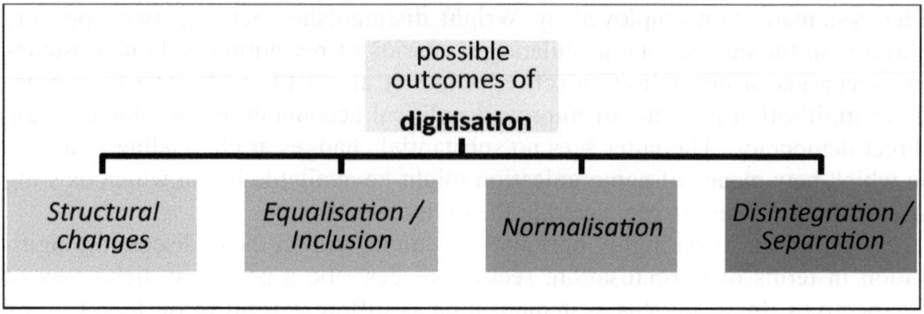

Fig. 4: Possible outcomes of digitisation; scenarios described in systematisations of the scientific debate on the phenomenon and its implications.

According to several authors (e.g. Papacharissi, 2009; Raupp, 2011; Ward & Gibson, 2009; Wright, 2012), there is also an observable time factor, i.e. a trend towards more sceptical accounts on digitisation, one that tends, over the time, to steer away from early positions of cyber-optimism.[12]

Based on this structural overview of the debate– which is a simplification of a complex subject to some extent of course – the following subchapter now discusses some central accounts on the process of digitisation and its potential implications. It will do so following the structure of four basic scenarios.

2.1.2 Literature Review

The implications digital technologies might have for politics and political communication have been subject to debate since the mid-1990s. The question is whether or not a theoretical enhancement of communicative possibilities leads to an actual alteration of the very patterns of political communication (cf. Emmer & Wolling, 2010, pp. 37-41). In the following, some central accounts on digitisation and its implications are reviewed and discussed.[13] The literature review is

12 Chadwick (2009, pp. 11-12) also describes a time-factor within the debate but differentiates even further, pointing out that: "scholarship has proceeded through several waves, from early enthusiasm to pessimistic reaction, and to the recent, more balanced and empirically driven approaches of the post-dotcom era."

13 As indicated, centrality should to be understood in this context primarily in terms of visibility within the debate.

structured according to the systematisation of perspectives presented in the preceding subchapter.

Structural changes

A strong form of cyber-optimism postulates an alteration of established structures of decision making and political communication due to digitisation. Here, the process is discussed in terms of direct democracy, e-deliberation and completely altered forms and patterns of communication. Such a perspective is prevalent in early accounts, especially in those from a practitioners' perspective.

Gore (1994) – at that time incumbent Vice-President of the United States – argues in such terms. The proliferation of ICT, here described as the establishment of a so-called Global Information Infrastructure (GII), is discussed as a major alteration to politics and political communication. It is postulated that this process would actually lead to the rise of a 'new Athenian Age of democracy', making the GII 'a metaphor for democracy itself' (Gore, 1994). From this perspective, ICTs enhance democracy by challenging established patterns; unhindered access to information and free speech are fostered by new technological possibilities. In general, the assumed impact of digital technology in the fields of politics and political communication is tremendous:

> "To promote; to protect; to preserve freedom and democracy, we must make telecommunication's development an integral part of every nation's development. Each link we create strengthens the bonds of liberty and democracy around the world" (Gore, 1994).

A similar perspective on digitisation is taken by Morris (2001), who, as a political consultant, again argues from a practitioner's point of view. Morris discusses rising levels of accountability and the introduction of new feedback-patterns for the electorate. He indicates a trend towards direct democracy that he deems unstoppable, ultimately leading to "a system of governance that pays closer heed to public views and tethers more closely to the opinions of the people" (Morris, 2001, p. 1034).

According to this account, digitisation would induce a drastic decline in production costs in the field of political communication due to new and cost-effective channels. Political mobilisation and democratic pluralism would then both profit from these developments (Morris, 2001, pp. 1041-1045). Accordingly, special interest groups would become less dependent on their financial resources, a process that would lead to greater equality among them. New modes of online-voting are described as effective means to increase participation without being vulnerable to misuse, since the checks and balances imposed by the constitution and various courts and the electorates' respect for authority would still prevail (Morris, 2001, pp. 1049-1052).

The perspective taken here again assumes a very large impact of the proliferation of digital technology in the neighbouring fields of politics and political communication. As Morris states: "The Internet offers a potential for direct democracy so profound that it may well transform not only our system of politics but also our very form of government" (Morris, 2001, p. 1033). From this point of view, digitisation alters actual patterns of power and communication.

The perspective these authors take is one connecting digitisation to fundamental changes to the ways in which politics and political communication function. Representation is to be replaced by patterns of direct democracy, patterns made feasible by the proliferation of digital means of communication. Such a degree of cyber-optimism appears to be a domain of practitioners,[14] especially prevalent in accounts from the early stages of digitisation. There are however scientific accounts approaching structural changes induced by digitisation, primarily in the form of e-deliberation.

Deliberation itself is a relatively prominent theoretical concept within the social sciences. Since the very notion of deliberation, or, to be precise, of deliberative democracy, has first been postulated,[15] scholars have approached it from various perspectives. They have done so in affirmative and depreciating terms, in the postulation of normative ideals, in the formulation of (critical) theoretical works and in the empirical enquiry into the actual feasibility of the very concept. Deliberation as part of democratic process indicates an emphasis on the collective reasoning of the people, on processes of public consideration and reflection and on opinion-forming. Gastil points out that "when people deliberate, they carefully examine a problem and arrive at a well-reasoned solution after a period of inclusive, respectful consideration of diverse points of view" (Gastil, 2008, p. 8).

The notion of deliberation is often connected metaphorically to the marketplace in ancient Athens, to the place where free citizens met to discuss affairs of importance, where they gathered for collective reasoning (cf. Habermas, 1990;

14 The account by Rheingold (1993) which was brought forward in the very early stages of digitisation is often cited as an example for scientific over-enthusiasm. However, one can clearly ascertain a profound discussion of possible distortions in it (especially in chapter 10), an attribute that clearly distinguishes it from the purely enthusiastic accounts brought forward by various practitioners.

15 In the case of 'deliberative democracy', it is generally accepted that this was first done by Bessette in his 1980 article 'Deliberative Democracy: The Majority Principle in Republican Government' (cf. Bessette, 1980).

Ruzé, 1997).[16] Deliberative democracy describes a form of government in which central affairs are dealt with by public deliberation executed by the members of society. The people gathers together and has an enlightened debate, a collective reasoning about the issues at stake (Scheyli, 2000, pp. 37-39).

Some scholars, perhaps most noteworthy Habermas (1997), have described these mechanisms as vital parts of democratic systems; the legitimacy of a democracy stands and falls, from this point of view, with the amount of its discursiveness or, as Page (with an admittedly weaker normative impetus than Habermas) puts it:

> "A vigorous democracy cannot settle for a passive citizenry that merely chooses leaders and then forgets entirely about politics. Such a citizenry would not know what it wanted its public officials to do or what they were actually doing. An ignorant public would have no way to hold its officials to account. There would be a very attenuated sort of democracy, if any sort at all. In order that the public as a whole can actively control what its government does, the public, collectively, must be well informed. Some kind of effective public deliberation is required that involves the citizenry as a whole" (Page, 1996, p. 5).

Proponents and advocates of deliberative democracy emphasise that it is the most suitable way to deal with plural contemporary societies, the best way to foster societal integration and to produce collectively binding norms of enhanced quality (Rauschenbach, 2010, pp. 71-76; Scheyli, 2000, pp. 40-42). However, it has also been repeatedly pointed out that its feasibility is at least questionable. According to the critics of the concept, this is especially due to reasons of scale.[17] It has been indicated that processes of deliberation might be manageable in relatively small settings such as town meetings within small communities while they become more and more difficult with a growing number of participants. Deliberative discussion in a classic sense is, according to a variety of authors, simply not practicable in contemporary societies (cf. Gastil, 2008, pp. 49-50; Page, 1996, p. 3; Xenos, 2008, p. 485).[18]

---

16 The affairs that were to be discussed by the citizenry were in fact widely spread; as Held puts it, areas and issues such as "the legal framework for the maintenance of the public order, finance and direct taxation, ostracism and foreign affairs (including assessing the performance of the military and navy, forming alliances, the declaration of war, the concluding of peace) came before the assembled citizens for deliberation and decision" (Held, 2006, p. 17).

17 There are of course other limitations mentioned in this regard. Young for example refers to barriers of either structural (that is mostly due to socio-economic inequalities), theoretical or psychological nature (Young, 2004, pp. 26-42). For a comprehensive overview of possible limitations of deliberation and of criticism regarding the theoretical conception as such, see Ryfe (2005).

18 An interesting calculation in this regard has been made by Page. With reference to the feasibility of deliberation in the United States, he points out that: "If, for example, a nation of 250 million

However, according to some recent arguments regarding potential implications of digitisation, technological change might have the potential to alter unfavourable conditions for deliberation, maybe even for deliberative democracy. From this perspective, deliberative spaces might emerge online. Digital means are said to foster fast and inexpensive access to political information and to easily enable citizens to take part in political processes, to communicate easily and unhindered. People become able to communicate as equals online, every issue regarded as salient is principally debateable. The majority of scale-related problems would be solved, the digital sphere would expand boundaries of space and time.

E-deliberation as a theoretically more demanding case of cyber-optimism is hardly postulated as a general outcome of digitisation,[19] yet there is in fact a multitude of scientific enquiries into the feasibility and actual emergence of the phenomenon.

In an international overview Coleman and Gøtze (2002, pp. 36-45) refer to a number of case studies regarding the deliberative usage of ICT in a variety of countries. They point out that the examples all tend to be at an experimental stage and that they usually suffer from two unfavourable factors: a small degree of public awareness and a lack of integration into government policy processes. Nevertheless they underline that even at a relatively early stage of digitisation one could indeed ascertain various attempts towards public online engagement. Further (and more recent) evaluation of e-deliberation is available with regard to the deliberative potential of online forums (e.g. Chadwick, 2009; Kies, 2010; Misnikov, 2010) or microblogs (e.g. Thimm et al., 2012), to patterns of dialogue in MPs or candidates weblogs (e.g. Auty, 2005; Trammell, Williams, Postelnicu, & Landreville, 2006) or to the chances and limits for user participation in parties' websites (e.g. Jackson & Lilleker, 2009).

The findings of these empirical studies differ: while some express cautious optimism, highlighting potentials of digitisation that have at least to some extent been realised (e.g. Trammell et al., 2006), others indicate a state in which their

citizens devoted twenty-four hours to fully equal collective discussion of some political issue, each citizen would get less than .0004 - less than four thousandths - of one second to talk. If each citizen insisted, instead, upon a rather modest two minutes of speaking time, the discussion would take five hundred million minutes: that is, 347,222 days, or 950 years" (Page, 1996, p. 3).

19 E-deliberation is to be understood as theoretically more demanding case of cyber-optimism in so far as 'common' cyber-optimism generally tends to focus on patterns of direct democracy, on the ease of access to political debates for interested citizens, while digital deliberation it is more far-reaching. This becomes clear with regard to the very notion of democracy: deliberative democracy is not only direct or aggregative but determined by a series of very specific characteristics. To put it the other way round: integrating strata of the population into patterns of decision-making (or altering these patterns in ways that allow for more direct forms of voting) does not necessarily constitute deliberative democracy.

realisation is more of a chimera. Here, potentials are (often intentionally) not utilised in the theoretically assumed way (e.g. Jackson & Lilleker, 2009, pp. 235-236). In some cases patterns of deliberation do indeed become visible online, yet these often constitute special cases due to the nature of forum and audience and are far from generalisable (e.g. Kies, 2010, pp. 136-142).

A test of potential examples of e-deliberation within the *Twitter* microblogging service against the Habermasian criteria of accessibility, equality of discursive opportunity, rationality, knowledgeability and controversy again reveals mixed results. The authors point out that the latter three might be met relatively easily online while accessibility and the equality of discursive opportunity might be hindered by technical barriers and digital divides (Thimm et al., 2012, pp. 290-291). Empirical findings indicate advanced general accessibility. Digital divides do not seem to cause larger distortions, even though they might hinder participation in some cases. The situation is different with regard to communicative parity. Due to a highly unequal distribution of attention, a minority of certain (central) actors gets the majority of attention. Rationality is again described as potentially problematic, however, due to a lack of generally accepted criteria for quality, the authors do not see any possibilities to evaluate on this criterion. Further findings suggest that the structure of *Twitter* enables deliberative processes but that the short length of the single *tweets* (max. 140 characters) tends to foster the distribution of information rather than the emergence of profound discussions. Therefore *Twitter* is, according to the authors, rather to be seen as a valuable tool for the spreading of information (which can potentially enhance deliberation) but not necessarily as a deliberative space in itself (Thimm et al., 2012, p. 302).

Equalisation / Inclusion

The second cyber-optimistic position is different from the first one in so far as it does not focus on the alteration of fundamental structures and patterns within the fields of politics and political communication. Here, the scenario describes an improvement of traditional (representative) structures through digitisation. Digital means function as means of equalisation, established structures become more inclusive but they do not vanish.[20]

[20] For a differentiation between these cyber-optimistic positions see inter alia Anstead and Chadwick (2009, pp. 58-59): "The relationship between institutions and the case made by internet optimists is more difficult to disentangle, largely because they do not form a single school but can be divided into two broad categories according to their attitudes to representative democracy. Most applicable to the American experience is what can be termed representative democracy optimism. This approach does not argue that the internet will destroy all representative institutions

Again, this position has so far often been taken by political communication practitioners, as for example by Trippi (2004). He describes digitisation as a process primarily benefiting citizens by allowing them to express mutual interests and strive for common goals. Digitisation enables them to exert pressure on actors in the centre of the political system, forcing their representatives to make decisions according to their interests (Trippi, 2004, pp. 223-224). The Internet is regarded as having the potential to unleash 'populist power' and therefore potentially able to fix the perceived shortcomings of politics from a pre-digitised era. These include the disengagement of citizens, the dumbing down of the electorate, the corruption of politics through the influence of wealthy donors and media trends such as attack ads and 'celebrity politics'. From this perspective, the Internet is regarded as the ideal medium for politics, much more suitable than television which, as Trippi states with regard to a popular TV series, is "great for *Law and Order*. It's not so good for making laws and keeping order" (Trippi, 2004, p. 226).[21]

Additionally, from this perspective digitisation is also said to affect the media sphere. The emergence of the blogosphere is said to offer great opportunities for civic journalism, fostering muckraking approaches and bringing enlightenment to areas traditional media outlets generally refrain from covering (Trippi, 2004, pp. 227-233).

Discussions surrounding the integrative and equalising potentials of digitisation are not the sole domain of communication practitioners. Scholars also argue on this position – though in a more balanced and reflected way.

Coleman and Blumler (2009) provide an extensive discussion on the challenges democracy faces at the beginning of the 21st century and on the potentials digitisation might have in coping with these. They point out that while democracy as a model of government is anything but out of favour, citizens tend to feel increasing gaps between them and those who govern. From the public's point of view, democratic government becomes remote and out of touch, (perceived) political efficacy is very low (Coleman & Blumler, 2009, p. 1). Digitisation is, according to the authors, in this context often regarded as a potential solution for this dilemma; new channels of communicative exchange should foster civic

---

but instead claims that it has the potential to reform and rehabilitate indirect vehicles of democratic participation, most notably political parties and elections. This approach has been accompanied by a second: the view that the internet will actually undermine representative institutions." [Italics retained from the original version]. As a matter of fact, Anstead and Chadwick cite the accounts by Morris (2001) and Trippi (2004) as examples for the two different cyber-optimistic positions.

21 Italics retained from the original version. Trippi is referring to NBC's legal drama "Law and Order" here.

participation and political integration. Coleman and Blumler carefully align themselves to this position, though clearly pointing out that there are necessary preconditions and that integration through ICT should not be taken for granted by any means:

> "We take the position that the Internet possesses a vulnerable potential to revitalise our flagging political communication arrangements by injecting some new and different elements into the relationship between representatives and represented and governments and governed. But we argue that such potential will be squandered without imaginative policy intervention designed to shape and nurture democratic opportunities provided by the Internet" (Coleman & Blumler, 2009, pp. 9-10)

Coleman and Blumler criticise common conceptions of the potentials of ICTs in regards of improved political communication and democratic processes stating that:

> "Too often e-democracy has been promoted in the name of convenience: vote from bed, text-message your MP while you're on the bus, press red buttons as a substitute for articulated opinion. There is hollowness about much of this interactivity – more like the dead-end languor of a south-coast amusement arcade than the vibrancy of empowered citizenship" (Coleman & Blumler, 2009, p. 167).

The argument focusses in particular on three main assumptions: a) that relations between power holding political elites and the general public are in flux, in a sense that the demand for accountability is increasing while established political actors are often unable to cope with this; b) that there is an 'inexorable impoverishment of mainstream political communication', meaning that established means of communicative exchange between those governing and those governed become (especially from a normative point of view) increasingly insufficient; and c) that new digital means of communication have the potential to alter established structures of communication, to improve them and to thereby enrich democracy as such. This potential however is to be regarded as vulnerable insofar as its realisation is highly dependent on the provision of an adequate infrastructure, of an integration of digital media into established political patterns (Coleman & Blumler, 2009, pp. 10-11).

The position taken by Coleman and Blumler is cyber-optimistic insofar as it clearly emphasises the democratic potentials of digitisation. Digital media are discussed as a potential solution to 'classic' dilemmas of representative democracy such as an increasing distance between those governing and those governed, low levels of general participation and perceptions of low political efficacy. Yet at the same time, the potentials of digitisation are described as vulnerable; while digital media clearly possess the ability to improve governance and relations between government and citizens, it is far from clear that this will happen automatically. The infrastructure will have to be utilised in a way that is actually likely to promote democratic citizenship; in contrast, not each and every (commercial) usage is suitable for promoting democratic values. Coleman and Blumler (2009, pp. 40-41) make recourse to concepts of e-deliberation, although their approach focuses on ways of altering currently existing democratic systems in a way that will make these more deliberative. It is, in contrast to radically cyber-optimistic positions, not about the replacement of representative democracy with some sort of pure e-deliberation but about the improvement of existing patterns in terms of accountability, integration and responsiveness.

Normalisation

As a non-cyber-optimistic position, the normalisation thesis argues towards a replication of offline structures in the online sphere. Brought forward at a very early stage of digitisation in the late 1990s, it negates the idea of larger societal and political effects of the proliferation of digital technology. According to this line of argument, the process of digitisation has, despite all potentials of digital technology, steered in a direction in which patterns of power and structures of communication in the online sphere are largely indistinguishable from their offline counterparts.

Resnick – the thesis' original author – postulates that the early Internet was comparable to a 'Lockean state of nature'. At this stage users were free and equal, the roles of producer and consumer were not differentiated and altruism could be regarded as the predominant ideology (Resnick, 1998; I, 9). Then transformations similar to those that ended the 'Lockean state of nature' happened in the online sphere. Commercialisation and the connected emergence of legislation, politicisation and institutionalisation created a digital world dominated by certain actors and characterised by functional differentiation. These developments (based on technological innovation) have led to a "transformation of the Internet from a virtual state of nature to a virtual pluralistic civil society" (Resnick, 1998; I, 13).

Politics and the online sphere are connected in three regards (described here as 'politics within the Net', 'politics which impacts the Net' and 'political uses of the Net') and all of these are affected by normalisation (Resnick, 1998; IIa-c). The first dimension, 'politics within the Net', relates to the online sphere and its structures, rules and standards, it represents a form of intra-net politics. According to Resnick, these used to exist in a state that 'inspired utopian speculation' simply because of its revolutionary egalitarian approach. However, this has neither been subjected to proliferation as a model for politics in general nor has it been adapted by new users after the initial stages of digitisation. Furthermore, an early state of 'almost total laissez-faire' has been replaced by external regulation (Resnick, 1998; IIa, 25).

The second dimension relates to 'politics which impact the Net', i.e. those actions that established political entities such as nation states take and that directly or indirectly affect the digital world. Here, an encroachment of established (state-) actors into the online sphere has led to substantial transformations:

> "The regulation of cyberspace is part of normalization – of transforming a marginal frontier into a populous settled territory of advanced industrial society. For some people this transformation marks the loss of freedom, but settling the frontier means establishing law and order; it means building fences and rounding up outlaws (…)" (Resnick, 1998; IIb, 34).

The last dimension relates to 'political uses of the Net', i.e. the employment of digital means by political actors in order to influence political processes in the offline sphere. Inter alia this covers communicative activities such as campaigning, lobbying and mobilisation. Here, digitisation might enable new actors to participate in political communication but sooner or later this effect will be undermined by an emerging predominance of already established players in the digital world, especially due to questions of resources (Resnick, 1998; IIc).

In principle, the normalisation thesis underlines a potential of digital means to yield major changes in the fields of politics and political communication:

> "If democracy entails equal opportunity to participate in politics, then the Internet creates that opportunity. Computer-mediated communication (CMC) technology provides individual citizens, interest groups, and public officials with the information necessary to decide questions of politics and public policy, and it provides them with the communication tools necessary to organize themselves for collective action. An 'electronic' agora actually seems possible, in which the ordinary citizen's voice can be amplified cheaply and broadcast as widely as the voice of the richest plutocrat" (Margolis & Resnick, 2000, p. 25).

According to this argument, the population of the Internet often largely resembles the general population, driving ICT usage away from being a pure elite-phenomenon. Yet at the same time those actors who are predominant in the offline world tend to achieve power-holding positions in the online world again. This is due inter alia to the commercialisation of the digital sphere and to the amount of resources necessary for the maintenance of a successful web presence (Margolis & Resnick, 2000, pp. 53, 60). Potentials are not necessarily realised:

> "The Internet does have the potential to change the nature of American and even world politics, but the evidence does not indicate that it will. Instead, commercial interests and mainstream politics are likely to dominate the WWW or its successor in the way they presently exert dominance in other mass media. Citizens who can afford it will have better access to information about

products and services and about a multitude of subjects, including politics, and most people will act as high-tech consumers rather than as political activists" (Margolis & Resnick, 2000, p. 74).

Replications of offline structures are then also to be found in the media sphere. Established offline news providers tend to dominate the Internet, even though digitisation offers potentials for new media outlets as well. Yet again these can hardly be realised. It is especially emphasised that the unsolved question of payment for online content harbours the danger that news and information will be presented 'in a manner that panders to low tastes of both advertisers and audience', thereby not making use of the potentials of digitisation (Margolis & Resnick, 2000, pp. 109-115).

The normalisation thesis is not to be qualified as purely cyber-pessimistic, since it acknowledges the possibility of effects of digitisation that would be regarded as positive from a normative perspective. However, it is sceptical about the actual implementation of the potentials of digitisation, often differentiating between realistic changes and unrealistic or even utopian scenarios (Margolis & Resnick, 2000, pp. 207-222).

Patterns of normalisation emerge in a variety of empirical studies. Inter alia these cover the representation of political parties in the Internet (e.g. Gibson, Margolis, Resnick, & Ward, 2003; Schweitzer, 2011; Small, 2008). More recently party politicians' representation in social network sites such as *Facebook* has been addressed (e.g. Gulati & Williams, 2013), again indicating a predominance of already established actors in this sphere. Other studies indicate a replication of offline modes of communication on social media sites, both for party politicians (e.g. Ross, Fountaine, & Comrie, 2014) as well as for actors from the state sphere (e.g. Kocks, Raupp, & Schink, 2014).

For Germany, findings regarding online campaign communication indicate that the offline standing of political parties determines their online communication, there is a replication of patterns of top-down communication online (Schweitzer, 2011, pp. 323-324). Similar patterns again replicate within the online communication of state actors (Kocks et al., 2014, pp. 82-83). Findings indicating normalisation then also emerge for the media sphere: Analyses of debates in off and online media show a spectrum of actors online that is both narrow and quite similar to its offline counterpart. The debates emerging online are seldom if ever more critical than their offline counterparts and the framing utilised on and offline is hardly distinguishable (Gerhards & Schäfer, 2007, pp. 224-225).

Disintegration / Separation

A further perspective on digitisation discusses the phenomenon with regard to emerging distortions and widening gaps. Here, the proliferation of digital means of communication is considered a potential threat to political and communicative inclusion and described as a process that tends to profit only a few. Often these accounts make recourse to the concept of digital divides or to its theoretical precursor, the knowledge gap hypothesis.

Originally formulated in 1970, the knowledge gap hypothesis postulates that, contrary to popular belief, knowledge gaps might actually be increasing in society. The information flow via the mass media is described as leading to differential growth in knowledge, to a state in which the growth of knowledge is relatively higher for those strata of the population that already have a high degree of formal education. The individual socio-economic status determines the individual gains in knowledge (Tichenor, Donohue, & Olien, 1970, p. 160). This primarily concerns political as well as scientific knowledge, whereas sectors of information such as sports, catastrophes and miscellaneous news are hardly affected (Bonfadelli, 2002, p. 569).

The concept of digital divides then transfers this conceptualisation to the digital age. It postulates that digitisation might lead to widening or deepening gaps within society. Groups tend to profit in different ways and, more importantly, to vastly different amounts from the new means of communication available. The acquisition of profit, for example in terms of political information, is relatively greater among the higher status segments of society.

Empirical analyses show digital divides between countries or regions (e.g. van Dijk, 2009) or between genders (e.g. Cooper, 2006; Liff, Shepherd, Wajcman, Rice, & Hargittai, 2004). More often they do so with regard to divides occurring due to varying levels of formal education – again understood as an indicator for socio-economic status – and cognitive capacities (e.g. Bimber, 1998; Iske, 2005; van Dijk, 2005).

Despite the importance of available technology in the online age, the phenomenon of digital divides must not to be reduced to mere questions of technological accessibility, but rather should be understood as a multi-level phenomenon:

> "The ensuing remark is that people framing the digital divide as a technological problem suggest that access to the technology concerned is able to fix existing social problems, among them problems of social inequality, democracy, freedom, social relationships and community building. This is a remnant of the Internet hype of the 1990s. Giving someone a computer and an Internet connection does not solve any of these problems. It might be more correct to say that is when they begin" (van Dijk, 2005, p. 5).

With recourse to Bourdieu's theory of social capital, this argument is also stressed by Dudenhöffer and Meyen (2012). In a five-step argument, they point out that (1) the effort people put into the acquisition of capital online depends of their perception of the Internet's importance and that (2) this perception of importance is directly related to their social position, with a higher one for individuals of elevated status. Subsequently (3) the cultural and social capital that has been acquired online directly improves the social position. Vice versa (4) refraining from acquiring this capital online tends to lead to a demotion of the social status which culminates in (5) a spiral leading to further societal disintegration (Dudenhöffer & Meyen, 2012, p. 13).

The concept of digital divides describes phenomena of stratification in various regards and societal fields. All of these phenomena are connected to the process of digitisation, but not merely to questions of technological availability. Digital divides are a multi-level phenomenon with both technological and social roots.

This concept partially underlies the account by Brundidge and Rice (2009). It focuses on two scenarios connected to digitisation: a possible increasing of knowledge gaps and an eventual fragmentation of society, i.e. a state in which the like-minded become more similar. With regard to the possible emergence of knowledge gaps they point out that while the Internet might offer new forums for deliberation,

> "the processes involved tend to be biased toward those with extensive civic skills, including a good vocabulary, the ability to communicate in English, a sense of personal efficacy, the ability to write or speak well, and the cognitive wherewithal to draw on previously existing knowledge" (Brundidge & Rice, 2009, p. 147).

Their argument indicates a digital divide in which e-deliberation is a phenomenon accessible for and prevalent among those actors that already enjoy a high socio-economic status, while fringe actors and marginal groups remain excluded. Furthermore the latter groups are subjected to a higher level of political leverage by the news media and other elites. This is achieved by agenda-setting and framing, i.e. by the influencing of "the kind of issues citizens think about and the way they think about them" (Brundidge & Rice, 2009, p. 148).

The second phenomenon then regards a possible fragmentation of society. Here enclaves of like-minded people become (internally) more and more similar while strongly differentiating themselves from other groups at the same time. Due to selective exposure to information and a general weakening of social boundaries in the digital age, like-minded people are brought closely together while the overall contact with different positions (i.e. the exposure to disagreement) diminishes. This development then leads to widening gaps between societal groups (Brundidge & Rice, 2009, pp. 149-152).

The interconnection of these phenomena then determines the implications digitisation has for politics and society. Decreasing knowledge gaps combined with an increase in exposure to disagreement would lead to an environment of e-deliberative democracy, while decreasing knowledge gaps and a simultaneous decrease in exposure to disagreement would result in polarised enclaves. Increasing knowledge gaps and decreasing exposure to disagreement would lead to a state of ideological domination "whereby minority and less educated groups are not even aware of alternative perspectives" and an increase of both knowledge gaps and exposure to disagreement would result in elite demagoguery, "whereby knowledgeable political elites can manipulate meanings and salience of alternative perspectives" (Brundidge & Rice, 2009, p. 154). According to Brundidge and Rice, findings of empirical research (for example regarding the United States in 2003), often support the latter scenario.

Such developments towards a separation between actors in the political centre and those on the periphery are also observed in other contexts, leading to a state in which "early enthusiasm has given way to more sober or pessimistic assessments of the Internet's potential for reconnecting political elites to citizens or party members" (A. Davis, 2010a, p. 747).

With regard to the United Kingdom, analysis shows two contrasting trends: On the one hand, communicative links between those in the very centre of the political system and those that find themselves surrounding it are increasing. More political information is available and the means for mutual exchange are at hand. Traditional channels which often fostered exclusion can easily be bypassed; this leads to an expansion of the very core of the political system, bringing together actors from the centre and those surrounding them. On the other hand there is a further distancing of inactive and fringe groupings. The mass of citizens finds itself farer away from the political centre. A decline in political coverage by the mass media and a trend towards fragmentation in the Internet, further intensified by divides in ICT usage, drive the periphery away from the core of the political system (A. Davis, 2010a, pp. 756-757). Accordingly the centre of the political system is becoming inclusive in some regards, integrating actors which surround the focal ones, and thereby is actually starting to enlarge itself. However, simultaneously the distance between this centre and the periphery, the ranks of inactive or excluded actors, is actually growing.

Apart from such empirically driven accounts, one also finds a variety of polemics arguing on potential downsides of digitisation. These focus inter alia on the problems ever increasing demands for political transparency online bring to political efficacy (e.g. Trankovits, 2011, 2012) or on the perils digitisation might bring to culture (e.g. Keen, 2007) or democracy as such (e.g. Lanier, 2006; Noam, 2005).

Noam (2005, pp. 57-58) specifically argues against four cyber-optimistic assumptions. He dismisses the idea that the Internet will facilitate political participatory action for reasons of scale and resources, arguing that the digital sphere is, or at least will soon be, conquered by those actors that already hold powerful positions in the offline world. He then points out that an increase in the quantity of political dialogue online does not necessarily foster its quality, but might even lead to more information clutter and to political communication that is rather 'distorted, shrill and simplistic'. A third argument states that direct access to public officials will become possible in the digital age; this is again dismissed by Noam, mainly due to reasons of scale. The final argument refers to the increased availability of political information online and to its potentially helpful effects for democracy. Noam admits that access to information might indeed foster the undermining of totalitarianism but at the same time points out that "it undermines pretty much everything else, too, including political parties and stability. (…) Democracy requires stability and stability requires a bit of inertia" (Noam, 2005, p. 58).

Lanier's (2006) polemic goes even further, discussing the advent of a 'digital Maoism' under the conditions of digitisation. In this scenario, a digital 'hive' (i.e. the collective) is 'all-wise' and therefore ultimately replaces both representative democracy and meritocracy. A collectivist system based on an idea that "has had dreadful consequences when thrust upon us from the extreme Right or the extreme Left in various historical periods" emerges online and then offline (Lanier, 2006).

There is a variety of rather pessimistic perspectives on the implications of the digitisation of politics and political communication. These focus on divides occurring due to the unequal distribution of wealth and technology or differences in access to formal education or on phenomena of societal disintegration and elite segregation. The latter regards the emergence of closed circles of elites that communicate (almost) exclusively among themselves and strictly apart from non-elites. It is emphasised that political online communication might – contrary to optimistic belief – become rather simplistic and shrill and that processes of digitisation might even destabilise established patterns of democracy, possibly paving the way for unwanted outcomes. In contrast to the normalisation thesis, the approaches subsumed under this category do not postulate the replication of real-world structures online but rather focus on the reinforcement of already existing inequalities, on new distortions and the undermining of democratic principles as a consequence of digitisation. The argument is not that digitisation will not account for changes at all but that it will in fact account for changes of a rather negative nature.

Excursus: Counter Public Spheres

In the digital age, the emergence of counter public spheres is a salient topic of discussion. Yet accounts subsumed under this notion are far from being unanimous about the implications of digitisation related to this phenomenon. Some frame it as evidence for the potential ICT has for fringe actors, enabling them to have their say online. Others focus on the fragmentation of the public sphere that might be connected to the emergence of counter public spheres, i.e. to phenomena of societal disintegration (cf. Wimmer, 2007, pp. 12-13).

In its fundamental understanding, a counter public sphere can be conceptualised as a partial public that is opposed to a hegemonic one and structured around a specific point of view or societal discourse (Krotz, 1998, p. 653). Such publics have at least been described since the 1960s, in a context of new social movements and alternative media outlets (Engesser & Wimmer, 2009, p. 44; Wimmer, 2007, pp. 153-154). Examples are to be found in many regards, among these contexts such as feminism (e.g. Fraser, 1990), indigenous peoples' movements (e.g. Salazar, 2003) or African American culture (e.g. Pough, 2004). In contrast, the role of digitisation in this context is still somewhat under-explored despite some recent approaches in this direction (Engesser & Wimmer, 2009, p. 44).

Downey and Fenton (2003, p. 200) attribute digitisation with great potential to foster the emergence of counter public spheres. From this perspective, ICT potentially destabilises the public sphere and simultaneously generates fragmentation and solidarity. Digitisation potentially enables fringe actors to have their say in a way that is ascertainable for large audiences. Those that appear to be excluded from the traditional networks of political communication can make themselves heard through new communicative means:

> "It is clear that the internet permits radical groups from both Left and Right (…) to construct inexpensive virtual counter-public spheres to accompany their other forms of organization and protest. The opinions of these groups have traditionally been excluded or marginalized in the mass-media public sphere. The internet offers them a way not only of communicating with supporters, but also the potential to reach out beyond the 'radical ghetto' both directly (disintermediation) and indirectly, through influencing the mass media" (Downey & Fenton, 2003, p. 198).

The emergence of counter public spheres (online) is again closely connected to fringe political actors – often also new social movements – and alternative online media, subversive projects aiming at the undermining of mainstream communication (Wimmer, 2007, p. 193). Digitisation potentially enables fringe political actors to engage in low-cost networking and coalition forming. In principle, it also allows them to articulate positions and to distribute information to their audiences. On the media side, counter public spheres can be understood as spaces in which alternative schemes of interpretation and discourses are prevalent, in which marginal topics can become issues of debate (Engesser & Wimmer, 2009, p. 49).

Empirical findings indicate an antagonistic relation between quality and scope of a counter public sphere. One can assume a decline in scope whenever the quality of a counter public sphere, the amount to which a means of communication constitutes an alternative space of communication, rises. Digitisation does foster the emergence of counter public spheres, yet at the same time it also leads to further stratification; what emerges is not a counter public sphere but a multitude of counter public spheres (Engesser & Wimmer, 2009, pp. 58-59).

So far, the connections and exchanges between the traditional public sphere and emergent (online) counter public spheres have been described as under-explored (Wimmer, 2007, pp. 215-222). However, notwithstanding their theoretical potentials, counter public spheres are often considered a peril for societal cohesion. When fringe actors (solely or at least predominantly) communicate in alternative channels – thereby absenting themselves from the general public sphere they originally strived to gain recognition in – they still remain excluded from public communication. They are enabled to communicate, but their communicative space is segregated from the centre of society, constituting a fringe sphere itself. Alternative media channels there are only of small outreach, leading to a state in which communications by fringe actors inhabiting counter public spheres do not reach significant audiences anymore (Engesser & Wimmer, 2009, pp. 59-60; Wimmer, 2007, p. 228). In principle, discourses from counter public spheres have the potential to spill over into the general public sphere, yet it is not sure that they actually do so (Emmer & Bräuer, 2010, pp. 322-323; see also: Mathes & Pfetsch, 1991).

The emergence of counter public spheres has become a salient topic in the debate on the process digitisation and its implications. Applying the model of potential outcomes, these phenomena could be subsumed both under the category of structural changes or of societal disintegration. The degree to which discourses in these spheres succeed in influencing the mainstream debate determines the categorisation.

2.1.3 Summary: Implications of Digitisation

The process of digitisation and its implications for the fields of politics and political communication have been subject to controversial debate almost ever since the proliferation of digital means of communication began. Positions are often described as polarised, sometimes even as overly polarised.

The systematisations discussed here all seek to approach the spectrum of positions that characterises this debate. All agree on a basic contraposition of cyber-optimistic and non-cyber-optimistic positions. The former emphasise the potentials digitisation offers for democracy, the latter tend to be more critical in this regard, either negating any substantial effects of digitisation or referring to potential perils. However, as comparison shows, the systematisations discussed are not necessarily unanimous with regard to the actual spectrum of positions described or to the differentiations made between them.

Ward and Gibson (2009) differentiate between three scenarios (structural changes, equalisation and normalisation) right from the beginning, while other systematisations start with a contraposition of optimistic and rather pessimistic accounts. Papacharissi (2009) and Raupp (2011) then both put special emphasis on additional subdivisions within these groups, differentiating between further cyber-optimistic and non-cyber-optimistic positions.

In sum, it is possible to identify four scenarios in the debate on digitisation and its implications. A decisively cyber-optimistic one discusses digitisation with regard to structural changes to politics and political communication. Established patterns of representation are replaced, forms of e-deliberation introduced. A second cyber-optimistic scenario argues in terms of equalisation and inclusion. Established structures are not replaced but become more inclusive, leading to greater equality between actors in these fields. As a non-cyber-optimistic scenario, the normalisation thesis negates any larger effects of digitisation. Despite technological change, established patterns of communication and power are said to remain largely unaltered here. A fourth scenario then argues in terms of possible distortions emerging under the conditions of digitisation. The process is discussed as potentially endangering societal cohesion and political legitimacy.

The emergence of counter public spheres – often described as a salient phenomenon under the conditions of digitisation – can be framed both in terms of structural alterations as well as in terms of emerging distortions. This process does not constitute a scenario in itself but rather a phenomenon that can be subsumed under one of the categories described here.

Critical analysis of accounts on digitisation then indicates that cyber-optimism is, as pointed out in various systematisations, indeed a phenomenon that is prevalent in early accounts from a practitioner's perspective. This applies both to the actual postulation of structural alterations on a large scale and to forms of strong optimism regarding equalisation and inclusion. Especially in science, there is now an observable trend towards more sceptical accounts; empirical analyses lead to critical reflections on the actual potential of ICT to either replace or alter established patterns (cf. Chadwick, 2009, pp. 11-12; Ferguson & Griffiths, 2006, p. 373; Francoli & Ward, 2008, p. 25). Sometimes the polarisation of the debate has been criticised for setting an overly high threshold for actual alterations, thereby inducing rather negative findings (Wright, 2012, pp. 250-253). However, this does not alter the overall observation of a trend towards accounts that are – with strong empirical support – more sceptical with regard to the actual potentials of digitisation.

2.2 Political Media Relations in the Digital Age

Digitisation has been discussed as a process potentially affecting both politics and political communication. Political media relations as a specific sub-field of political communication make no exception here. One could expect that the relations and interactions between communicators from politics and the media would be would be affected by the proliferation of new digital means of communication.

As indicated, digitisation is also one of the trending topics in political science and communication studies. Therefore there is a great and ever increasing variety of empirical studies concerning politics and political communication and the degree to which they are affected by digitisation.

The following state of research first briefly focuses on studies that enquire into the digitisation of political communication by analysing political online presences. Subsequently attention is drawn on selected empirical studies on political media relations, specifically those on elite actors and their networks in the field.

Political online presences

Analysing the state of research concerning the online activities of different types of political actors, one finds a relatively large body of research on the online presences of political parties and party politicians and the ways in which political communication professionals utilise these. This inter alia regards the employment of social media and micro-blogging by political parties (e.g. Elter, 2013; Kalnes, 2009) or the weblogs (e.g. Auty, 2005; Francoli & Ward, 2008) or online presences (e.g. Jackson & Lilleker, 2004; Ward & Lusoli, 2005) of individual

UK members of parliament. Recent approaches focus on the proliferation of *Facebook* among US congress candidates (e.g. Gulati & Williams, 2013) and New Zealand members of parliament (e.g. Ross et al., 2014).

Generally, the digitisation of election campaigning (the so-called e-campaigning) is to be considered a salient topic here. Empirical studies focus on e-campaigning in the US and Canada (e.g. Latimer, 2007; Small, 2008), in Germany (e.g. Schweitzer, 2008, 2011; Schweitzer, 2012; Zittel, 2009) or, with an additional focus on e-participation, on digitised campaign communication in the United Kingdom (e.g. Jackson, 2006; Jackson & Lilleker, 2009). Comparative empirical approaches then confront findings regarding e-campaigning in different national contexts such as Germany, France, the United Kingdom and the United States (e.g. Gibson et al., 2003; Zielmann & Röttger, 2009).

In general, these studies show that political parties and party politicians are fairly active in the online sphere. There are however findings for the United Kingdom that indicate the utilisation of online presences as so-called 'cyber safety valves', i.e. a pattern of usage in which a presence is occupied but not maintained (Jackson & Lilleker, 2009, p. 247). This pattern is not found in other national contexts; however shortcomings in questions of participatory options within party online presences are a common phenomenon. Despite this, political parties and party politicians show high levels of activity online, this holds especially true for those actors that enjoy an elevated standing in the political sphere (Gulati & Williams, 2013, p. 585). Often enough, patterns of offline communication are replicated within these online presences (Schweitzer, 2011, pp. 323-324).

The body of research concerning governmental communication online is comparatively smaller; the field as such is often considered an under-researched area of communication studies (Canél & Sanders, 2012, p. 85). There are however some empirical studies focusing on topics such as the online presences of state actors in Germany (e.g. Kocks et al., 2014) and on the employment of Web 2.0 applications by governmental bodies in Canada and the United States (e.g. Wigand, 2010). Research also focuses on the overall digitisation of governmental communication (e.g. Chen, Gibson, Lusoli, & Ward, 2007), also from a comparative perspective (e.g. Sanders, Canél, & Holtz-Bacha, 2011).

Other studies analyse the communicative exchange between governmental bodies and individual citizens online, mostly at a local level (e.g. Edwards, 2008; Kies, 2010). A larger body of research regards the digitisation of administrative and governmental functions, often subsumed under the notion of e-government (e.g. Chadwick & May, 2003; Sweeney, 2007; Wong & Welch, 2004).

In general, these studies indicate that governmental bodies are active in the online sphere, yet to a comparatively lesser degree than political parties and party politicians. They show distinct patterns of communication, often characterised by relatively low levels of interactivity. Governmental communication in Germany appears especially formalised (e.g. Kocks & Raupp, 2014a; Vogel, 2010), potentially due to a high degree of legal regulation (cf. Holtz-Bacha, 2013; Kocks & Raupp, 2014b; Schürmann, 1992). Yet in sum existing empirical research describes both forms of political online communication – by political parties, party politicians and governmental bodies – as fairly digitised with regards to maintained online presences and digital representation.

Communicative relations

Media relations and the potentially shifting distributions of power in them have been repeatedly approached empirically. Accordingly, a considerable number of studies and accounts now focus on shifting patterns of power between the two sides involved in this arrangement, on the question who actually leads the Tango-dance between them (e.g. Bennett et al., 2007; Reich, 2009; Strömbäck & Nord, 2006; Van Aelst & Vliegenthart, 2014).

In contrast to that, the particular context of media relations under the conditions of digitisation and the role of elite actors in them have so far not been subject to larger amounts of in depth empirical research. This especially holds true for approaches of social network analysis in this field (cf. Raupp, 2011, p. 82).

The following state of research therefore seeks to provide some comprehensive discussion of selected empirical studies on elite actors and their networks in the field of political media relations under the conditions of digitisation. It seeks to do so with regard to national contexts similar to the German one (i.e. countries that inter alia have representative democratic political systems, freedom of press and functioning media systems) or to Germany itself. Relevant subjects of study might be politicians, political spokespersons and political journalists; special attention is drawn to those approaches that make empirical recourse to social network analysis.

Accounts on digitised political communication that are fundamentally different from the research conducted here regarding inter alia their methodological approach (e.g. Bennett, 1990; Lewis, Williams, & Franklin, 2008), their subjects of study (e.g. Emmer, Vowe, & Wolling, 2011) or their theoretical framework and overall research interest (e.g. Dohle & Bernhard, 2013; Dohle, Blank, & Vowe, 2012; Håkansson & Mayerhöffer, 2010; Lesmeister, 2008) are set aside. The same goes for studies conducted so early that they do not deal with very current developments of media change (e.g. B. Pfetsch, 2003; Rinke, Schlachter, & Agel, 2006).

Due to the contemporary nature of the phenomenon, the accounts discussed all derive from recent years; new publications have been taken into account up to November 2014.[22]

Recent studies on political media relations have approached the phenomenon with regard to a variety of national contexts and focusing on different sets of actors. While some studies approach political media relations concentrating on the interaction of politicians and political journalists (e.g. A. Davis, 2009; A. Davis, 2010a; Ross, 2010; Schwab Cammarano, 2013; Schwab Cammarano et al., 2010; van Aelst, Sehata, & van Dalen, 2010), others integrate political spokespersons into their focus (e.g. Burgert, 2009; Heinze, 2012; B. Pfetsch & Mayerhöffer, 2011; Wenzler, 2008). A recent approach based on social network analysis concentrates on the networks surrounding elite journalists in Germany (Krüger, 2013).

A central field of interest for most of these studies is the actual relations between the actors involved; they often concentrate on questions of closeness and distance in this regard. Burgert (2009) for example analyses political communication cultures in France and Germany, focusing on political journalists and governmental spokespersons. Findings indicate differences between the communication cultures in Germany and France in so far as the relation between journalists and political spokespersons is significantly closer in France. Professional and social interactions are clearly characterised by this. Closeness is also deemed a necessity for the gathering of information in France; journalists often lament unequal distributions of this depending on the quality of the relationships between them and the political spokespersons in question (Burgert, 2009, pp. 253, 296, 301).

But close contacts are not only valuable for media professionals seeking to gain information for political coverage, spokespersons heavily rely on these as well. Especially when German speakers seek to widely distribute important messages, they often make recourse to elevated media outlets in their personal network; contacting them and then relying on effects of inter-media agenda-setting is considered a highly effective strategy (Burgert, 2009, p. 340).

---

22 Communication options such as social networks (e.g. Facebook), video hosting sites (e.g. YouTube) and microblogging services (e.g. Twitter) are often attributed with potentials to fundamentally alter patterns and structures of political communication and political media relations. They are now considered central elements of digitisation. It is therefore important to focus on those studies analysing (networks within) the respective field that have been conducted after the establishment of such options. The line is drawn here in the year 2007, i.e. three months after Facebook was made available to the general public and in the very year in which Twitter (founded in 2006) faced the first significant increase in usage.

Krüger's (2013) analysis of leading political journalists, their communication networks and the ways in which their embeddedness into certain circles and networks potentially reflects in their coverage largely confirms this picture of political media relations. Findings indicate a multitude of connections between leading journalists and elites from the fields of politics and the economy; mutual membership in various organisational bodies, clubs and circles is common. Apart from encounters as part of their everyday work routine, over a third of these media professionals are in direct contact with political and economic elites through background circles, foundations, think tanks, policy discussion groups or non-public conferences.[23] This applies especially for the fields of foreign and security politics, where the study finds direct connection between leading journalists from major national newspapers and structures connected to the United States, the German government and NATO. Journalists connect to leading elites, thereby gaining valuable contacts for their coverage but also becoming involved in the formation of policies and actual political measures (Krüger, 2013, pp. 149-150, 256-257).

Other studies provide further differentiation on issues of closeness in media relations. A study by Davis (2009) on British MPs (both from the House of Commons and the House of Lords) and on political journalists from national newspapers as well as from national broadcast, wire service and online journalism indicates differences in the contact networks of front and backbench MPs. While the former connect with national political and policy specialist reporters and additionally also with local journalists, the latter only have established contact with local media personnel, political backbenchers are generally unable to connect with higher ranking journalists. The willingness of political journalists to establish communicative links is accordingly far higher when it comes to government ministers than to backbench politicians; their observation of Opposition actors tends to be less critical. Political backbenchers can – according to Davis' findings – only overcome the media threshold by the exploitation of 'populist news values' (A. Davis, 2009, pp. 208-210).

A second study by Davis (2010a) confirms these findings indicating the emergence of relatively close networks of communicative exchange between British politicians and political journalists. It complements data from the preceding study with 20 additional interviews with government officials. Here, findings suggest two contrasting trends: On the one hand, links between those in the very centre of the political system and those that find themselves surrounding it rela-

23 Recently, Krüger's empirical approach has been subject to criticism for equating this form of closeness between journalists and political elites with an actual influencing of journalists by elite actors (cf. Neuberger, 2014).

tively closely are indeed increasing. On the other hand there is also an increasing distance between the mass of citizens and the political centre (A. Davis, 2010a, pp. 756-757).

Findings show an advanced state of digitisation in the field of political communication in the UK. A large majority of interviewees makes use of ICTs both to gather information and to publish it. Journalists gain more space for their coverage and bloggers are able to cover topics of their own interest. Especially backbench MPs emphasise the usefulness of digital media in their struggle to keep up with their colleagues of a more elevated standing, even though both groups generally make comparable use of new means (A. Davis, 2010a, pp. 750-752). There is more political information available, traditional channels and their exclusive potentials can be bypassed. The very core of the political system is expanding. Even so, and this clearly emerges from the interviews, the evolving networks are of a rather exclusive nature. Online discourse networks are made up of elite actors, audiences for new media channels largely derive from privileged and politically oriented backgrounds. A decline in political coverage by traditional media outlets and a trend towards fragmentation online, further intensified by digital divides, drive the periphery away from the core of the political system (A. Davis, 2010a, pp. 754-755). The distance between the political centre and the ranks of inactive or excluded actors is growing.

A study by van Aelst, Sehata and Dalen (2010) also yields similar results. Findings resulting from a survey among members of parliament and political journalists in five European countries – subsumed under Hallin and Mancini's (2008) democratic corporatist model – indicate that regardless of the national context an elevated status of political actors markedly affects their contacts with professional journalists. Their position toward the media is directly influenced by their overall political standing (van Aelst, Sehata, & Dalen, 2010, p. 321); institutionalised political power enables them to overcome media thresholds. It is emphasised that, at least in the short run, journalistic attention is to be understood as 'a consequence rather than a cause of political power', though journalistic attention might also have long term influences on the position of political actors (van Aelst, Sehata, & Dalen, 2010, p. 322). Political actors compete for journalistic attention, especially in countries with large political fields. Existing elite status is deemed a valuable resource in this competition since circles of communication tend to be quite exclusive.

Schwab Cammarano's (2013) findings for Switzerland then show an ambivalence regarding the intertwining of political journalists and politicians: She first identifies four types (i.e. clusters) of role behaviour. These are either characterised by formal distancing, antagonism, high contact frequencies or collegiality; 61% of the journalists belong to the rather distanced first two categories, politicians fit in there by 56% (Schwab Cammarano, 2013, p. 159). Further analysis shows distinct differences between these groups according to individual status. MPs with elevated status and the highest ranking journalists both show significantly higher rates of contacts than others, yet both also describe relations as more conflict-laden than their counterparts with lower status do. Politicians prefer to interact with print journalists (as opposed to those who work for electronic media) and print journalists are more often directly connected to politicians. Yet again, the relations between them are described as being characterised by (regular) conflicts.

A further factor according to Schwab Cammarano's findings is the position of politicians in the political spectrum; the highest contact rates are to be found among right wing politicians, the lowest among those that belong to the centre of the spectrum. Last but not least findings indicate an effect of gender: male politicians and male journalists have more contacts and higher contact rates than their female counterparts (Schwab Cammarano, 2013, pp. 180-181).

In terms of closeness and distance between politics and the media, Wenzler (2008) differentiates between different policy fields. Findings for Switzerland indicate two partially different cultures of interaction; the field of energy politics is characterised by a comparatively more stable and dense type of communication network between the various groups of actors. Informal interactions are regarded as the medium of choice here; personal meetings still exceed other forms of communicative interaction in their importance. The less stable and dense system in the field of cultural politics is characterised on the other hand by a prevalence of formal structures of interaction; informal contacting is only of minor importance there (Wenzler, 2008, pp. 172-173).

Conflicts between actors occur, but when it comes to journalists and PR professionals it is predominantly between those that find themselves in different groups (i.e. between journalists and spokespersons but not between spokespersons and also not between journalists) (Wenzler, 2008, pp. 239-241). Policy networks are regarded as the medium of choice for advocating political positions and the pursuit of specific interests. It is by networking with other powerful players in a specific field that actors gain the ability to deal with existing constraints, political communication is characterised by the mutual pursuit of individual interests. Again, the difference between energy- and cultural politics emerges; the higher professionalisation ascertainable in the former field leads to (perceptions of) a higher importance of professional networking and more stable flows of communication (Wenzler, 2008, pp. 253-255).

Analysis of existing studies on political media relations indicates a further difference in terms of distance and closeness according to national communication cultures. While some of these, such as for example the French one, generally yield a very close interaction between politics and the media, others, like Germany, show a greater amount of (professional) distance between the fields (cf. Burgert, 2009; Maurer, 2011). Communication cultures in Switzerland and to some extent also in New Zealand seem to be characterised by a comparatively even higher degree of distance between the sets of actors; networks of political media relations appear less dense (cf. Ross, 2010; Schwab Cammarano, 2013; Schwab Cammarano et al., 2010; Wenzler, 2008).

The communicative exchange underlying these relations between politics and the media takes place both in formal and in informal ways; studies suggest that both are important, again with divergences due to different national communication cultures (Burgert, 2009, pp. 305, 330-332). As indicated, this exchange is generally perceived as bringing mutual benefits. While politicians tend to profit in terms of the promotion of themselves and their policies, journalists gain valuable information for their coverage and prestigious contacts that elevate their status within the media field. Journalism is far more than merely fulfilling publicity functions for political actors, reporters are, as results for the United Kingdom suggest, often regarded as sources of information. This change of roles generally tends to elevate their status within the field of political communication and subsequently also their influence on political processes (A. Davis, 2009, pp. 208, 215).

In the case of Germany, perceptions of such relations are somewhat inconsistent. While a larger fraction of politicians describes them as harmonious, a large majority of journalists disagrees with this perspective. Over a fifth of them even goes so far as to describe them as conflictual. Political spokespersons on the other hand appear to have very good relations with the media or at least they perceive them as such. Two thirds of this group describe media relations as purely harmonious, thereby even exceeding the perceptions expressed by politicians (B. Pfetsch & Mayerhöffer, 2011, p. 54).

The media is still regarded as an important arena of political communication here. Pfetsch and Mayerhöffer (2011, pp. 49-50) point out that elites from the field of political communication (regardless of their specific background) widely agree in their perception of a declining importance of the parliament as the main arena for political discourse. Instead the mass media has – according to these perceptions – become the central arena. Employing mass media outlets is widely regarded as the most effective strategy for gaining public attention for policies. There is however disagreement between politicians and political journalists regarding the most effective media channels in this regard.

From this perspective political communication in Germany is becoming increasingly dominated by media logic. Relations between the political and the journalistic field appear to be harmonious at first sight, yet differences and disagreements are clearly ascertainable. This casts doubt on popular conceptions of solid and stable relations between them. Political spokespersons have emerged as a third important group in the field of political communication, a group whose members show distinct differences from politicians but have so far not been subjected to greater amounts of in depth research (B. Pfetsch & Mayerhöffer, 2011, p. 57).

Maurer's (2011) findings, which draw on the same project background as those of Pfetsch and Mayerhöffer – though taking additional political communication cultures into consideration – confirm this picture. Findings indicate that both politicians and political journalists perceive a high media influence on political careers. In three national contexts (with the exception of Spain) this influence is regarded as being even stronger than the one on political agendas. Positive media coverage is generally perceived as a decisive factor for the acquisition or preservation of elite status in the political field. Yet there are differences between the countries. While France scores very high means (ranging around four on a five point scale), Germany shows comparatively lower values, ranging around three on a five point scale, thereby constituting the lowest values in this comparison (Maurer, 2011, p. 38). Political elites perceive the media as an important factor for their work and try to adjust their (public) activities to the needs of this group. Furthermore they seek to establish stable cooperation with them, especially with those journalists that are in leading positions (Maurer, 2011, p. 44).

Civic actors on the other hand do, as Heinze (2012) points out, perceive large distances between them and the core of the political system, the (perceived) political efficacy is rather low. Direct elite-to-citizen communication (i.e. the bypassing of traditional media outlets) is in this context not seen as a bridging of existing gaps but as an attempt to 'sell' political messages. Compared with news from a journalistic background, these messages are met with far higher levels of scepticism and distrust (Heinze, 2012, pp. 201-202). The rather positive perceptions elite communicators have of their communication (especially with regard to dimensions such as the enabling of dialogue and general openness and accountability) is not in accordance with the perceptions of their addressees. The latter see significant shortcomings in these regards (Heinze, 2012, p. 206).

Findings indicate that those communications that directly address citizens (i.e. those that bypass established media outlets) are common among resource rich actors such as large federal ministries that devote substantial funding to their communicative activities. Smaller actors on the other hand still opt for traditional channels. Another factor explaining the usage of new means of direct communication is to be seen in the perceptions spokespersons have of processes of mediatisation and media change. The more importance they attach to these, the more often they (complementary) try to bypass established media outlets. A perceived increase in media power and changing media environments are met with new strategies of direct communication aiming at citizens (Heinze, 2012, p. 165).

Apart from questions of distance, closeness and interaction, empirical research also focuses on other aspects of political media relations. This inter alia regards the professional roles of the individual actors involved and furthermore also their perceptions of these roles.

Burgert (2009, pp. 333-335) finds that in contrast to their French counterparts German journalists often perceive themselves as active entities within the political process. They strive to co-create outcomes they regard as desirable by influencing the course of politics. At the same time, spokespersons in Germany also perceive their role as much more active in comparison to their colleagues in France; they actively seek to represent their organisations in the public.
Schwab Cammarano's data then suggests that communicative exchange between journalists and their counterparts in political organisations has developed away from regular mutual exchange to a clear division of roles. Politicians and political spokespersons are those that account for the provision of information, journalists on the other hand are those that demand it for their coverage. Survey data shows that the role of journalists as the providers of political information is only of marginal importance (Schwab Cammarano et al., 2010, pp. 38-39).[24]

Heinze approaches questions surrounding the changing of one's professional role. It turns out that professional experience in the journalistic field does not affect the strategic portfolio of political spokespersons, i.e. there is no difference between the strategies of ex-journalists and of those spokespersons that have not worked on the other side (Heinze, 2012, p. 158).

In sum, what emerges from the discussion of the various empirical approaches here is firstly the finding of an increasing importance of elite-elite interaction. As the studies by Davis (2009, 2010a) clearly show, leading British politicians overwhelmingly opt for mutual exchange with leading journalists. Parliamentary backbenchers are often excluded from their communication networks and find it hard to overcome the media threshold. The findings by Heinze (2012) support this assumption with regard to the situation in Germany; outsiders clearly express perceptions of closed elite networks. Maurer's (2011) and Krüger's (2013) studies also confirm a tendency of elite actors to stick together closely in regard of political communication. The findings for Switzerland show a differentiated picture in which the closeness of elite-elite interaction differs between political

---

24 This stands in contrast to Davis' (2009, pp. 208, 215) findings for the United Kingdom, where the mutual exchange of information – one that involves journalists as actual providers – is to be considered a clear trend in journalist-source relations.

fields (Wenzler, 2008), in New Zealand it generally seems to be slightly lower (Ross, 2010).

Secondly, the interaction between journalists and political communicators (i.e. politicians or political spokespersons) can generally be understood as one that brings (informational) profits for both sides. Burgert (2009) names the value of central media outlets for political communicators as one key factor. According to this line of argument inter-media agenda-setting is to be regarded as a central component of the communication strategies of political elites. According to her findings German journalists on the other hand are often inclined to actively exercise influence in the political process, they therefore seek interaction with political actors of elevated status. Davis (2009) confirms these findings for the United Kingdom; communicative exchange is perceived as bringing benefits for both sides. Journalists are able to elevate their status through the prestige of their contacts and can gain valuable information; politicians gain the ability to promote themselves and their positions. Furthermore journalists often function as valuable sources of information for actors from within the political system. Maurer (2011) largely confirms this picture, pointing out that especially actors from the political field tend to profit from their (good) relations with media professionals.

Findings that journalists function not only as demanders but also as sources of information differ between countries. While Davis' (2009) findings clearly identify this as a salient phenomenon in the United Kingdom, empirical analyses of the situation in Switzerland indicate a continuously clear division of roles there (Schwab Cammarano et al., 2010).

The third field of interest is the usage and employment of digital means of communication. Davis' (2010a) findings indicate that especially those political actors that do not have the most elevated status (i.e. backbenchers) tend to see ICTs as a means of overcoming media thresholds and communicating their messages directly to the electorate. Yet in sum, elite actors do make comparable use of new means. Heinze's (2012) findings indicate that especially those actors that are already rich in resources invest in direct communicative exchange with the electorate, mostly through digital means. Bypassing media outlets as instances of selection (i.e. as gatekeepers) is a strategy employed by central political actors in this perspective. ICTs are far from being only a medium of choice for those that are excluded from structures of 'classical' political communication.[25] However, it emerges from several studies (B. Pfetsch & Mayerhöffer, 2011; Schwab

[25] Findings concerning the advanced state of ICT-diffusion in this sphere are also supported by a variety of studies focusing specifically on the ICT-equipment of such actors. See inter alia: Auty, 2005; Ferguson & Griffiths, 2006; Jackson & Lilleker, 2004, 2009; Kalnes, 2009; Kocks, Raupp, & Schink, 2014.

Cammarano et al., 2010) that so far digitisation has not led to an erosion of the significance of 'classical' journalism for political communicators. Mass media outlets (in Switzerland especially those from the print sector) are still of elevated importance in this regard.

Apart from these three groups of findings, there are also solitary findings that deserve attention: On the one hand this regards the strategy of bypassing media outlets. It is not only described as a strategy of political communicators but also analysed from the perspective of its addresses (i.e. the electorate). Findings indicate that messages distributed through such channels are quite common – that the phenomenon as such is salient – and yet it is widely met with scepticism. Rather than being regarded as an additional informational option, they are often perceived as attempts to sell political messages (Heinze, 2012).

In addition it considers the relationship between network-building and professionalisation / professional standards. From the perspective of the actors in question findings indicate that there is hardly any contradiction between professionalism and networking. In some cases higher levels of professionalisation even lead to comparatively higher network densities (Wenzler, 2008). Journalists prefer to interact with high ranking political counterparts, yet their coverage tends (at least in the United Kingdom) to be more favourable towards opposition politicians (A. Davis, 2009).

Last but not least, some studies refer to the growing importance of professional spokespersons in the field of political communication. Professional communicators increasingly dominate communicative exchanges with political journalists; they shape patterns of political communication (Schwab Cammarano et al., 2010).[26] However, the role of professional spokespersons in political communication has not been analysed to an extent comparable to the analyses regarding political journalists and politicians and their roles in this field (B. Pfetsch & Mayerhöffer, 2011).

2.3 Summary and Interim Conclusion

It has been postulated that in a classic understanding, political media relations could be considered a form of communicative interaction between relatively few professionals of elevated standing. As a brief analysis of relevant literature concerning media source relations in political communication illustrates, the arrangement generally tends to be fairly exclusive here; high ranking journalists

26 In this context see also Lesmeister's (2008) reflections on the importance of political spin-doctoring.

communicate with their counterparts from central political organisations and vice versa.

Several studies indicate that these relations can at times be conflictual and many authors describe them as characterised by a constant competition for leadership; the actors involved take part in a sort of 'danse macabre' (Ross, 2010) in which patterns of power often shift and in which it is not always clear who is actually leading and who is lead (cf. Bennett et al., 2007; Reich, 2009; Strömbäck & Nord, 2006; Van Aelst & Vliegenthart, 2014). Nevertheless, the classic understanding remains the same: political media relations are an exclusive arrangement and their exclusiveness is generally beneficial to both sides involved.

Digitisation, the proliferation of new means of communication is then considered a potential process of change. As a review of relevant literature shows, it can indeed be regarded as a very salient topic. The proliferation of digital means, especially in the fields of politics and political communication, is regarded as a highly relevant issue, from a societal, political and scientific point of view.

The implications of digitisation have been subject to debate ever since the proliferation of such means began. Potential effects and their actual strength (i.e. the degree to which they might affect patterns of politics and political communication) have been debated in a controversial way. Arguably, the debate has sometimes even shown an overly high degree of polarisation.

Closer inspection brings forward four basic scenarios connected to the proliferation of digital means of communication. These either argue from a cyber-optimistic or a non-cyber-optimistic point of view. A very cyber-optimistic one discusses digitisation focusing on structural changes to politics and political communication. From this perspective digitisation leads to the replacement of established patterns of representation and forms of e-deliberation are introduced. Another cyber-optimistic scenario mainly argues in terms of equalisation and inclusion. Here established structures are not replaced but become more inclusive, inducing greater equality between actors. The non-cyber-optimistic normalisation thesis negates larger effects of digitisation. Established modes of communication and patterns of power are said to remain largely unaltered here, despite all forms of technological change. A fourth scenario then argues in terms of possible distortions. From this perspective, the process of digitisation is discussed as potentially endangering societal cohesion and political legitimacy.

Observation of the debate over time indicates a trend towards more cautious or even sceptical accounts. Pure forms of cyber-optimism are a domain of practitioners from the field of communication and especially ascertainable in their early accounts. Scientific accounts generally tend to discuss potential benefits of digitisation more carefully. This is especially the case with more recent accounts on the phenomenon and its potential implications.

Political media relations as a particular sub-field of political communication are also affected by the proliferation of digital means. Yet at the same time, political media relations online still remain a comparatively under-researched area; this holds especially true for enquiries into the interaction between political public relations and journalism under the conditions of digitisation.

As a review of empirical research shows, most political parties and party politicians show high levels of activity online, this holds especially true for those actors that enjoy an elevated standing in the political sphere. Yet at the same time, their online presences often replicate patterns of offline communication. Governmental bodies also appear to be quite active in the online sphere, yet to a comparatively lesser degree than political parties and party politicians. They often show distinct patterns of communication, mostly characterised by relatively low levels of interactivity and communicative reciprocity.

As a further review of relevant empirical studies shows, political media relations online (still) appear to be largely characterised by the interaction of leading actors from the fields of politics and the media, i.e. by a form of elite interaction. This interaction is generally regarded as mutually beneficial to both sides. Close networking is generally not considered a violation of professional standards by the actors in question but rather regarded as a necessity. In some cases higher levels of professionalisation even lead to comparatively higher network densities. Generally, journalists prefer to interact with high ranking political counterparts.

Journalism itself has a somewhat ambivalent role. Some studies indicate that journalists no longer act exclusively as demanders of information but also serve as valuable sources for their counterparts from the political field. Yet this finding is not unanimously confirmed.

The proliferation of ICT appears advanced among those actors that constitute the field of political media relations in the various national contexts analysed. All actors tend to be active in the online sphere, even those of high standing sometimes utilise digital means to bypass established media outlets in their gatekeeping function. However, despite the generally high impact of digital means, established networks are still considered important by the actors in question. Digitisation has so far not led to an erosion of the significance of 'classical' journalism for political communicators, mass media outlets are still highly important.

In general, the findings concerning political media relations in the digital age emerging from these studies are very much in accordance with the overall course of the debate concerning the implications of digitisation. Technological change clearly affects this field of communication, but established patterns and structures have not altered markedly so far. The postulations of (radical) cyber-optimism do not hold true in this field, studies generally find only minor alterations to the spectrum of active actors. Political media relations still remain dominated by established actors of high standing – at least according to the analysed empirical studies,

They are not an analogue phenomenon; digital means have seen proliferation and actually impacted patterns of communication. However, according to the studies analysed, this does not seem to largely impact the spectrum of actors.

Since the field is in constant motion and arguably still under-researched, especially with regard to the interaction between political spokespersons and political journalists, there is still a need for further research. The actual diffusion of ICT in political media relations in Germany has to be analysed as well as the constellations of actors and their actual interactions in this field. It still has to be clarified whether political media relations in Germany in the online age can (still) be considered an elite phenomenon. Furthermore, the ways in which those actors that have so far shaped the field of political media relations actually perceive the process of digitisation is largely unexplored as well. This constitutes a need for additional research on perceptions and actual adaptations of digitisation in the field of political media relations in Germany.

3 Political Media Relations as an Elite Phenomenon: Theoretical Considerations and Implications

Elites are often considered actors that largely influence the actual ways of society (cf. Lasswell et al., 1952). Accordingly, they and the communications surrounding them are of course considered a subject of political communication research. Studies focus inter alia on the representation of elite discourse in the media (e.g. Bennett, 1990; Krüger, 2013), on the connections between individual elite actors in the fields of politics and the press (e.g. Hoffmann, 2003; Krüger, 2013; Maurer, 2011; B. Pfetsch & Mayerhöffer, 2011) or on the privileged access of corporate elites to the political centre (e.g. A. Davis, 2002).

Yet despite a multitude of approaches focusing on elite actors in political communication, actual elite theory has so far been largely neglected by political communication research (Savage & Williams, 2008, pp. 1-3). However, given the persistent influence of these actors in mediatised politics, they and the communications surrounding them could be considered important starting points for political communication research; sociological elite theory would then have to be understood as a potentially fruitful paradigm in this discipline (A. Davis, 2003, pp. 669-670, 672).

Sociological elite theory approaches a large variety of questions concerning elites, their compositions, their societal standing and functions and their actual interests and strategies (cf. Wasner, 2004, pp. 23-25). Analysing political media relations in the online sphere regarding their potential nature as an elite phenomenon, questions concerning elites and their ideologies and interests and then also their operating principles and strategies are of elevated importance. Sociological elite theory has the potential to ground and substantiate analyses here.

Yet sociological elite theory is not to be considered a middle range theory that directly generates hypotheses that can be empirically investigated. In their original conceptualisation, approaches towards sociological elite theory aim more at the description and explanation of societal phenomena on a larger scale (Daloz, 2007, pp. 27-34). Accordingly, sociological elite theory as a theoretical foundation is to be understood as a theoretical heuristic, as a perspective from which an explanandum is to be considered (cf. Abbott, 2004, pp. xi, 80-81, 250). Here, the purpose of this theoretical background is the provision of a perspective from which political media relations under the conditions of digitisation are to be considered.

Sociological elite theory is not to be understood as one unitary grand theory. As a matter of fact, there is a variety of distinct approaches, ranging from classical ones over a functional school of thought to those approaches that are generally subsumed under a notion of critical elite theory.[27] These share a large set of common assumptions but are also distinct in certain theoretical aspects.

The following sub-chapters argue on the elite status of those actors that shape the field of political media relations online and then discuss classical, functional and critical approaches towards sociological elite theory. They do so with regard to some central questions of elite sociology focusing on elite interests and their actual communicative strategies (cf. Wasner, 2004, pp. 23-25). Central lines of argument are then employed as a heuristic analytical frame for subsequent analyses of actual adaptations of digitisation.

3.1 Political Media Relations and the Actors Defining Them

Political media relations can be conceptualised as the communicative relations between politics and the media. Accordingly, the set of organisational actors present in this field consists of political organisations (e.g. governmental bodies, political parties) and media outlets (e.g. newspapers, broadcasters and some forms of online media). The field of political media relations has no natural boundaries, it needs to be delimitated based on theoretically guided decisions.

As the term 'political media relations' implies, the neighbouring fields of politics and the media are both involved here. Accordingly delimitating the field of political media relations requires defining relevant sets of actors from the fields of politics and the media. Politics, in a wide understanding, generally relate to the influencing of actions and policies and to the achievement or preservation of positions of power. From this perspective, a large variety of organisational actors could be considered 'political' in principle. A more narrow understanding would then limit this to actors that are primarily occupied with daily politics, i.e. to political intermediaries, political parties and governmental bodies. A further narrowing might even exclude (some) intermediaries and focus on political parties and governmental bodies alone. In any given understanding, these organisa-

27 This widely accepted classification of approaches towards sociological elite theory follows a systematisation originally employed by Hartmann (2007; see also: F. R. Pfetsch, 2012). Other systematisations utilise a stronger geographical focus (e.g. Wasner, 2004), yet Hartmann's systematisation succeeds in highlighting not only historical developments but also the lines of argument distinguishing the various approaches.

tions would have to be considered focal political inhabitants of the field of political media relations (cf. Raupp, 2010, pp. 211, 217).

Delimitating the set of actors in the field of the media poses a similar problem. Understandings of the notion of 'media' differ strongly between relatively wide ones and those that employ a comparatively narrower perspective. This problem has become increasingly salient with the advent of new forms of online media under the conditions of digitisation. Yet even relatively narrow understandings of the notion of 'media' generally include newspapers, broadcasters and established online media platforms (such as for example the online variants of established newspapers). Again focusing on actors that could be considered focal inhabitants of the field of political media relations, attention would primarily draw on national newspapers and political magazines, leading broadcasters (both public service and private) and leading online media outlets.

Employing an organisational perspective and a narrow understanding of political media relations, one would accordingly have to consider political parties and governmental bodies on the one hand and national newspapers, political magazines, leading broadcasters and leading online media outlets on the other as organisational inhabitants of the field of political media relations.

Yet below this organisational level, there are identifiable individual inhabitants of the field. Most often, they belong to focal organisational inhabitants. On the media side, this generally regards leading political journalists working for leading media outlets. They provide political coverage and are therefore, as indicated here beforehand, to be considered important partners of communicative exchange for their counterparts from the political field. On the political side, existing empirical studies have often concentrated on actual politicians as individual actors (e.g. A. Davis, 2009; Schwab Cammarano, 2013; Schwab Cammarano et al., 2010; van Aelst, Sehata, & van Dalen, 2010). Yet to an increasing degree, professional political communicators have now become a group of interest for analyses of political media relations (e.g. B. Pfetsch & Mayerhöffer, 2011; Wenzler, 2008), with some studies even focusing primarily on them as the main representatives of political actors in this field (e.g. Burgert, 2009; Heinze, 2012). Political communication becomes increasingly professionalised and functionally differentiated (cf. Holtz-Bacha, 2007); processes of mediatisation strengthen the role of political spokespersons, further accentuating their importance for the field (cf. Kamps, 2007, pp. 117-127; see also: Raupp, 2009). Notwithstanding their elevated importance – arguably even their decisive role for political communication and politics – they remain a somewhat under-researched group of actors in the field of political communication and of political media relations in particular (Raupp, 2010, p. 210).

Focusing on political journalists and political spokespersons, it remains to argue on their potential elite status. While some classical approaches towards the identification of elites would be critical in identifying such actors as elites, this does not hold true for positional approaches (cf. K. U. Mayer, 2006; Mosse, 1987). In a positional understanding, elite becomes a category under which those elements are subsumed that occupy positions of elevated status within relevant entities (Paris, 2003, p. 60); it is, according to Maurer and Vähämaa (2014, p. 59) "based on the premise that influence in any societal domain is bound to formal leadership positions within organizations." From such a perspective, leading political journalists are often labelled elite actors in the field of political communication and political media relations (cf. Blumler, 1998, p. 94; B. Pfetsch & Mayerhöffer, 2011), the same also holds true for those spokespersons and communication managers that account for the (external) communication of focal political organisations (Håkansson & Mayerhöffer, 2014, pp. 130-131). The decisive category here is the field of political communication as one inhabited by identifiable focal organisations; accordingly individuals holding leading positions within these organisations are to be considered positional elites inhabiting the field of political media relations.

3.2 Theoretical Considerations

Elite theory as a theoretical concept within the discipline of sociology can be traced back to the 19th century. Its origins lie at the beginning of the industrial age and of industrialised mass society.

It was a time in which Western societies faced strong political and social changes. With mass migration into the developing industrialised cities, a new type of society began to emerge, the mass society of the industrial age. Intellectuals and scholars were highly sceptical of these developments.[28] Various critical accounts of the characteristics of masses (which, from this point of view, were regarded as primitive, characterised by irrationality and high levels of impressionability, and given to affects rather than to critical reflections) were brought forward at this time (e.g. Le Bon, 1960).

Parallel to these approaches concerning masses, others began to concentrate on the opposite societal group, i.e. the elite. Early sociological approaches towards elite theory are in fact directly related to those on masses. The two topics

28 An interesting account on such resentments against masses prevalent among intellectuals is to be found in Carey's (1992) work on elitist prejudices among the literary intelligentsia between 1880 and 1939.

represent two sides of the same coin, two notions within the same debate, one with extremely positive connotations and the other in a strictly pejorative understanding (Hartmann, 2004b, pp. 13-16). Elite theory in this era was determined by what has been described as a 'fin de siècle' sentiment (F. R. Pfetsch, 2012, p. 403), by an atmosphere of fierce scepticism regarding societal developments such as the emergence of masses in industrialised cities. These sentiments often lead to an idealisation of elites.

Accordingly, early accounts often show strong affirmative tendencies. Later accounts become more neutral, in some cases also more critical. They either focus on the societal functions of elites or criticise unequal distributions of power and societal distortions.

Classical approaches

Systematisations of sociological elite theory generally trace back its origins to the works of three theorists: Mosca, Pareto and Michels. Despite later criticism regarding some of their concepts and strong dissociations from some of their political ideas, traces of their works are to be found in virtually every approach towards sociological elite theory (Hartmann, 2004b, pp. 19-41; Nye, 1977; F. R. Pfetsch, 2012, pp. 403-449). Quite often, contemporary approaches are still regarded as directly related to these early theoretical conceptualisations (Rebenstorf, 2009, p. 22). Here, these early works are discussed under the notion of classical approaches.

The approach brought forward by Mosca at the end of the 19th century describes the contraposition of a governing class and one that is governed as a fundamental characteristic of all political entities. Regardless of its state of development, be it in an economical or a cultural sense, every society is, according to Mosca, in fact characterised by the existence and antagonistic positioning of these two classes. The governing one is smaller in numbers while at the same time monopolising political power and enjoying various privileges while the governed majority is subjected to direction and regulation (Mosca, 1953, p. 78).

Mosca distinguishes between two groups of people,[29] between a small governing class and their numerous counterparts. In this understanding, history is regarded as characterised by struggles between distinct minorities over political power. New aspiring minorities strive either to mingle with the established governing classes or to replace them. While the foundation of the governing class

[29] There is, and this has often been subject to criticism regarding Mosca's approach, no further subdivision of the two distinct groups, they are rather regarded as unitary actors (cf. F. R. Pfetsch, 2012, p. 408).

can, dependent on the respective historical era, lie in different fields such as material wealth, religion, art, science, military might or political skills, the degree of organisation of a group of people is always of prime importance. Organised groups inevitably dominate their unorganised counterparts (Mosca, 1953, pp. 82-83). At the same time, governing classes never admit to their power but rationalise or hide it behind certain formulas and dogmas, behind patterns of their external communication. In this understanding, the reference to concepts such as 'human rights', 'popular sovereignty' or 'liberty, equality and fraternity' is a mere masking of elite dominion. These concepts are to be understood as 'political formulas', as generally accepted feelings or beliefs that justify the existing power relations within a society or a state (Mosca, 1962, pp. 386-387).

The ascent of members of the governed class into the governing one is dependent on the ability of ascenders to adapt quickly and comprehensively to the characteristics of established elites. Exchange between these two classes is to freshen the governing minority and not to assimilate it to the majority (Mosca, 1962, pp. 391-393).

The understanding of elites and their societal role prevalent in Mosca's approach is sometimes labelled inherently anti-democratic. Nye (1977, p. 20) emphasises this with reference to Mosca's 'tacit endorsement of a manipulative conception of elite political authority' and his 'essentially pragmatic definition of the political utility of popular illusions'. Albertoni (1987, p. 52) however rejects this understanding of Mosca's approach, pointing out that:

> "Another concept which recurs in the *Elementi* is that of organized minority. In our opinion, it should not be interpreted as a diabolical contrivance, the conspiracy of a minority to impose its will on the majority. In some parts of Mosca's work the concept does in fact take on this particular connotation; however, careful analysis shows – as we have already seen – that the expression is used by Mosca, in the sense it has here, to refer in particular to minorities which organize elections. (…) More precisely, the concept of organized minority must be related to that organization of society in which the intermediary layer, by nature bureaucratic, occupies most of the power structure".[30]

Hartmann (2004b, pp. 19-24) then emphasises the critical perspective Mosca generally takes on representative democracy. He refers to Mosca's argument according to which organised minorities dominate the majority here as well and elected representatives do not represent a majority that only temporarily delegates its power to them but act as members of a ruling minority.[31] From this

[30] Italics retained from the original version.

[31] It has been underlined that terminological inaccuracies in the translation of this argument by Mosca often account for accusations of inherent anti-democratic thought (cf. Albertoni, 1987, p. 52). The original argument states: "Quel che avviene colle altre forme di Governo, che cioè la

perspective, Mosca's approach is not regarded as fundamentally opposed to democracy but as highly critical of its actual representativeness.

The approach by Pareto, brought forward in the early 20th century, concentrates on the circulation of elites, of elected classes ('circolazione della classe eletta'; Pareto, 1964b; § 2042). Again, society is understood as being divided into two distinct classes, the elected one and the non-elected one. The former constitutes the political elite. It determines the course of society and state and is – out of a multitude of potential elites in various fields – to be regarded as the decisive elite group (Pareto, 1964b; § 2033). This political elite itself is then again divided into two subgroups: the power-holding elite and the elite that strives for power without currently holding it. Especially in democratic systems, both groups compete for the favour of the non-elite majority to secure or ameliorate their own position (Pareto, 1964b; §§ 2026-2059), yet without necessarily seeking to actually represent this majority (Pareto, 1964b; § 2244).

Pareto (1964a; § 870) explains elite circulation by making recourse to a concept of social residues, a psychological category corresponding to prevalent schemes of action and interpretation (cf. Bongiorno, 1930, pp. 360-361). Non-power-holding elites primarily characterised by class one residues (i.e. those of cleverness and intelligence, metaphorically described as fox-residues) conquer power-holding positions by evolutionary means while elites characterised by class two residues (i.e. those of force and violence, metaphorically described as lion-residues) do so by revolutionary means.[32] To achieve stability and maintain its position, a power-holding elite must combine residues of both classes. This is only possible through constant openness for renewal, understood as the potential ascent of members of the majority into the ruling minority. Elite seclusion ultimately endangers elite status (Pareto, 1964b; § 2057; see also: F. R. Pfetsch, 2012, p. 418; Zauels, 1968, pp. 22-29, 42-46).

Communicative measures are considered an important instrument for both power-holding and non-power-holding elites. Appealing to schemes of interpretation prevalent in the non-elite majority functions as a strategy to secure their

---

minoranza organizzata domina la maggioranza disorganizzata, avviene pure, e perfettamente, malgrado le apparenze contrarie, col sistema rappresentativo. Quando si dice che gli elettori scelgono il loro deputato, si usa una locuzione molto impropria; la verità è che il deputato si fa scegliere dagli elettori (…)" (Mosca, 1953, p. 205); [What is happening in other forms of government, that an organised minority is dominating the unorganised majority, is happening also and to perfection, whatever the appearances to the contrary might be, under the representative system. Saying that the voters choose their representative means employing an inexact description. The truth is that the representative has himself chosen by the voters (…); translation by the author (JNK)].

32 Force and violence are not to be understood in a purely physical sense here but also more figuratively in one of 'energy' or 'vigour' (F. R. Pfetsch, 2012, p. 420).

favour; communications potentially also mask existing gaps and distortions and argue towards an identity of the elite interests and those of the governed majority. From this perspective, adapting actual (political) communication to popular demand and preferences is necessary to ensure its efficacy. The communicator has to address relevant residues and rationalise politics behind specific derivations (Pareto, 1964a; § 868; 1964b; §§ 1397, 1746, 2250; see also: Zauels, 1968, pp. 28-29, 49-55).

The approach by Michels, also brought forward in the early 20th century, does not argue about society as such but focuses on an organisational level. Here, organisation is considered a fundamental principle of modern mass society; individual actors are necessarily organised in collective bodies to pursue their economic and political interests (Michels, 1949, pp. 21-22). Nevertheless, organisations do also have an inherent tendency towards oligarchy, towards the emergence of internal organisational elites:

> "Organization implies the tendency to oligarchy. In every organization (...) the aristocratic tendency manifests itself very clearly. The mechanism of the organization, while conferring a solidity of the structure, induces serious changes in the organized mass, completely inverting the respective position of the leaders and the led. As a result, of organization, every party or professional union becomes divided into a minority of directors and a majority of directed" (Michels, 1949, p. 32).

Organisations breed elites for both administrative and intellectual reasons. Direct and unmediated representation is regarded as dysfunctional, delegation and institutionalised leadership is considered necessary. Effective administration calls for inner-organisational elites (Michels, 1949, pp. 23-41). From an intellectual perspective, individual members of organisations actively search for leadership and guidance; they select assumingly intellectual superiors to guide the organisational bodies to which they belong (Michels, 1949, pp. 49-68).[33]

Organisational elites on the other hand are characterised by a desire for institutionalised power within their specific organisations. A superior rhetoric and the skilled utilisation of mass communication for the direction and guidance of non-elites serve as means to secure these positions of institutionalised power (Michels, 1949, pp. 69-90; see also: Wasner, 2004, pp. 53-57).The emergence of inner-organisational elites is then always considered to be the product of organi-

33 The understanding of non-elites that coins this conceptualisation is of a somewhat derogatory nature; members of this group are portrayed as impressionable, idealistic and not entirely politically conscious (cf. Nye, 1977, pp. 28-31; F. R. Pfetsch, 2012, pp. 434-435).

sational characteristics and those of both organisational elites and non-elites: "*Oligarchy = F (Org., Ch.*$_{Elite}$*, Ch.*$_{Mass}$*)*" (F. R. Pfetsch, 2012, p. 435).[34]

In sum, the approaches by Mosca, Pareto and Michels – subsumed here under the notion of classical approaches – all allow for the identification of elites, their interests and their actual communicative strategies, thereby answering three central questions of elite sociology (Wasner, 2004, pp. 23-25).

Mosca describes elites as minorities exercising power and control over majorities. They are characterised by a high degree of organisation which accounts for their elevated societal position, for their elite status as such. The foundation of their position can be localised in different fields. Depending on the respective historical era, fields such as material wealth, religion, art, science, military might or political skills can be the decisive factor in this regard. Pareto then identifies two groups of elites: power-holding elites and elites that strive for power. Here, elites are mainly conceptualised in a political understanding. The sphere in which they maintain an elevated position is the political one and they are characterised as those that determine the way in which society and state function. Pareto admits to the existence of other elites as well, nonetheless the political ruling class is the central category for his conceptualisation and merits in other fields do not necessarily grant access to it. Michels focuses on intra-organisational elites, pointing out that (political) organisations tend to breed a bureaucratic elite, a small fraction of members that directs the large majority and exercises control over the organisation as such.

The central interest of elites lies, according to Mosca, in maintaining their elevated societal standing. Elites strive to hold their elite position, to conserve established structures. Societal and political stability are only achieved by means of stable elites that at the same time allow a few non-elites to ascend into their sphere. Pareto again differentiates between power-holding and non-power-holding elites. The former group seeks to uphold its elevated position, the latter strives to conquer it. The decisive category in both cases is power, mainly understood in a political sense. To keep or conquer a position in which it can be exercised over the governed classes is the key interest of every (political) actor. It is emphasised that elite seclusion endangers elite status; elites have to allow for the ascent of non-elites. Michels then describes organisational elites striving for positions in which they can exercise control over the mass of members. Again, these actors are characterised by a desire for power.

Mosca emphasises that elites do not admit to their power but rather rationalise it behind certain formulas and dogmas. The emphasis put on popular notions

---

34 Read: Oligarchy is to be understood as the three factor function of the characteristics of the organisation, the leading elite and of the led mass.

is part of a greater communicative strategy utilised by elites; masking elite dominion is in their vested interest. Elites strive to maintain their elevated societal standing; the employment of communicative strategies can be seen as a central factor in doing so. Nonetheless they do not generally hinder the ascent of smaller strata of the governed classes into their sphere. Pareto also describes communicative measures as a means of upholding elite status. Members of the ruling class address feelings or residues prevalent within the wider population; they make recourse to already existing patterns of thought and common ideals in order to exercise political control and mask elite dominion. Both groups of elites seek to exercise influence over the governed classes, they aim to address and influence them by communicative means. Michels puts special emphasis on communicative strategies, inter alia describing a superior rhetoric as a central and necessary characteristic of elite actors. Furthermore he points out that the skilled utilisation of the press for the direction and guidance of the masses is of prime importance within the overall strategy pursued by elites.

Functional approaches

During the 20th century, elite theory underwent further developments, conceptual refinements and diversifications. The postulation of pluralistic functional elites – originally brought forward by Mannheim in the 1930s – and subsequent corresponding theoretical developments are often described as a first decisive step in this direction (Hartmann, 2004b, pp. 42-46; F. R. Pfetsch, 2012, p. 457).[35] Functional approaches characteristically assume the simultaneous existence of several elites in different fields of society; this distinguishes them inter alia from their 'classical' predecessors. They coin a notion of pluralistic functional elites.

Here, three functional approaches are discussed. They are selected for their applicability in a context of political communication. The one by Mannheim is actually deemed to have founded the functional current of elite theory while Lasswell's approach is regarded as closest to contexts of (political) communication. Keller's approach is then generally described as outstanding in terms of analytical precision concerning the identification of elites and their interests (cf. Ettrich & Utz, 2002).

In his early approach Mannheim points out that society has faced fundamental changes in the formation and construction of elites, specifically naming four processes of change: "(1) The growing number of élite groups, and the conse-

---

35 The description of the following approaches as 'functional' follows the terminology employed by Hartmann (2004b) (and also by Reitmayer (2010)); Wasner (2004) uses the term in a different understanding, limiting it only to the approach brought forward by Stammer (1965). Since this whole chapter makes recourse to Hartmann's systematisation, it also adapts his nomenclature.

quent diminution of their power. (2) The destruction of the exclusiveness of the élite groups. (3) The change in the principle of the selection of these élites. (4) The change in the internal composition of the élites" (Mannheim, 1954, p. 86).

The first argument refers to an increase in the number of groups within society that can be regarded as elites under the conditions of liberal democracy. According to this, traditional models in which only a small and clearly delimitated minority exercises the vast share or even the totality of control are overturned, first in favour of models of greater variety, but in the end giving way to diffuseness: "Indeed, the more élites there are in a society the more each individual élite tends to lose its function and influence as a leader, for they cancel each other out" (Mannheim, 1954, p. 86).

The second argument postulates a decrease in the exclusiveness of elites. In this understanding, societal and political conditions that are generally more open lead to the breaking down of barriers between elites and non-elites, thereby depriving the former groups of their exclusive status. While this may be desired in the interest of societal evolution and democracy in the first place, it inevitably also has dire consequences both in the cultural and political field. A decline in the exclusiveness of elites might even lead to the emergence of anti-democratic tendencies and populism:

> "We must recognize further that it is this general lack of direction in modern mass society that gives the opportunity to groups with dictatorial ambitions. If such groups succeed in achieving some sort of political integration, they can carry out their programme without any great resistance from the other groups in society. They meet with no real resistance because all the élites from whom values, tastes, and standards of judgement could emanate, have cancelled each other out" (Mannheim, 1954, p. 87).

Mannheim's third argument then refers to processes of change regarding the selection of elites. According to this, there are three principles governing the selection of elites; these are either based on blood (predominant in aristocratic societies), property (predominant in bourgeois societies) or achievement, the latter being predominant in contemporary democratic societies. Selection by achievement is described as a dynamic principle, potentially fostering societal advancement but on the other hand also with the potential to undermine stability and continuity (Mannheim, 1954, p. 91).

The last line of argument regards changes in the formation of societal elites. Mannheim (1954, p. 96) contrasts established principles of positive selection of outstanding individuals and contemporary developments towards different modes of selection. He sees the societal function of elites endangered by new modes of negative selection, arguing in terms of provincialism and a decline in cultural taste and moral values.

In general, Mannheim regards the existence of leading elites as a necessity to maintain high cultural and political standards. Their guidance and leadership ensures the functioning of democratic societies(cf. Wasner, 2004, p. 77).[36] The societal and political conceptualisation here is one of planned democracy. Accordingly, the exercising of political influence by a leading minority over the majority is considered necessary, be it by political direction and communication or be it by education or propaganda (Mannheim, 1951, p. 8).

The approach by Lasswell again strictly distinguishes between elite and mass. Mass is defined ex-negativo in contrast to elite: "The influential are those who get the most of what there is to get. Available values may be classified as *deference, income, safety*. Those who get the most are *elite*; the rest are *mass*" (Lasswell, 1951, p. 295).[37] Lasswell's approach is generally characterised by a critical perspective on the mass as such (cf. Hartmann, 2004b, pp. 46-47), yet it also distances itself from an overly affirmative understanding of elites. Elite studies are understood as serving democracy by enabling a better understanding of power and those who exercise it (Lasswell, 1966, pp. v-vi).

Elites are considered existent both in democratic and non-democratic societies. The main difference between democratic elites and those in authoritarian states lies in the base from which they are recruited; in democracies it is rather broad, in authoritarian systems they derive from a narrow base (Lasswell et al., 1952, p. 6). Out of a multitude of elites, the political elite is regarded as the most central elite group, as the one that actually holds power.

Power is understood as the ability to make 'severely sanctioned choices' and exists both in an actual way and in a potential one, i.e. among those that do not actually inhabit power-holding positions but are at least in contention to these. The elite consists of those that form the political leadership and of the social formations from which these leaders come, 'to which accountability is maintained, during a given generation'. The political elite is, in this understanding, the class of power and influence (Lasswell, 1966, pp. 12-28; Lasswell et al., 1952, pp. 7-13).

Political communication is of elevated importance for political elites. It involves defining generally accepted symbols, notions and concepts:

---

36 Keller (1963, pp. 13-16) points out that Mannheim distinguishes between two different types of elites, an integrative elite and a sublimative variant. While the latter is made up of moral-religious, aesthetic and intellectual leaders and serves as a means to the sublimation of the psychic energies of a people, the former group consists of political and organisation leaders and serves integrative functions while primarily working through formalised organisational bodies.

37 Italics retained from the original version.

> "Any elite defends and asserts itself in the name of symbols of the common destiny. Such symbols are the 'ideology' of the established order, the 'utopia' of counterelites. By the use of sanctioned words and gestures the elite elicits blood, work, taxes, applause, from the masses. When the political order works smoothly, the masses venerate the symbols; the elite, self-righteous and unafraid, suffers from no withering sense of immorality. 'God's in heaven – all's right with the world.' 'In union there is strength' – not exploitation" (Lasswell, 1951, p. 311).

Often, political communication is even understood as a necessity in the preservation of elite-power. This applies in an international context, where affirmative contact is sought with audiences within the frontiers of other powers, as well as in a national context, where the ideology of the elite is strengthened and opposing ones are derided through communicative measures (Lasswell, 1948, pp. 45-46). Elites seek to control their environment, especially in communicative regards; they seek to set agendas and coin interpretative frames (Lasswell, 1951, p. 444).

While ruling elites are generally equipped with institutionalised power, non-power-holding elites are more reliant on communicative measures. Challenging the position of actual power-holding elites depends on the ways in which these non-power-holding elites succeed in influencing and setting public agendas:

> "The problem of a revolutionary propagandist is to guide miscellaneous insecurities into channels suitable to his seizure of power. He seeks to control the projection of love, destructiveness, guilt, and weakness with reference to a [sic] utopia capable of becoming ideology" (Lasswell, 1951, p. 445).

Lasswell's approach conceptualises political analysis as elite analysis; focusing on the ruling groups is regarded the key to the understanding of politics and society as such. It concentrates on the ways in which elites secure their dominion, focusing primarily on the employment of communicative measures. Elites utilise communication to gather intelligence, to create sympathy for them and their decisions and to mask and stabilise their dominion. Non-power-holding elites are especially dependent on such measures to pursuit their goals and strengthen their position and standing.

Keller's approach then employs a strictly functional understanding of elites. According to this, elites are to be understood as:

> "(…) a minority of individuals designated to serve a collectivity in a socially valued way. Elites are effective and responsible minorities – effective as regards the performance of activities of interest and concern to others to whom these elites are responsive. Socially significant elites are ultimately responsible for the realization of major social goals and for the continuity of the social order" (Keller, 1963, p. 4).

Elites are differentiated between segmental and functional elites; while there can be a multitude of groups of elevated standing within society, only a small fraction of them is also of high significance for society as a whole. Segmental elites occupy high positions within certain delimitated segments of society while strategic elites are of importance for the entire society (Keller, 1963, p. 20). Strategic elites have a sustained societal impact; their actions and decisions have direct consequences for larger groups within society. Yet their actual existence is not limited to the political field. In fact, Keller identifies strategic elites within various other areas of society, among these the economy, culture and science (Keller, 1963, p. 20, 1983).

In contrast to older (classical) approaches, Keller negates the idea of a unitary ruling class. Contemporary society is not conceptualised as one hierarchical pyramid capped by an elite but by the parallel existence of several pyramids and therefore also several capping strategic elites. The diversification and autonomy of societal sectors breeds diversified strategic elites (Keller, 1963, pp. 82-83). These different elites set societal and political rules and goals, provide the necessary means for their achievement, offer guidance and integration and uphold societal solidarity and morals (Keller, 1963, pp. 88-104; see also: Parsons, 1952). In principle, they are open to ascent from non-elites, individual actors can become part of one of the strategic elites based on their specific merits (Keller, 1963, pp. 186-193, 198-221).

Elites generally strive to maintain their elevated position in their fields and in society as such. However, this is dependent on their strategic adaptations to their environments:

> "In summary, several prominent factors are operative in the failure of elites to survive: their inability or reluctance to reproduce themselves when inheritance of elite position was the expected pattern; the degeneration of their creative powers due either to the inbreeding of incapacity or to the selection of unsuitable candidates; and certain social afflictions such as conservatism and excessive social distance from the mass of men and their problems" (Keller, 1963, p. 250).

The preservation of elite status goes together with the preservation of communicative links with the broader population; elites need to be alert to the needs, feelings and desires of the public. It is their duty to cope with the demands of the classes over which they cap in the various pyramids of society. Communication is understood here mainly as observation and dialogue and it is considered necessary for the preservation of elite status. In contrast to other approaches, it does not function as a means to mask the elite dominion but as one of mutual exchange between those in an elevated position and those that lack this status. Nonetheless it again functions as a central measure in the pursuit of elite interests.

The approaches by Mannheim, Lasswell and Keller – subsumed here under the notion of functional approaches – again all allow for the identification of elites, their interests and their actual communicative strategies, thereby answering three central questions of elite sociology (Wasner, 2004, pp. 23-25). Their main focus is on the functions elites have for society and its subsystems; they often consider them a necessity.

Mannheim's approach distinguishes between elite and mass. It describes the former group as the one that serves as the central planning instance within a planned democracy, as the one whose guidance and leadership ensure the functioning of society and political system. The exclusivity of the elite is considered important; the ascendancy of non-elites is only functional when these adapt to the fundamental standards of existing elites. In this understanding elites are the upper strata of society, the idealised minority opposed to the often vilified majority. They exist in three forms: as political and organising elites, as intellectual and artistic elites and as moral and religious elites (cf. Hartmann, 2004b, p. 44). Lasswell then defines elites in terms of great influence and large available resources such as deference, income and safety. Differences between elites and non-elites are considered existent in democracies as well as in authoritarian systems. Among the variety of different elites, political elites are the central group. They are often equipped with large resources of power, understood here as the ability to make severely sanctioned choices, or they are in a position where they aim to gain this power by replacing the current power-holding elite.

Keller's approach defines elites as a minority of individuals designated to serve society in a socially valued way. They are responsible for the realisation of societal goals and for the continuity of the social order. Elites are not considered unitary; there is a multitude of strategic elites. Different groups of strategic elites set societal and political rules and goals, provide the necessary means for achieving them, offer guidance and integration and uphold societal solidarity and morals.

The conceptualisation of elite broadens in functional approaches. While classical theorists mainly utilise an understanding of elites limited to the leading political actors, functional theorists focus on various societal groups and describe their respective leaders as elites. There is no longer a single pyramid capped by one unitary elite but a multitude of pyramids capped by a multitude of elites. Elites are existent in various societal fields, ruling a particular area while not necessarily being equipped with comparable privileges in other fields. As Scott (2008, p. 36) puts it:

> "Elites can exist at various levels of a society and so are distinguishable by their degree of power. The commanding elite within a golf club, for example, may have autocratic control over club employees and other club members, but it will have little influence in the wider society unless its

members individually have positions of power within other, more salient organizations and institutional hierarchies. Their power may also be enhanced if the golf club becomes a means of access to other channels of power (…)".[38]

Functional approaches aim at enquiring into and explaining the functions of elites for and within society and consider elites to be a societal necessity. They often employ a rather affirmative evaluation of their overall value for the greater community. The very interests of elites are comparatively seldom in their main focus of attention. There are however some references to the goals pursued by elite actors. Lasswell's approach in particular allows for elite interests to be identified. According to this, those elite actors that occupy a power-holding position strive for its preservation while opposing elites strive for its conquering. Groups at the very top of societal pyramids find themselves in opposing roles and thereby in competition over the occupancy of power-holding positions. From a functional perspective, the ability to exercise power is again considered an elite interest.

Power is understood here to be the ability to make severely sanctioned choices or, as Scott puts it: "Power, in its most general sense, can be seen as the production of causal effects and social power is an agent's intentional use of causal powers to affect the conduct of other agents" (Scott, 2008, p. 29). Classical elite theory regards power as the central point of interest for elites; Pareto's circulation of elites is characterised by a constant battle over power-holding positions as a prime mover. Functional elite theory principally agrees on that. The elite that has power does everything necessary to keep it, the non-power-holding elite strives for it.

According to Mannheim, exercising influence is considered part of the planning, management and supervision of the exercising of power, of the actual societal function of elites. To exercise such influence over the governed majority, elites employ communicative strategies. They do so in different forms, including political direction, political communication, propaganda and education. Lasswell regards communication as an absolute necessity in the preservation of power. This holds true both from an international understanding, where affirmative contact is sought with foreign audiences in order to facilitate the gathering of intelligence, as well as in a national context, where the ideology of the elite is strengthened and opposing ones are derided through communicative measures. Elites can only ascend and persist when they succeed in controlling their environment, especially through communication. According to Keller, political

38 Scott is cited here for his clear definitions (which correspond with the works discussed and provide further clarifications and explanations) and descriptions of historical developments in the field of elite theory. Yet Scott's approach itself is not part of functional elite theory.

communication is also to be considered a means for securing the elite status. However, from this perspective the preservation of communicative links with non-elites is of utmost importance. Maintaining dialogue with these groups, thereby being aware of their needs, feelings and desires, is the societal function and duty of elites. Therefore the necessary communicative strategy of elites involves the fostering and preservation of mutual communicative exchange with non-elite actors.

Communication is considered a central strategy of elite actors, both in terms of unidirectional communication that seeks to exercise influence and in terms of mutual exchange with non-elite actors. It fosters inter alia dialogue, campaign purposes in the competition of opposed elites, the securing of institutionalised elite power and then also the masking of elite dominion behind generally accepted formulas and images.[39]

Critical approaches

Critical approaches are different from their functional counterparts in so far as they do not consider elites with regards to their function for society but from a more critical perspective, focusing on societal inequalities and distortions. Mills and Bourdieu are often cited as having coined this approach towards elite theory; furthermore it is closely related to the works of inter alia Domhoff, Scott and Krysmanski.

A large proportion of critical approaches focuses on patterns of elite reproduction, i.e. on the conditions under which individuals are educated and socialised to become members of the ruling elite (e.g. Bourdieu, 1982). These approaches are often not applicable for the identification of elites, their interests and their communicative strategies. In other cases, the rejection of vilifications of the mass and of overly affirmative perspectives on elites leads to opposite extremes. It then tends to bring forward accounts that lack theoretical sophistica-

[39] In this context see also Westerbarkey (2004), who extensively discusses the employment of so-called 'Tarnkappen' (magic hoods) in the masking of elite interests and elite dominion: "Wer Macht hat und behalten möchte, muss daher zwar egoistisch handeln, aber Altruismus bekunden, um gesellschaftlich akzeptiert zu werden, denn sonst gedeihen Missgunst, Neid und Angst. Daher ist denen, die ihre Interessen hinter bewährten Gemeinwohlphrasen verstecken, grundsätzlich eine bewusste Täuschung ihrer Adressaten zu unterstellen und nicht etwa bloß eine mehr oder weniger raffinierte Selbstdarstellung" (Westerbarkey, 2004, p. 37); [Who has power and wants to preserve it must though act egoistically, but publicly manifest altruism in order to be accepted socially, because, otherwise, hostility, envy and fear prosper. It is therefore that one should allege those that hide their interests behind phrases referring to the greater common good with the intentional deception of their audiences rather than with a more or less ingenious way of self-representation; translation by the author (JNK).]

tion and vilify elites as such, making a judgement on any intertwining between leading strata of societal fields. Critical elite theory is sometimes difficult to apply in contexts of political communication research.

However, there are some theoretically sophisticated approaches that are also applicable for identifying elites, their interests and their communicative strategies. This primarily concerns the works of Mills but also those of Bourdieu that do not specifically focus on patterns of elite reproduction (cf. A. Davis, 2010b, pp. 84-86).

Mills' (1956) approach primarily aims at an identification and analysis of patterns of power within society. Brought forward in the 1950s, it specifically focuses on the interwoven interests of the leading strata of the military, corporate and political fields of society. It suggests a state in which only a few elements exercise power while the individual member of society is subjected to manipulation by these actors; a line of argument also elaborated in some of Mills' later works:

> "For among the means of power which now prevail is the power to manage and to manipulate the consent of men. That we do not know the limits of such power, and that we hope it does have limits, does not remove the fact that much power today is successfully employed without the sanction of the reason or the conscience of the obedient" (Mills, 1958, p. 29).

The power elite is made up of outstanding individuals. It is, according to Mills (1956, pp. 3-4) "composed of men whose positions enable them to transcend the ordinary environments of ordinary men and women; they are in positions to make decisions having major consequences." He goes on to point out that: "Whether they do or do not make such decisions is less important than the fact that they do occupy such pivotal positions: their failure to act, their failure to make decisions, is itself an act that is often of greater consequence than the decisions they do make" (Mills, 1956, p. 4). Being a part of the power elite means occupying a position in which personal influence and – most important – the ability to exercise power is almost unlimited. Members determine and shape political and societal processes without necessarily becoming active. They have the ability to control access to their circles, to allow ascent into them or to close them hermetically (cf. Wasner, 2004, pp. 90-91).[40]

Changing one's professional role, the transition from one of the leading fields into another one, is regarded as a special form of distinction here. Those that succeed in this are regarded as 'the core members of the power elite' due to them having the possibility to personally unify normally delimitated fields. Mills

---

40 In contrast to Pareto, Mills assumes a closed circle of elites rather than a succession or circulation of elite groups (Mills, 1968, pp. 247-248).

points out that those 'professional go-betweens' belong to the inner core due to their function as unifiers of the power elite (Mills, 1956, pp. 288-289).

According to Mills' approach, elites do not necessarily strive for the advancement of society but rather focus on their own interests (Mills, 1968, pp. 230-231). These often concern the preservation of pivotal power-holding positions, allowing them to alter structures positions within these structures and the ways in which these positions are utilised (Mills, 1956, p. 24).

Political communication is primarily understood as the influencing of non-elites; ruling classes sustain their position by exercising control over communication and ideas (cf. A. Davis, 2003, pp. 669-670; Kornhauser, 1968, pp. 42-44, 50). Elites compete over the exercising of unidirectional communicative influence:

> "But in the mass society of media markets, competition, if any, goes on between the manipulators with their mass media on the one hand, and the people receiving propaganda on the other. Under such conditions, it is not surprising that there should arise a conception of public opinion as a mere reaction – we cannot say 'response' – to the content of the mass media. In this view, the public is merely the collectivity of individuals each rather passively exposed to the mass media and rather helplessly opened up to the suggestions and manipulations that flow from these media. The fact of manipulation from centralized points of control constitutes, as it were, an expropriation of the old multitude of little opinion producers and consumers operating in a free and balanced market" (Mills, 1956, p. 305).

Such trends are then further reinforced by an increase in political indifference among non-elite actors which renders them passive audience open to unidirectional communicative influences (Mills, 1968, pp. 245-246).

Yet communication does not only serve as a means of influencing between elites and non-elites, it is also employed between elite actors as a means of inter-elite coordination. Elites from different fields and with different goals coordinate their efforts to pursue their individual interests in a better way:

> "But it is to say that as the institutional mechanics of our time have opened up avenues to men pursuing their several interests, many of them have come to see that these several interests could be realized more easily if they worked together, in informal as well as in more formal ways, and accordingly they have done so" (Mills, 1956, p. 20).

Coordination and belonging to elite circles in which several actors might pursue their several interests collectively become valuable resources and central points of elite strategy. Occupying a power-holding position which allows influence to be exercised over non-elites, politics, the economy and society as such is of prime interest to elites, and inter-elite coordination is a central means to that end.

In reflecting on elite networks and the role of mass communication in contemporary democracy, Bourdieu also argues towards a critical understanding of elites in politics and political communication.[41]

In this context, the concept of social capital is of elevated importance. This can be understood as a type of capital that is based on relations and ties between individuals. It is the aggregate of resources (either of actual or potential nature) that are related to the possession of a network of institutionalised relationships of mutual acquaintance and recognition. Social capital can be described as the resources that one has due to group membership. The actual amount of social capital available to an actor depends on two key factors: on the one hand this is the actual amount of relations that an actor has (i.e. the size of the personal network) and on the other hand it is the amount of capital (either of economic, cultural or symbolic nature) that the other members of the network have (Bourdieu, 1992, pp. 63-64; see also: Jansen & Diaz-Bone, 2011, pp. 75-76). Membership in a large network of actors that are equipped with large amounts of (various forms of) capital provides access to gains in dimensions such as power, prestige or wealth.

Preserving or acquiring high amounts of social capital is regarded as being highly desirable. Being integrated in a network of actors that are rich in resources guarantees an elevated standing; in contemporary societies one can hardly have (or maintain) a power-holding position without being related to other powerful actors. According to Bourdieu's approach, actors now strive for integration in networks that are characterised by a resource-rich membership (Bourdieu, 1992, p. 67). They seek to have strong ties with nodes that account for high amounts of economic, cultural or symbolic capital. Such groups of actors then strive to define their borders to the 'rest' of society; delimitating their networks is of elevated importance to them (Bourdieu, 1992, p. 66).

Mills defines inter-elite coordination as central for elite actors insofar as it allows for the pursuit of several interests in one coordinated effort. Belonging to elite circles in which several actors pursue their several interests collectively is regarded as both a valuable resource and a central point of elite strategy. Bourdieu's approach is similar to this line of argument. Belonging to elite networks (conceptualised as networks of actors possessing various forms of capital) is equivalent to possessing high amounts of social capital, which is a necessary condition for the acquisition or preservation of other forms of capital and of political power. Elite actors constantly invest resources (i.e. work) in the maintenance of their relations with other elite actors; the higher the standing of an actor,

41 The discussion of Bourdieu's approach under this critical notion again follows the systematisation by Hartmann (2004b, 2007; divergent opinion: Wasner, 2004).

the higher the profit gained from this investment (Bourdieu, 1992, p. 67). Here, profits are significantly higher for those who already possess.

The concept of social capital is of importance insofar as it stresses and further deepens Mills' argument on the importance of inter-elite coordination for the acquisition and preserving of power-holding positions. This applies especially to elites from the fields of politics and the media and the interplay between them.

Bourdieu (1997, p. 182) compares politics and the communications surrounding them to a game of chess that is taking place between experienced players. In this understanding it is inter-elite communication that is of central meaning for politics. The electorate's role is one of spectators. Mass media (especially television) provide a soundboard for the political debate that is taking place; their rules and structures are adapted by political actors (Bourdieu, 2010, pp. 291-293). Political communicators seek to gain attention for their policies and viewpoints, they engage in debate (according to Bourdieu often in pseudo-debate) to achieve this. Journalists provide them with the necessary space for this, competing over market share and public attention they then gain from this as well (Bourdieu, 1998, pp. 41-49). Political communicators profit from their connections to each other since these provide them with valuable resources and they profit from connections with journalists since, inter alia, these facilitate public visibility. Journalists profit from connections to political communicators since they provide them with valuable resources in the form of topics for coverage which are of decisive importance in the competition for market share and visibility (Bourdieu, 2010, pp. 294-295).

From this point of view, the communication network between politics and the media is regarded as being a network which allows for the acquisition of large amounts of social capital by means of membership. Having connections to its central nodes is regarded as being (extremely) desirable when it comes to preserving or acquiring a power-holding position. Interacting in such a network allows several elite actors to pursue their several interests mutually. Defining the boundaries of such a network (i.e. excluding a large proportion of non-elite actors) is a necessity in order to preserve structures that benefit the current membership; the reproduction of the elite from the sphere of political communication (as opposed to the erosion of this group) is only achieved by close interaction.

The elites described by Mills are the elites of early Cold War America; identified in the fields of politics, economy and the military. They are primarily interested in the preservation of their elevated position; having power is deemed desirable and those that have it strive to preserve it. Non-power-holding (oppositional) elites do not play a major role in this approach.[42] Mills focuses on actors at the very top of societal pyramids. A changing of spheres or professional roles is however capable of further elevating one's elite status; those that have belonged to several elite groups are even more advantaged (due to their potential to personally unify normally delimitated fields).

Elites employ communicative strategies in the pursuit of their goals. They try to exercise influence over their non-elite counterparts, in some cases they even seek to manipulate them. Since non-elites show increasing degrees of political indifference, exercising communicative control over them is comparably easy. Furthermore elites employ communication to coordinate with each other, to allow the mutual pursuit of several goals by several elite actors. Being well connected to other members of the elite is regarded as an asset in this conceptualisation.

Bourdieu considers such connections within an elite-network as valuable sources of social capital. Elite actors strive to have large amounts of social capital since its possession is a necessary condition for the acquisition or preservation of other forms of capital and of political power. Belonging to elite networks and delimitating these networks against outsiders is very much in the interest of elite actors since it guarantees the preservation of their elevated societal, political and economic position. This applies for elites from the sphere of political communication which seek connections with each other to allow the mutual pursuit of individual goals such as media attention, public visibility or gaining market shares.

3.3 Summary and Implications

Sociological elite theory is not a middle-ranged media theory. It does not directly provide hypotheses that can be empirically investigated. Sociological elite theory should be seen more as a grand theory that aims to describe and explain societal phenomena on a larger scale (Daloz, 2007, pp. 27-34). Nevertheless it is able to substantiate a theoretical heuristic, a perspective from which empirically observable phenomena can be considered (cf. Abbott, 2004, pp. xi, 80-81, 250).

There is no unitary sociological elite theory; approaches differ in their conceptualisations of elites and their societal role, and in the functions and freedoms they attribute to them (cf. Hoffmann-Lange, 1992, pp. 22-24). Approaches to-

---

42 The fact that it very much sets aside the notion of opposing elites, concentrating on the idea of a unitary power elite has in fact been one of the major points of critique regarding Mills' argument (cf. Bell, 1958).

wards sociological elite theory have to be considered together, weighed according to their explanatory value and adapted to the specific context of the explanandum for which they function as a heuristic (Mills, 1968, p. 247).

Nevertheless, the elite perspective – and accordingly also its theoretical foundation – persists with analyses of politics and power; questions concerning the role of elites have not lost their importance (F. R. Pfetsch, 2012, pp. 464-465). This also holds true in an organisational context, when not only the role of individual elite actors but also that of central organisational 'command posts' is considered, inter alia in terms of policy making and implementation (Zald & Lounsbury, 2010, pp. 964-965, 980-982). Elite analysis serves as a means to understand organisational relations and its effects on political processes (Reed, 2012, pp. 206-208).

In an age of mediatisation, the interconnectedness of politics and media is apparent (cf. Kepplinger, 2002; Mazzoleni & Schulz, 1999), the media is in some regards even described as a political institution (Allern & Blach-Ørsten, 2011, pp. 92-93). Therefore, the field of political communication – and specifically its sub-field of political media relations – is central to the analysis of political processes and both media outlets and individual political journalists should be considered important players in the political field. The interaction between politics and the media or, more specifically, between political communication/ public relations and political journalism becomes a central focus of analysis (A. Davis, 2002, pp. 171-181, 2010b, pp. 67-81). Political media relations are central for politics – a field that persists in being considered from an elite perspective – and thereby become an explanandum for this heuristic themselves.

Approaches towards sociological elite theory describe elites as minority groups inhabiting or at least potentially inhabiting power-holding positions. They exist in society, both in authoritarian and democratic systems, but also emerge within political organisations. In general, the political field is – due to the institutionalised power available – considered the field inhabited by the most central and important elites, even though elites also exist in other sectors of society. Within the increasingly important field of political media relations, those that account for the communication of central organisational actors and those that provide political coverage for major media outlets form a positional elite; their organisations are focal organisational actors.

Sociological elite theory mostly cites power as the central interest of elite actors. Mosca describes history as a process shaped by struggles between distinct minorities over political power. From this perspective, elites strive for dominion, they try to maintain existing distributions of power. Pareto argues similarly, describing the circulation of elites as a form of competition for power-holding positions. Power is understood as the central resource, its preservation or conquering is the central interest of elite actors. Michels sees a natural desire for power as the central characteristic of organisational leaders. He emphasises that inner-organisational bureaucratic elites constantly strive to maintain their elevated standing; occupying a position in which power can be exercised over the majority is considered desirable.

Functional elite theory does not primarily focus on elite interests. Furthermore, the autonomy that elites have is smaller; elites are described as minorities that find themselves tightly woven into societal and systemic structures and they are primarily described as a societal necessity. Mannheim sees the advancement of society as one of the prime functions of elites. According to his argument negative elite selection might undermine societal advancement, so elites should, from a normative point of view, strive for the preservation of their power-holding positions in order to provide guidance and leadership. Keller also concentrates on the societal functions of elites. Elite interests are only of minor importance in her approach, yet she also describes power as a desired resource. Lasswell is clearer in his identification of elite interests. According to his argument, elites that find themselves in power-holding positions strive for their preservation while opposing elites constantly try to achieve these. Those that are at the top of societal pyramids are competing over power.

Critical approaches attribute greater freedom to elites. Again, power is a central category in their description of elite interests. Occupying power-holding positions is considered especially desirable. It allows influence and control over politics and society to be exercised. Power allows existing structures to be altered and existing constraints to be overcome, and it is in the very (selfish) interest of elites that they possess it.

Despite some differences in their understanding of elites and their role, the approaches discussed unanimously cite power as the central elite interest. Power in such contexts lacks a generally accepted definition yet there is "a core complex of its meaning, having to do with the capacity of persons or collectives to 'get things done' effectively, in particular when their goals are obstructed by some kind of human resistance or opposition" (Parsons, 1963, p. 232). Power is regarded as the ability to produce causal effects, to bring about consequences and to affect the conduct of other actors (Scott, 2001, pp. 1-2, 2008, p. 29); it is the ability to make 'severely sanctioned choices', actually or potentially (Lasswell, 1966, pp. 12-28; Lasswell et al., 1952, pp. 7-13). Power means control, ideally (quasi-) monopolistic control (Reed, 2012, pp. 208-213).

The elevated standing elite actors enjoy equips them with power; it allows them to pursue their goals relatively regardless of obstacles. Maintaining power is related to maintaining elevated positions and their standing as elites. This holds true not only for individual positions but also for the standing of organisations that ground the importance of their leading representatives. Apart from further actor-specific interests (e.g. in terms of votes, circulation numbers etc.), power and its preservation are central for elite actors.

In pursuing their interests, elite actors often employ communication as a strategy. Mosca argues the ways in which elite power is rationalised behind communicative formulas: referring to popular notions is utilised as a means to justify elite dominion to non-elites. Pareto argues similarly: here ruling classes make recourse to feelings or residues that are prevalent among the wider population, thereby exercising control and masking their dominion. Circulating elites rely on communicative means to exercise influence on the governed class which – especially in democratic systems – is of elevated importance for the preservation or conquering of a power-holding position. Michels then refers to superior rhetoric and skilled utilisation of mass media as important characteristics of inner-organisational bureaucratic elites, thereby again emphasising the importance of (mass-) communication for elite actors.

Functional approaches also focus on the employment of communicative measures by elites, yet their descriptions of the ways in which these utilise political communication differ. Mannheim argues that the leading minority exercises control over the governed majority and also – from a more affirmative understanding – plans democratic processes by communicative means. In this understanding, political communication, propaganda and education secure the societal influence of elites. Lasswell draws a stronger focus on political communication and its importance for elites, describing it as an absolute necessity in the preservation (or conquering) of power. From this perspective, ruling and oppositional elites both make strong recourse to communicative measures, the latter are even more dependent on these. Both utilise communication to gather intelligence, to strengthen their own ideologies and to deride opposing ones. Communication secures elite dominion and sometimes masks it as well. Keller's understanding of the role of communication for elites again differs from these positions. Here the preservation of communicative links with the broader population is described as its most important function. Elites need to be alert to the needs, feelings and desires of the public. Communication is understood here mainly as dialogue and observation and it is regarded as an absolute necessity for the preservation of elite status.

Critical approaches also focus on communication and its importance for elites and their strategies. Mills primarily argues in terms of mass influencing. Political, military and corporate elites usually employ means of communication such as the mass media to influence non-elites; they often do so in a persuasive way. The broader population is subjected to suggestions and manipulations distributed via the mass media, ruling classes control communications and ideas. Public opinion is largely shaped by these processes. This is facilitated by an increasing amount of political indifference that is prevalent among non-elites. Mills also makes reference to another aspect of communicative elite strategies: inter-elite coordination. Being a member in elite circles allows the pursuit of interests to be improved and coordination within these circles means that several actors can pursue several interests more easily than would be the case without coordinated effort. To communicate with other elites and to maintain close links with them is considered a central part of elite strategy. Bourdieu describes public (pseudo) debates as one of the central means employed by political elites when these strive for public attention for their policies and viewpoints. The media function as soundboards, and both sides benefit. The main focus of interest though is in (communicative) networking. It is the linking between elite actors – especially the communicative linking – that increases the available amount of social capital, of a resource that inter alia allows for the acquisition of wealth and the preservation of (political) power and prestige. Maintaining strong ties with nodes that account for high amounts of capital secures elite status. Again, communication serves two functions: it permits public representation and coordination and networking with other elites.

Sociological elite theory approaches three forms of communication employed by elite actors: elite to non-elite communication, elite with non-elite communication and elite with elite communication. Elite to non-elite communication – discussed by most approaches – is to be understood as the unidirectional distribution of messages to non-elite actors; this form of communication is non-reciprocal. It can involve influencing or information. Elite with non-elite communication then implies communicative exchange. Elite actors and non-elites interact and potentially even engage in dialogue.[43] This bidirectional form of political communication serves two functions: on the one hand it allows close observation of public demands and needs, and on the other it allows leading non-elites to be integrated into the elite sphere. Elite with elite communication as the third variant then sets aside non-elite actors. This form of communication is concerned with inter-elite coordination and networking; elites engage in communicative exchange with other elites and build exclusive networks of communication. These networks serve as a means of coordination and secure access to resources; being connected to powerful nodes means possessing large amounts of

[43] The varieties of elite to non-elite communication and elite with non-elite communication as conceptualised in sociological elite theory show some similarities to the four models of public relations described by Grunig and Hunt (1984). Elite to non-elite communication is corresponding to one-way communication, either in the form of publicity or information. Elite with non-elite communication is corresponding to two-way communication and potentially exists in both asymmetrical and symmetrical form.

social capital, which is an important resource for elite actors. Communicating with other elites means that efforts can be coordinated; being connected to those that have power ultimately increases one's own power and standing.

4 Empirical Analyses: Perceptions and Adaptations of Digitisation

Digitisation renders new means of communication increasingly ubiquitous. The process is now inducing vast technological changes in a variety of societal fields. Arguably, this also affects the field of political communication in general and the sub-field of political media relations in particular.

The question is however, how do those actors that are potentially affected (i.e. leading political spokespersons, communication managers and journalists) perceive such processes of digitisation and their implications for politics and political communication? Which importance do they attribute to the proliferation of new means of communication? From their point of view, which effects might digitisation have and in how far might it lead to in- or exclusion into or from communicative networks in this field?

Furthermore: How do leading political communication professionals and their specific organisations actually adapt to processes of the proliferation of ICT? How do political organisations organise their external communication under the conditions of digitisation? Through which channels do spokespersons and journalists interact? And last but not least: How are communication networks in the field of political media relations constructed under the conditions of digitisation?

The following empirical analyses enquire into these questions, thereby seeking to analyse the field of political media relations in Germany. A first complex of analysis focuses on individual perceptions of digitisation. A second complex of analysis then takes actual adaptations into consideration, both on an individual and an organisational level. In fact, both levels are interwoven here – and then ultimately also related to a super-ordinate macro level which constitutes the specific political communication system or culture (Quandt & Scheufele, 2011, p. 12). Spokespersons and communication managers account for the organisational communication of political parties and governmental bodies and are simultaneously individually influenced by their organisational culture. Despite their comparatively higher levels of autonomy, political journalists are also rooted within their specific media organisations (Altmeppen, 2006, pp. 115-131). In both cases, the interconnectedness of analytical levels is apparent.

The following subchapters constitute the empirical part of this thesis. After an initial rationale for the sampling employed and a methodological reflection, analyses on perceptions of digitisation are presented and briefly discussed. Subsequently, the focus of analysis is drawn on actual adaptations. As indicated, these are analysed with regard to three specific fields of interest; findings are again briefly discussed afterwards.

4.1 Methodology

The empirical analyses conducted here employ a combination of several empirical methods to approach the subject of political media relations under online conditions. The following first seeks to provide a rationale for the actual sampling and then briefly presents and discusses the methods employed.

Sampling

The analyses conducted here seek to enquire into the perceptions and actual adaptations of digitisation by elite actors, i.e. by individual actors of authoritative standing within focal organisational inhabitants of the field of political communication in Germany, and then also by these organisations. A first step of sampling therefore seeks to identify focal organisations in the field of political communication in Germany. This considers both political actors and media outlets.

On the political side, federal governmental bodies and major political parties are taken into account. The federal government is considered to be the centre of the political executive and arguably also the most influential constitutional body in Germany (Kloepfer, 2012, pp. 81-83). Government then necessarily implies a principle of institutionalised publicness (Canél & Sanders, 2012, p. 86), rendering regular engagement in political communication mandatory. As part of the most central and important constitutional body with a mandatory engagement in political communication, governmental bodies are to be considered focal organisational actors in the field of political communication in Germany.

Political parties are equipped with special competences and privileges by the German constitution (Art. 21 GG). Not being constitutional bodies, they are nonetheless considered institutions of constitutional right, a classification giving them rights similar to those of actual constitutional bodies in several regards (BVerfGE 4, 27; 85, 264). German democracy has often been described as a party democracy (e.g. Decker, 2013; Gabriel, 2001), a notion that does – despite all recent debates surrounding potential processes of disintermediation (cf. Hornig, 2013) – underline the elevated importance (major) political parties have for daily politics and the German democracy. The communication undertaken by (major) parties is considered central for the field of political communication, they are to be understood as key actors (Donges, 2008, pp. 27-28).

Given the high number of parties in the German political system – many of these on extremely fringe positions and with hardly any substantial base – it is of course necessary to focus on major parties, on those that have some standing in the political field. The criterion employed here is representation in the German parliament in the 2009-2013 legislative period. These parties are considered to be focal organisational actors in the field of political communication in Germany.

Even though Germany is sometimes described as a state that shows some corporatist tendencies (Rudzio, 2011, pp. 82-85), other intermediary organisations are not included here. Intermediaries exercise influence in their specific fields; their communications are highly field specific (Rudzio, 2011, pp. 57-65). The definition of elite actors employed here is relatively narrow; it makes recourse to their authoritative standing within focal organisational inhabitants of the field of political communication in Germany. This implies a focal standing of these organisations in the 'whole' field and not just in a certain sector. Therefore other intermediaries are – despite their overall importance in the German democracy – not included.

On the media side, the sampling takes major media outlets into account. This criterion covers those outlets that are generally considered to be leading or especially prestigious quality media outlets (cf. Jarren & Donges, 2006, pp. 86-92). An indicator for leadership and prestige is to be found in the number of citations a media outlet claims.[44] On the other hand the circulation figures or audience ratings of those media outlets that provide some form of political coverage are taken into account to integrate those that claim a high degree of distribution.[45]

In sum, the application of these criteria leads to a sample of 18 governmental bodies and six major political parties. All of their online presences are subjected to content analysis, interviews are then conducted with 16 spokespersons and communication managers (response rate: 67%).[46] On the media side interviews

44 These citations are here evaluated through the citation index of 'Media Tenor'.

45 Circulation figures and audience ratings are taken from the German handbook of public life (Oeckl, 2011).

46 Interviewees accounting for the external communication of political actors had jobs described both as spokespersons and communication managers; these are not differentiated here, i.e. figures referring to spokespersons are of course meant with regard to both kinds of political communicators.

are conducted with 29 journalists representing 25 media outlets.[47] Analysis distinguishes between on- and offline media outlets (i.e. the online version of a newspaper is treated as a separate node within social network analysis), which generally reflects organisational structures in media outlets and perceptions by political communication professionals communicating for the political actors in question. Accordingly, social network analysis here initially focuses on a sample of 41 organisational actors from the field of political media relations in Germany. Subsequently, other actors named as important organisational contacts by the interviewees (but not interviewed themselves, mostly due to their representatives' refusal to take part in the study) are also taken into consideration; the same goes for 'new' (i.e. non-established) actors named as part of a network sampling conducted within the interviews.

All individual actors identified here in the initial sampling either account for the communication of the political actors in question – gaining their elite status from their authoritative standing within these focal organisations (cf. Maurer & Vähämaa, 2014, p. 59) – or work as high ranking political journalists within the leading media outlets identified. Such journalists are regarded as being elite actors (cf. Blumler, 1998, p. 94), again even more so due to the focal standing of their organisations.

Methodology

The first empirical analysis conducted here focuses on perceptions of digitisation and is therefore guided by the research questions 1a-1d. Methodologically, it draws on 45 personal (semi-structured) interviews with political spokespersons and communication managers and political journalists.

The necessity for such interviews here derives from an understanding of perceptions as the results of processes of the organisation, identification and interpretation of sensually grasped stimuli. The enquiry is at this point interested in the ways in which leading spokespersons, communication managers and journalists perceive digitisation and its implications. Since these perceptions are the results of internal processes of the actors in question (be it on an organisational or individual level), they can only be analysed by making recourse to those that perceive. One has to ask the perceiving actors about their perceptions; there is no other way of accessing them.

---

47 Four media outlets (Der Spiegel, Die Welt, ZDF heute, ZDF heute.de) provided more than one interviewee when asked to participate in the 'Media Relations Online'-study; in these cases network data (which, as indicated, is analysed on an organisational level) was aggregated per organisation leading to 25 journalistic datasets.

These interviews were conducted by two interviewers (including the author). The questionnaires focus on four areas of interest: perceptions of technologically induced media change, perceptions of technologically induced organisational change, perceptions of technologically induced political change and informational relations and communication networks between actors present in the field of political media relations.[48] In each area, they employ a combination of closed and open questions, thereby allowing for an adequate degree of standardisation without hindering spontaneous in-depth answers, potentially providing further insights into the expert knowledge of the interviewees (cf. H. O. Mayer, 2004, pp. 37-38, 58, 90-94; Möhring & Schlütz, 2010, pp. 72-75; Schnell, Hill, & Esser, 2008, p. 323).

The conduction of the interviews as personal interviews is demanding, especially in terms of resources, but also allows for the elicitation of rich data, even concerning potentially sensitive issues (cf. Kocks & Raupp, 2016, pp. 253-254; Möhring & Schlütz, 2013, pp. 195-197). The 'classic' perils of personal interviews such as a lack of anonymity around potentially sensitive topics are not of importance here since interviews concern professional perceptions and professional network building rather than potentially shameful personal thoughts, feelings and experiences (cf. Irvine, Drew, & Sainsbury, 2013, p. 88; Shuy, 2003, p. 179). What might still be of influence though are interview effects such as for example phenomena of social desirability. These have to be reflected in the interpretation of the findings.

A pretest for the questionnaires was conducted between 04/2012 and 05/2012. Here four political spokespersons and journalists that did not make part of the actual sample were interviewed. The actual interviews were then conducted between 06/2012 and 05/2013. Their average duration was between 45 and 60 minutes (with one exception of 112 minutes); 43 of 45 interviews were audio-recorded with the consent of the interviewees.

For data evaluation, answers to closed questions (mostly given on five point scales) were compiled in an *SPSS*-dataset and then subjected to quantitative evaluation. Answers to open questions were transcribed and then subjected to an in-depth qualitative analysis.

The second empirical analysis then focuses on actual adaptations of digitisation. It is guided by the research questions 2a-2d. Methodologically, it utilises a combination of empirical methods. The online presences of political actors are subjected to a (quantitative) content analysis focusing on the means employed

48 Two separate questionnaires were employed for spokespersons and journalists. Questions are in concordance, yet (primarily in terms of wording) adapted to the specific work environment of the two groups of interviewees.

and on the actual patterns of their employment. The means utilised by political spokespersons and journalists in their communicative exchanges are evaluated based on data from the 45 interview conducted with these actors. Communication networks are then analysed by social network analysis. The data for the latter step again derives from the 45 personal semi-structured interviews.

The content analysis was conducted as a quantitative analysis of websites and social media presences of political actors in two waves (2011 and 2013) within the research project 'Media Relations Online'. The first wave was coded by three coders (including the author), the second wave by two coders (including the author). In both cases pretests were conducted with 10% of the overall sample. An additional content analysis focusing on the social media presences (*Twitter* and *Facebook*) of governmental bodies was conducted in 2013 by 17 coders (excluding the authors). Again, a pretest with approximately 10% of the overall sample was conducted beforehand.[49]

The instrument of the two waves of content analysis conducted within 'Media Relations Online' in 2011 and 2013 focuses on the websites of political actors, taking into account both their general section and – if available – their specialised press-section. It inter alia measures the frequency of updates, the availability of communicative and informative options and the overall usability. On a content related dimension it distinguishes between purely informational and mobilising website content on a five point scale (cf. Hirzalla, Van Zoonen, & de Ridder, 2010, pp. 2-3). Additionally, the instrument also seeks to analyse social media presences (including *Facebook*, *Google+*, *VZ-Netzwerke*, *Twitter* and *YouTube*). Again analysis focuses on frequency, the enablement of user dialogue and the identification of the type of content that is distributed as either informational or mobilising (again operationalised on a five point scale). The instrument of the additional content analysis of governmental social media presences (*Facebook* and *Twitter*) focuses on the content that these actors distribute through these channels. It distinguishes between different types of information (factual information, background information, and warnings), mobilising content, soft news, campaign communications and service communications, thereby allowing to gain further insights into the actual usage of social media platforms among governmental bodies.

As indicated, the next field of analysis here regards the communicative preferences of political spokespersons, communication managers and journalists. Since it is not feasible to monitor actual daily communications, especially due to the elevated status of these actors and to their professional secrecy, communica-

49 The reliability-threshold in all pretests for the three content analyses was set at a minimum of r(Holsti) >.80.

tive preferences and routines are enquired into within the personal semi-structured interviews conducted with them. Interviewees are questioned about their preferred channels of daily communicative exchange within political media relations and about potential.

The same semi-structured interviews also ground the subsequent social network analysis. Gathering data for social network analysis this way is generally considered demanding and time-consuming but often also regarded as one of the most promising methods (Borgatti, Everett, & Johnson, 2013, pp. 29-30, 54-56; Hollstein, 2011, p. 410; Kocks & Raupp, 2016, pp. 253-254; Ter Wal & Boschma, 2009, p. 748), especially due the possibilities that a further enriching of network structures by additional interview data offers (Stegbauer, 2001, p. 167).

Network interviews here first employ a closed list of potential contacts that is based on a theoretical sampling of important organisational actors from the fields of politics and the media. This is then supplemented by an open network sampling in which the interviewees are asked to name additional contacts of importance for their communicative work within political media relations. Analysis is conducted on an organisational level and bi-modal, focusing on inter-group relations between media outlets and political actors and not on intra-group contacts between spokespersons or between journalists only. All actors constitute network nodes, ties between them are first to be understood as communicative exchanges; further enrichment of these ties then adds dimensions such as the regularity of contact or (perceived) influence in the field of political media relations to the analysis. All network data derived from the interviews is digitised utilising *SPSS* statistics software and subsequently analysed utilising the network analysis software *UCINet* with *NetDraw*.

4.2 Assumptions

Reviews of relevant literature and reflections based on elite theory yield a variety of assumptions concerning potential perceptions and adaptations of digitisation in the field of political media relations.

The first complex of research questions focuses on the perceptions individual actors have of digitisation and on the related technologically induced changes affecting their organisations, their daily communicative exchanges and their communicative networks. It circles around one central research question:

RQ1: How do elite actors from the field of political communication in Germany perceive the process of digitisation and its implications and consequences?

Here the central point of interest is the way in which practitioners of political communication, a group potentially affected by digitisation in their daily work routines and organisational surroundings, perceive different kinds of technologically induced changes. In particular, analysis concentrates on perceptions of technological (RQ1a) and organisational change (RQ1b) and on those that regard patterns of interaction and actual networks of communication in the field of political media relations (RQ1c), with specific regard to the set of actors present in these (RQ1d).

As a review of relevant literature indicates, digitisation is generally to be considered a process of tremendous impact for various societal fields, among these of course also those of politics and the media. Empirical analyses of political communication under the conditions of digitisation show a strong impact of new digital means on this field; patterns of external communication and communicative interaction are often strongly affected by new technological possibilities. The interviewees as individual actors of elevated standing within focal political organisations and media outlets, as a positional elite for that matter, accordingly find themselves in a field which could be considered in permanent flux. Since they are not to be understood as completely remote elite groupings but rather as heavily involved actors, it is expectable that they will perceive a variety of technologically induced changes.

Furthermore, as existing empirical studies suggest, there are slight differences between the groups of interviewees to be expected. Since media outlets are generally considered comparatively stronger affected organisational actors, it is expectable that journalistic interviewees will express stronger perceptions of changes induced by digitisation. Assumingly, interviewees rooted in political organisations will have more positive perceptions of digitisation – generally a typical phenomenon for political communication practitioners – than their counterparts in political journalism which are often described as a slightly more sceptical group of actors in the field of political media relations.

Given the overall direction of the debate on digitisation however, both groups of interviewees should at least show some scepticism concerning the actual integration of new and formerly marginal actors into networks of political communication. From a theoretical perspective, monitoring current developments and debates in their field would be considered important for these actors, so it is expectable that their actual perceptions would, at least to some extent, reflect the general direction of the debate concerning the integration of new and formerly marginal actors into networks of political communication.

Further analyses then regard actual adaptations of digitisation by individual political communication professionals and their specific organisations. Potentially, these adaptations are often influenced by the perceptions these individual actors have (cf. Bader, 2013, p. 66; Donges, 2008, pp. 56; 140-151). Furthermore, a specific set of assumptions can be formulated based on the empirical state of research and on theoretical reflections. Here, the first research question (RQ2a) asks about political websites and social media presences: *How do organisational political actors construct their online presences? Which communication options do they maintain and in how far do they integrate reciprocal elements?*

Political online presences initially function as a means of elite to non-elite communication; they do however also offer some dialogic potential, principally allowing elite with non-elite communication. It is expectable that political actors will maintain professional online presences and seek to be present on a variety of social media platforms. From a theoretical perspective, elite to non-elite communication is generally deemed important; in contemporary democracies the distribution of information and making policies and concepts known are of great importance. This is especially true for those actors that are – unlike governmental bodies – not in long-term institutionalised positions of power.

Dialogic functions are feasible in technical terms yet more demanding in terms of resources; they would constitute channels of elite with non-elite communication. From a theoretical perspective, it is expectable that political actors would employ some dialogic functions within their online presences, yet still give priority to the distribution of information, especially if they find themselves in long-term institutionalised positions of power. Considerations concerning the legal constraints faced by governmental actors in Germany indicate greater communicative freedom for political parties, both in terms of content that is not entirely informational and online dialogue (cf. Holtz-Bacha, 2013; Jensen, 2006; Kocks & Raupp, 2014b). This again renders some differences between the online presences of governmental bodies and political parties probable. Assumingly the former will – despite a generally high state of digitisation – show greater communicative restraint.

The empirical state of research supports these assumptions. Findings generally indicate a high state of digitisation; political actors are present in the online sphere and they maintain professional presences. Dialogic channels are sometimes employed, yet priority is overwhelmingly given to means that rather distribute information, that serve as means of unidirectional communication. Slight differences between governmental bodies and political parties are also to be expected, as research into the situation in Germany in particular indicates.

The second research question (RQ2b) focuses on the actual communicative exchanges between individual communication professionals from the fields of media and politics: *Through which channels do individual actors from the field of political communication (i.e. political spokespersons and journalists) engage in communicative exchange in the online age?*

Actual communicative exchanges between political journalists and political spokespersons and communication managers would have to be considered elite with elite communication. Here individual elite actors interact directly. Often both sides are mutually dependent and – despite established role-conceptualisations – both act as demanders and providers of information (cf. A. Davis, 2009; Jarren & Röttger, 1999; van Aelst, Sehata, & Dalen, 2010). This interconnection of actors combined with a high degree of mutual dependency renders probable a scenario in which individual elite actors match their communicative preferences to a great extent. Greater differences in channel preferences between the two groups are improbable, mutual dependency calls for similar communicative preferences.

The third research question (RQ2c) then asks about network structures: *How are communication networks between politics and the media constructed under the conditions of digitisation?*

Again, this question primarily concerns elite with elite communication, i.e. an area to which the actors in question arguably attribute great importance. Network connections with (other) elite actors are regarded as a form of social capital (cf. Jansen & Diaz-Bone, 2011), it is therefore in the very interest of elites to build and maintain these. Actors from the media sphere depend on high ranking political actors as sources of information; privileged access and strong connections substantiate political coverage. Vice versa, actors from the political sphere depend on central media outlets and high ranking journalists to reach large audiences, both within politics (cf. A. Davis, 2003) and the broader population. Additionally, these media professionals potentially function as sources of information for political actors, providing them with knowledge about political processes and competing political elites (cf. A. Davis, 2009; Jarren & Röttger, 1999). From a theoretical perspective, strong connections between central elite actors are expectable. Leading political actors will seek close communicative connections to important media outlets, especially to those deemed important for the political field. Vice versa, media outlets and the journalists working for them will then also seek to maintain such connections to central political actors.

The state of research generally supports these assumptions. Admittedly, actual network studies on political media relations are still rare, yet the picture emerging so far is one of close connections between elite actors, of interconnectedness and mutual dependency. Existing studies often describe political media relations as a phenomenon largely dominated by leading actors from politics and the media.

The question though is whether or not these networks actually integrate new actors. This is approached by the fourth research question (RQ2d) which asks about integration into media relations networks: *Which role do new or formerly marginal actors play in political media relations under online conditions?*

From a theoretical perspective, the integration of non-elite actors into elite networks would be expectable, yet only on a small scale. Sociological elite theory considers the ascent of non-elites into the elite sphere a necessity to maintain established structures and distributions of power. Apart from all the normative considerations, some degree of non-elite ascent is in the very interest of elite actors who wish to maintain their elevated standing and their power-holding position. Adapted to a context of political media relations, one should expect to find some new actors (e.g. political blogs and bloggers or new political and civil society organisations) within communication networks that are however still largely dominated by established elite actors.

4.3 Perceptions of Digitisation

How do leading political spokespersons, communication managers and journalists perceive processes of digitisation and their implications for the fields of politics and political communication? Is the proliferation of ICTs considered important or regarded more as a phenomenon of only marginal impact? According to those that shape political communication in Germany, which effects might digitisation have and in how far might it lead to in- or exclusion into or from communicative networks in this field? Last but not least: Which kinds of implication and outcome of digitisation do those that actually inhabit the field of political communication perceive?

The first complex of analysis in this thesis focuses on perceptions of digitisation. It seeks to analyse the perceptions of those individuals that either account for the communication of political actors (i.e. governmental bodies or political parties) or that provide political coverage for leading media outlets. Individual actors occupying important positions in the field of political media relations are questioned regarding their perceptions of digitisation and its consequences for themselves, their organisations and the field as such.

It specifically focuses the first complex of research questions postulated here. These are related to one central question:

RQ1: How do elite actors from the field of political communication in Germany perceive the process of digitisation and its implications and consequences?

In particular, they ask about technological change and organisational political change, about changing patterns of interaction and network integration:

RQ1a: How do elite actors from the field of political communication in Germany perceive technological change under the conditions of digitisation?
RQ1b: How do elite actors from the field of political communication in Germany perceive organisational change under the conditions of digitisation?
RQ1c: How do elite actors from the field of political communication in Germany perceive changing patterns of interaction in their field under the conditions of digitisation?
RQ1d: Which changes do elite actors from the field of political communication in Germany perceive regarding the set of actors present and the patterns of influence prevalent in the field of political media relations?

As indicated, this complex of analyses draws on personal semi-structured interviews with political spokespersons and communication managers from governmental bodies and political parties represented in federal parliament and with political journalists who account for the political coverage of leading off- and online media outlets.

The following sub-chapters will now first approach some statistical data concerning the actual interviewees. Thereafter the interviewees' perspectives on their profession and their professional roles will be analysed. Both enquiries primarily serve as means of contextualisation, grounding further enquiries into perceptions of digitisation and – in subsequent analyses – also into actual adaptations of the process. Then the actors are asked how they perceive the importance of digitisation for themselves and their professional life, and attention is drawn to the effects they attribute to it regarding their own organisation and other actors in this field. Perceptions regarding implications of digitisation affecting political communication and politics as such are analysed; additionally, special attention is given to perceptions regarding the in- and exclusion of new actors into communication networks in the field of political communication. In sum, the analysis takes an individual, an organisational and a superordinate macro-level into account, enquiring into perceptions of political spokespersons, communication managers and journalists with regard to all of these.

Political spokespersons, communication managers and journalists are equally treated as inhabitants of the field of political communication. However, due to their different organisational surroundings (affecting both liberties and constraint structures), their different professional roles and last but not least their different professional socialisation, the findings are always differentiated between these two groups.

4.3.1 Communication Professionals and their Professional Roles

Who are the individuals that account for the communication of major political actors? Which journalists provide coverage for leading media outlets in Germany? What background do these persons have and how do they perceive professional roles within the field of political media relations? The following is an enquiry into some basic statistical data concerning the interviewees and into their perceptions of their own and neighbouring professional roles.

The sample here consists of 38 male and seven female interviewees, the latter group can be subdivided into four female journalists and three female spokespersons.[50] Accordingly the percentage of women in the whole sample is 15.6%; among the journalists we find 13.8% women, among the spokespersons the percentage is slightly higher at 18.8%. The age of the interviewees is measured in ten-year steps, the youngest group ranging from 22-32 years (in 2012), the oldest consisting of those that are over 63 years of age. It is widely accepted that the so called generation of digital natives is the one that was born after 1980 (Palfrey & Gasser, 2013, p. 1), therefore the lowest age group here should include these; there are not expected to be any interviewees below 23 years of age due to the senior positions in political communication that the interviewees have to have.

Age group	23-32	33-42	43-52	53-62	>63	n/a
n (N=45)	4	14	14	9	2	2

Tab. 2: Age of interviewees.

The high percentage of interviewees in the middle age groups is not surprising given the fact that the positions of interest for the interviews (i.e. leading politi-

50 A list of interviewees and their affiliations is to be found in the appendix.

cal spokespersons, communication managers and journalists) are hardly early-career positions.

Accordingly, many of the interviewees look back on a long career in their respective field. On average, journalistic interviewees have been in their job for 21.4 years and have worked for their current medium for 12.4 years. The average work-experience of spokespersons is comparatively lower at 8.9 years; they have worked for their current organisation for an average of 4.5 years. Both groups show a relatively high variance, standard deviations are 8.52 and 9.09 for journalists and 4.9 and 5.1 for spokespersons and communication managers. Extreme values (like the 45-year work experience of one senior political journalist) only slightly contribute to these results, even the employment of a measure that is robust against such extreme values confirms a picture of high work experience; the median values for journalists are 20 (overall work experience) and twelve years (current medium), those for political spokespersons six and three years. Again, given the fact that interviews were only conducted with high or highest ranking spokespersons and journalists and that German journalists in particular tend to start their careers relatively early (often as freelancers in their early 20s), these values appear plausible. Changing power relations and political office terms might – besides the fact that many spokespersons have indeed changed professional roles during their career – contribute to the comparatively lower values for political spokespersons.

As indicated, a change in professional roles is relatively common among those interviewees that work as spokespersons and communication managers; half of them can look back to previous work experience in the journalistic field (potentially also contributing to their comparatively shorter work-experience in their current field), however none of them still work (part-time) as journalists; as is to be expected, professional roles are clearly separated here. In contrast, journalists have hardly any experience in the field of (political) public relations; only three of the 29 journalistic interviewees have ever worked in PR previously.[51]

Most interviewees have an academic background; they show high levels of formal education. As a matter of fact there is only one journalist without any tertiary education. Most interviewees have graduated in either social sciences or arts and humanities; natural sciences are very uncommon.

51 Interestingly, these three interviewees occupy very high positions in leading media outlets, even in comparison to the other high-ranking journalistic interviewees: one is deputy editor in chief for a major tabloid, one deputy editor in chief for a major quality weekly newspaper and one is editor in chief for the online version of a major weekly magazine.

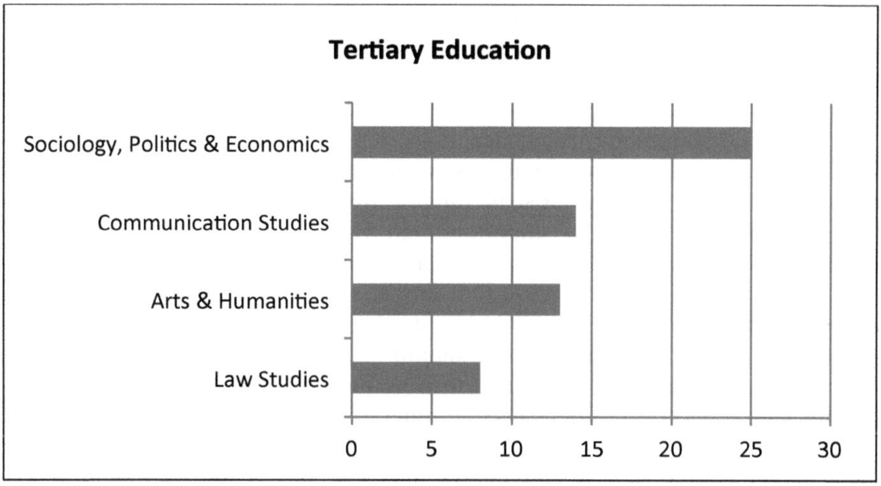

Fig. 5: **Tertiary Education: Interviewees per field of study;** multiple answers possible; [n (interviewees): 45; subjects with low numbers (such as natural sciences) have been erased; one interviewee refused to state his field of study].

Within their organisations, the interviewees do, as indicated, mostly occupy high or highest ranking positions; 60% of them work as heads of department, 7% even as heads of their respective organisational bodies (i.e. as editors in chief for their respective medium). A further 9% place themselves directly below their respective head of department, working in positions such as team leaders. The remainder mainly consists of journalists working as correspondents; these claim to have high degrees of autonomy and very much influence on political coverage, however, they do not necessarily occupy leading positions within their organisations. With regard to digital technology it emerges that the interviewees show a relatively high and long lasting affinity to such means. Asked about the beginning of their usage of a computer (either in their private or professional life), all named dates between 1975 and 1998. There is not a single interviewee with less than 14 years' experience in this field;[52] on average, interviewees have been using digital technology for about 23.8 years.

In sum, the interviewees are middle aged and highly educated professionals, and predominantly male. They can look back on a good many experience in their

[52] Values are missing for three interviewees here (two spokespersons and one journalist); these could not recall their first computer usage in the interview.

field and have – in the case of the spokespersons – also had experience in the neighbouring one. They mostly occupy leading positions within their organisations, affording them a high degree of influence in the field of political communication surrounding their respective organisational body.

Questioned about their role conceptions, the interviewees are asked to rate a variety of items related to the professional fields of journalism and political communication on a five point scale ranging from 'not important at all' via 'rather unimportant', 'somewhat important' and 'rather important' through to 'very important'. They are asked both with regards to their own professional group as well as the respective other group. In a further step, they are then asked to critically evaluate their organisation's performance against these standards; having pointed out how important an issue should be, they then have to indicate the importance that is actually attributed to it by their respective organisation. Last but not least, concerning the respective other group, they have to confront their expectations on how important an issue should be for the other group with their personal perceptions of how much importance the other group actually attributes to it (e.g. journalists are asked about how important an issue should be for political spokespersons and are then asked to evaluate the actual performance spokespersons show in this regard). The following aims to present some findings from this step in order to complete the picture of the interviewees with regard to their conceptions of professional roles and the importance of certain issues for political spokespersons and journalists.

How important do the interviewed journalists consider (= *desired importance*) a) distributing precise information to the public, b) selecting of information (gatekeeping), c) providing citizens with the chance to be heard by politicians, d) scrutinising and criticising politicians, d) setting political agendas and d) engaging in dialogue with citizens? How do they rank their medium's performance in these regards (= *actual importance*)?

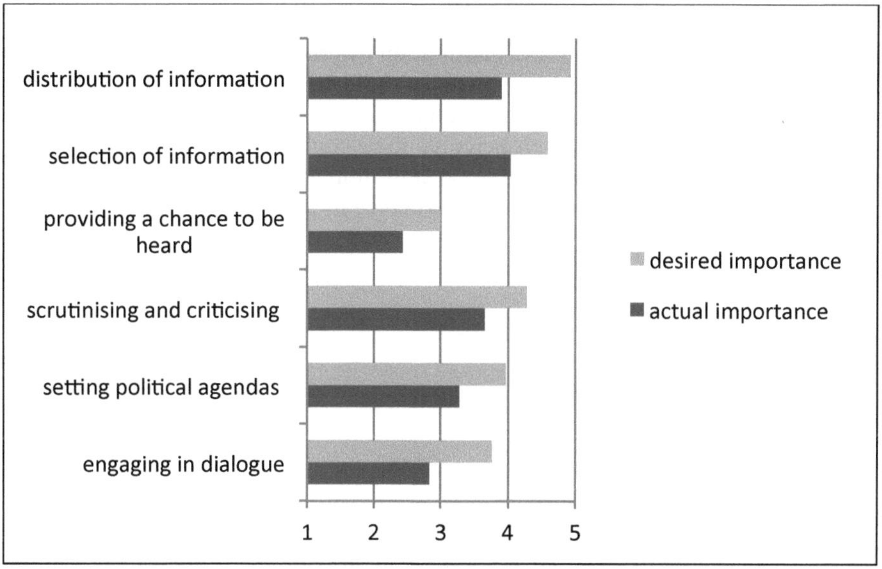

Fig. 6: **Journalistic role conceptions as seen by journalists: desired and actual importance;** (mean values for 29 journalistic interviewees; 1= not important at all, 5= very important).

It turns out that the interviewed journalists attribute utmost importance to the distribution of precise information to the public (M= 4.93), followed by functions such as the selection of information (M= 4.59) and scrutinising and criticising politics and politicians (M= 4.28). Functions normally associated with activist understandings of journalism are ranked considerably lower; accordingly the item 'providing citizens with a chance to be heard by politicians' only scores a mean of 3.00. The comparatively highest standard deviation here (SD= 1.31) indicates furthermore that there is in fact disagreement among journalists regarding the desired importance of this item.[53] Engaging in dialogue with recipients and citizens in general is also ranked comparatively low (M= 3.76).

Journalistic interviewees generally appear critical about their medium's actual performance regarding these items; in all cases they attribute lower values for actual importance than for desired importance. The comparatively highest values

[53] It is however not possible to identify any connection here between the organisational background of an interviewee (i.e. the medium that she or he works for) and the importance that is attributed to this item; the same goes for age and gender.

for actual importance are attributed to the gatekeeping-related item 'selection of information' (M= 4.03) and to the distribution of precise information to the public (M= 3.90), although the latter item is characterised by a relatively strong difference between actual and desired value.

How do these journalists then perceive their counterparts in political organisations? What are their expectations on how important an issue should be for them? How do they rate their actual performance in these regards?

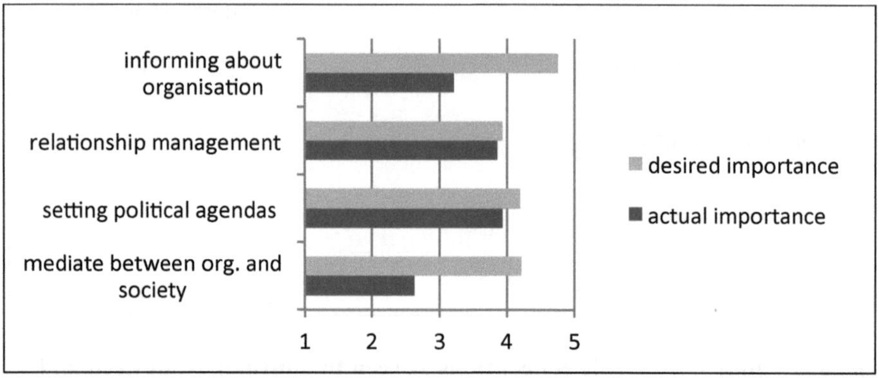

Fig. 7: PR role conceptions as seen by journalists: actual and desired importance; (mean values for 29 journalistic interviewees; 1= not important at all, 5= very important).

It emerges that journalistic interviewees overwhelmingly understand political public relations as the distribution of information about an organisation and its goals and policies (M= 4.75). This is closely followed by the mediation between organisation and society (M= 4.21) and the setting of political agendas (4.19). Relationship management is ranked fourth (M= 3.93). From a rather normative understanding of political public relations, journalists do expect political spokespersons to inform the public about what their organisation is doing and then to mediate between its particular interests and those of society.

Questioned about the actual performance of their counterparts in political communication, journalistic interviewees again appear very critical, often attributing lower values for actual importance than for desired importance. This is especially true for those items that they regard as central, namely informing the public (M= 3.21) and mediating between the public and the organisation (M= 2.62). They clearly indicate a (perceived) failure of political spokespersons to mediate. When it comes to relationship management and the setting of political agendas, however, the journalistic interviewees evaluate their counterparts as rather effective; there is no large difference between desired and actual values ascertainable here.

But how do the spokespersons in question see themselves with regard to these items? Which importance do they attribute to them and how do they rank their organisation's performance?

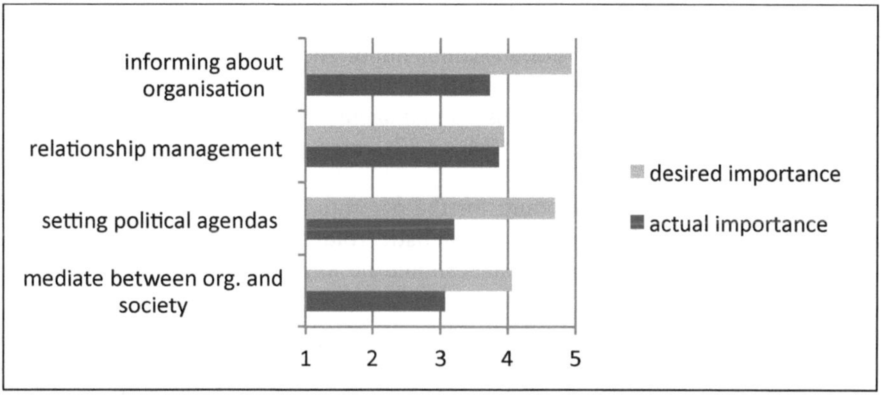

Fig. 8: **PR role conceptions as seen by spokespersons and communication managers: actual and desired importance;** (mean values for 16 interviewed political spokespersons; 1= not important at all, 5= very important).

Informing the public about the organisation and its goals and policies is regarded as the most important item here (M= 4.94), closely followed by political agenda-setting (M= 4.69). Mediation between the organisation and society is ranked in third place (M= 4.06), and relationship management comes after this (M= 3.94). It is apparent that the interviewed spokespersons generally regard all of these functions as important for their professional field (means hovering between rather and very important), yet they clearly give preference to information and agenda-setting.

The evaluation of actual performances in these regards shows that the interviewed spokespersons see considerable shortcomings in the importance their organisations give to political agenda-setting. While journalists have indicated (from an external perspective) that they perceive organisations as attributing high importance to this communicative task, the spokespeople in charge see it differently. With an actual importance of 3.20 (mean) in comparison to a desired importance of 4.69 (mean), this difference is apparent.

Admittedly however, while spokespeople generally tend to agree on a high desired importance, the perceptions of actual importance in this regard are far from unanimous, as a comparatively high standard deviation of 1.02 for this variable clearly emphasises. Critical evaluation of the actual importance is ascertainable in other fields as well as for example with regard mediating between organisation and society, where the interviewed spokespeople record a desired importance of 4.06 (mean) and an actual importance of 3.07 (mean). One can, however, identify relatively similar means for actual and desired performance with regard to the issue of relationship management, where spokespeople desire (M= 3.94) and actually perceive (M= 3.87) corresponding levels of attributed importance.

But how do those that account for the communication of political organisations view conceptualisations of journalistic roles? According to their understandings of journalism, which issues should be important and what importance is actually attributed to them?

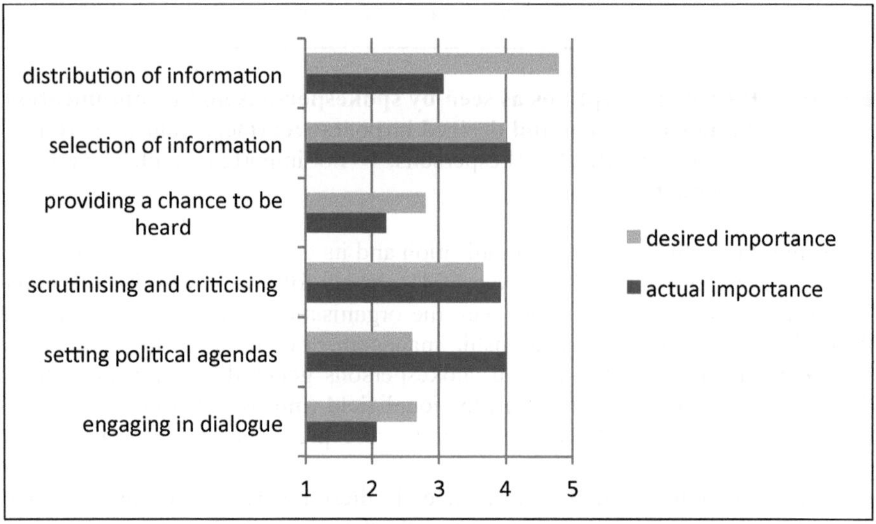

Fig. 9: Journalistic role conceptions as seen by spokespersons and communication managers: actual and desired importance; (mean values for 16 interviewed political spokespersons; 1= not important at all, 5= very important).

It emerges that the interviewed political spokespersons primarily understand journalists as distributors of information (M= 4.80). Their understanding of political journalism also puts emphasis on the selection of information (M= 4.00) and the scrutinising and criticising of politics and politicians (M= 3.67). Political spokespersons generally do not consider activist functions (such as providing citizens with a chance to be heard by politicians) as central parts of the journalistic role (M= 2.80), the same goes for any engagement in dialogue with recipients and citizens in general (M= 2.67) and also for political agenda-setting (M= 2.60).

However, when it comes to the perceptions spokespeople have of the actual performance of political journalists and media organisations in these regards, differing findings emerge. Interviewees generally agree that journalist attribute high importance to gatekeeping-functions, as a matter of fact, the values measured for actual importance (M= 4.07) here are even slightly higher than those for desired importance (M= 4.00). The same also goes (with in both cases slightly lower means) for the scrutinising and criticising of politics and politicians. An even greater gap between desired and actual values emerges with regard to agenda-setting functions: political spokespersons and communication managers regard this as an issue that should only be of minor (if any) importance for political journalism, yet they clearly point out that from their perspective journalists tend to attribute very high importance to this issue (desired importance: 2.60 (mean) vs. actual importance: 4.00 (mean)). On the other hand they clearly state that journalist tend to attribute too little importance to the distribution of precise information, while this is normatively considered an important issue (M= 4.80); according to the spokespersons interviewed, journalists only give medium importance to it (M= 3.07). From the perspective of spokespersons, activist and dialogic functions (normatively seen as rather unimportant) are not treated as issues of prime importance by political journalists; values for actual importance are comparatively low in both cases (M= 2.21 and M= 2.07 respectively).

In sum, the journalistic interviewees predominantly understand their professional role as one that is clearly dedicated to the selection and distribution of precise political information. They also put great emphasis on scrutinising and criticising politics and politicians. On the other hand, fostering dialogue with their audiences let alone acting as their advocates is a role concept that is not that widely accepted; the journalists interviewed place greater importance on their interaction with representatives of the political system. They generally appear to be critical about their medium's actual performance regarding these functions, yet point out that they largely succeed in gatekeeping and still place much (although not sufficient) importance on the distribution of information. Their picture of political spokespeople is characterised by an understanding of political public relations as the distribution of information about an organisation and its goals and policies, as the mediation between organisation and society and as the setting of political agendas. Spokespeople are supposed to be information brokers, mediators and influencers at the same time. Actual evaluation by political journalists however is critical, especially with regard to functions of information and mediation; they perceive their counterparts more as successful influencers and relationship managers.

Those interviewees that account for the communication activities of political actors see their professional role as being primarily characterised by the distribution of information about their organisation and its goals and policies and by political agenda-setting, They do however also attribute great importance to issues such as relationship management and mediating between the organisation and society. The evaluation of actual performances then shows that the spokespersons interviewed see considerable shortcomings in the importance their organisations give to political agenda-setting and, to a lesser extent, with regard to mediating between the organisation and society as well. They largely perceive the relationship management undertaken by their organisations to be in accordance with their expectations in this field.

Their picture of political journalism is characterised by an understanding of journalists as distributors of information and as professional gatekeepers, and to a lesser extent as professionals scrutinising and criticising politics and politicians too. They neither consider journalists to be civic advocates nor do they expect them to engage in or actually foster dialogue with audiences and citizens in general. Their actual evaluation of journalism and its performance in these regards leads to a differentiated image: spokespersons and communication managers acknowledge that journalists attribute high importance to gatekeeping and the scrutinising and criticising of politics and politician, but they also see considerable shortcomings regarding the distribution of precise political information. Even though they do not consider political agenda-setting as a journalistic task, they point out that journalists do in fact attribute high importance to this. With regard to dialogue and activism, they do not see any substantial importance devoted to these fields by professional political journalists.

4.3.2 Perceptions of Change

The preceding analyses were aimed at clarifying on the professional roles and understandings of the interviewees that account for the perceptions of digitisation and its effects that are to be analysed here. Findings are not representative for any larger group, let alone for political communicators as such but serve as a means of describing, contextualising and thereby understanding those whose perceptions are analysed here (i.e. the actual interviewees).

Interviews were conducted with 45 interviewees, 29 of them work as (leading) political journalists, 16 as political spokespersons and communication managers. These persons occupy central positions in the communication network between media and politics in Germany and, now that the preceding steps have clarified their socio-demographic characteristics, their professional and academic background and last but not least their role concepts and perceptions of these, the following will enquire into the perceptions of the digitisation of political communication that these 45 leading communication professionals have.

The first complex of interest concerns the importance of digitisation that the actors in question attribute with regard to themselves and their professional lives. Interviewees are asked to rate the importance of ICTs in their daily life, especially its professional part, on a five point scale, again ranging from 'not important at all' through 'rather unimportant', 'somewhat important' and 'rather important' through to 'very important'.

	Not important at all	Rather unimportant	Somewhat important	Rather important	Very important	*n*
Spokespersons and communication managers	**0**	**0**	**0**	**0**	**16**	*16*
Journalists	**0**	**0**	**0**	**6**	**23**	*29*
n	*0*	*0*	*0*	*6*	*39*	*45*

Tab. 3: Perceived importance of ICTs in daily (professional) life; (n=45).

Findings show that all interviewees attribute high importance to digital communication technologies; all spokespersons consider them 'very important', journalists overwhelmingly agree on that with only six of them seeing it as 'rather important'. There is no interviewee that ranks ICTs below that; the perception of high (or very high) personal importance is unanimous, regardless of age, organisational background or position.

The next questions concern the potentials digital media might have with regard to the distribution of (political) information and to their potential influences in the field of political coverage. Interviewees are asked to point out their degree of agreement to two statements regarding these possible effects of digitisation, they should do so on a five point scale ranging from one (completely disagree) to five (completely agree).

The first of these statements regards the potential of the Internet to replace established forms of mass media in the long run. Can ICT take over the functions of newspapers or television channels?

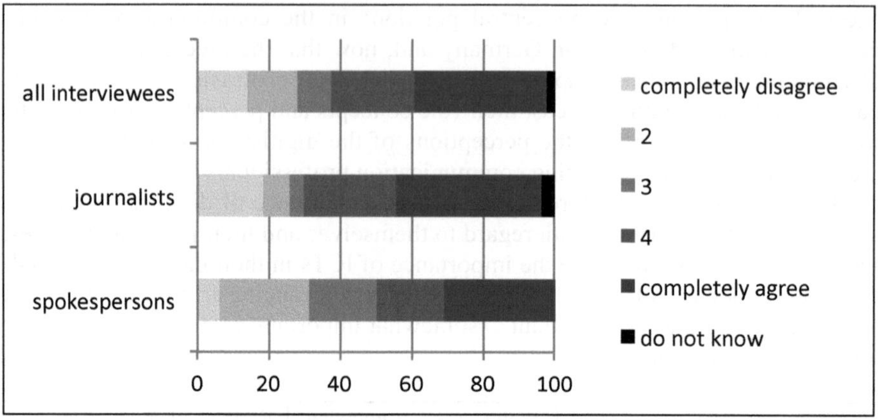

Fig. 10: 'The Internet can replace established forms of mass media in the long run' – degrees of agreement; (percentage; n=43(all) /27 (j) /16 (s); two journalists out of 29 did not answer, they have been excluded from the calculation here).

It emerges that both groups of interviewees show relatively high degrees of agreement here, attributing digitisation with potentials to largely re-shape the ways in which (political) information is communicated. 50.1% of the spokespersons and communication managers mostly or completely agree with the aforementioned statement on the possibility of such digitisation-related developments; of the 27 journalistic interviewees that answered the question, 60.5% did so too. There is in fact a majority in both groups that actually supposes strong potentials for digitisation to re-shape some established patterns of political communication. The second statement then regards the boundaries between the consumer and the producer of information. Popular assumption has it that digitisation might actually blur these, leading to a state in which people could simultaneously act in both roles, producing (political) information as well as consuming it. How do the interviewed political journalists and spokespersons see this? Do they agree with this assumption?

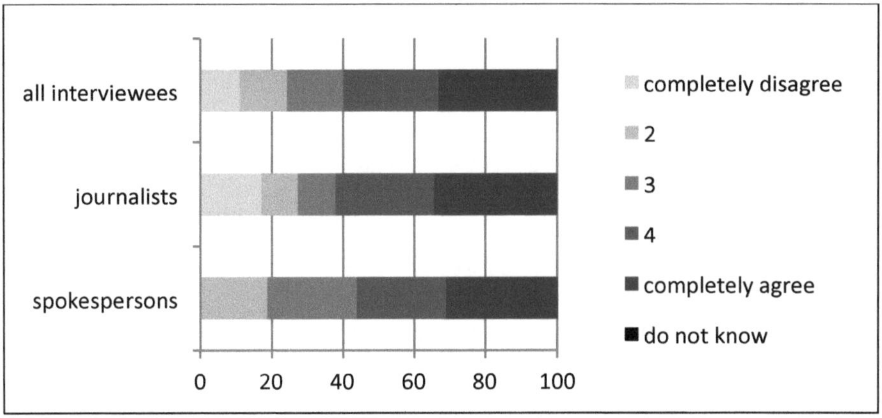

Fig. 11: 'ICTs increasingly blur boundaries between producers and consumers of information' – degrees of agreement; (percentage; n=45(all) /29 (j) /16 (s)).

Again one ascertains a majority in both groups that agrees to the postulation of strong digitisation-related effects on political communication. In fact, 62.1% of the journalistic interviewees here mostly or completely agree with this; among the political spokespersons and communication managers the rate is slightly lower, but nonetheless 56.3% still agree mostly or completely.

However, opinions are hardly unanimous when it comes to political news and transparency, i.e. to the question whether or not audiences could, under the conditions of digitisation, understand the origination process of political news more easily. While 53.5% of all interviewees totally disagree with this assumption, over a quarter (25.6%) of them say they mostly or completely agree. There is hardly any difference between the two groups of interviewees in this regard, except for the fact that the political spokespersons express even stronger disagreement, with 66.7% of them completely negating such assumptions compared with the 46.4% of journalists who do so.

So far, interviewees consider ICTs to have rather strong potential to change established patterns of political communication, yet they remain rather sceptical when it comes to the fostering of transparency in political news production.

Asked about potential changes to inter-organisational relationships and the exchange of information under the conditions of digitisation, interviewees again predominantly express perceptions of at least rather strong changes:

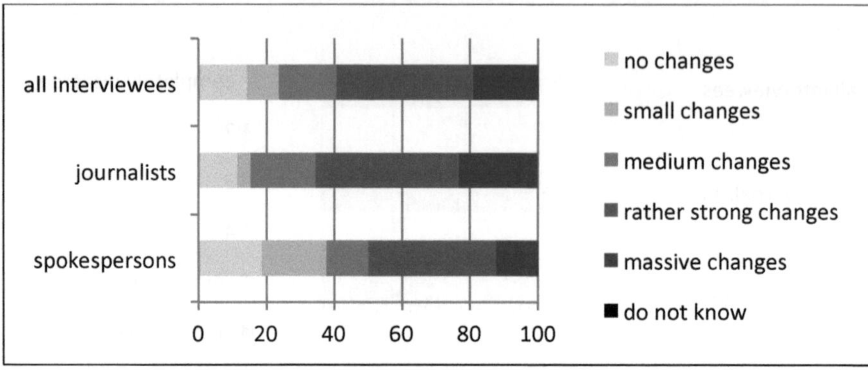

Fig. 12: 'Has digitisation altered inter-organisational relations and the related exchange of information?'; (percentage; n=42(all) /26 (j) /16 (s)).

Findings show that 50% of the interviewed spokespersons and communication managers actually perceive rather strong or even massive changes affecting inter-organisational relations and the related exchange of information. Among the 26 journalistic interviewees that answered this question, the rate is even slightly higher, with 65.4% expressing perceptions of either rather strong or even massive changes.

Having quantified their perceptions of changes to inter-organisational relations and related information exchanges, interviewees are then asked to be specific about this topic. Answers often concern issues such as scale, scope and timing; interviewees refer to altered conditions for information exchange.

In the first place, they do this with regard to simplified procedures of contacting their counterparts, referring to new ways of circumventing or avoiding extensive coordination with administrative offices and being able to reach persons of interest directly, inter alia via the social media (J12, §§5&13; J14, §13; J09, §17).[54]

Accordingly they often describe informational exchanges as increasingly direct and largely accelerated (e.g. J17, §27; J22, 17) and as becoming denser due to new communicative possibilities (J05, §13). As one journalist puts it:

> "More direct means that contact has become easier and is taking place in situations that are actually even crazier. Let me put it this way: Being at location Y, I can still remain in contact with a

[54] References refer to the code number of the interviewee and the specific paragraph (as sorted by MaxQDA) in their transcript of the interview.

chief whip who is currently at location X just by employing this form of 'wire'. And – how do I put this? – one gets a different perception of one another, above the level of mere exchange of content, an actual understanding of community" (J20, §33).[55]

The predominant perception of changing communicative exchanges is one of acceleration, often even to a comparatively large degree. All groups and subgroups of interviewees say the same (e.g. S03, §§30-33; S15 §17; J16, §5; J26, §§3-5). Journalists often connect specific expectations to this acceleration of communicative exchange, demanding concise answers to their questions in relatively short periods of time (J20, §9). At the same time they point out that these demands are often not yet met entirely by their counterparts in political media relations (J24, §5). Spokespersons confirm being confronted with increasing demand for fast and concise answers by political journalists (S15, §§3-5).

Both journalists and spokespersons also refer to the perils of accelerated political communication. This often regards an increasing amount of overall superficiality (e.g. J02, §§2-9); in some cases spokespersons also express concerns about a possible decrease in the quality of journalism (S16, §3; S13, §5) or in their own ability to communicate strategically (S06, §37).

Accelerated communication is welcomed on the one hand – especially by journalistic interviewees – as simplifying daily work routines and the provision of political coverage (e.g. J11, §13) but on the other hand is also deemed a potential threat to the overall quality of political communication. As one journalist puts it:

"To be frank, it is a constant – I almost called it a constant blathering. (…) You know what I mean: one finds an abundance of useless stuff there as well. One has to admit that: With such an abundance of content there is also a lot of rubbish. You can compare it to the bargain counter in a department store: you'll find something every once in a while but of course this is not always the case" (J15, §17).[56]

According to the interviewees here, information exchange has largely accelerated and in many cases become more direct due to the proliferation of ICTs. They feel

---

55 Original quote: „Also direkter heißt, man hat Kontakt leichter und in verrückteren Situationen. Also ich sag mal so: Ich kann ja, wenn ein parlamentarischer Geschäftsführer sich am Ort X aufhält und ich bin am Ort Y, kann man trotzdem auf diesem Draht miteinander in Verbindung bleiben. Und - wie soll man das beschreiben? - man nimmt sich auch anders wahr. Also das ist schon auch, sag ich mal, über die inhaltliche Beziehung hinaus dann mehr so ein Community-Verständnis."; [translation by the author (JNK)].

56 Original quote: „Also es ist schon ein ständiges - fast hätte ich gesagt Plappern. (…) Sie wissen was ich meine. Also es ist auch viel, viel nutzloser Kram dabei, nicht. Das muss man ja auch sagen. Bei so einer Fülle von Angebot kommt auch viel Schund. Das ist wie der Wühltisch im Kaufhaus. Da finden Sie mal etwas, aber eben nicht immer."; [translation by the author (JNK)].

that daily work routines are simplified but at the same time they also perceive a constant danger of superficiality.

The next field of interest regards the organisations the interviewees work for, be it in the form of governmental bodies or political parties, or media outlets, either on- and offline. To what extent do the interviewees see digitisation affecting these organisations and the work routines established within them?

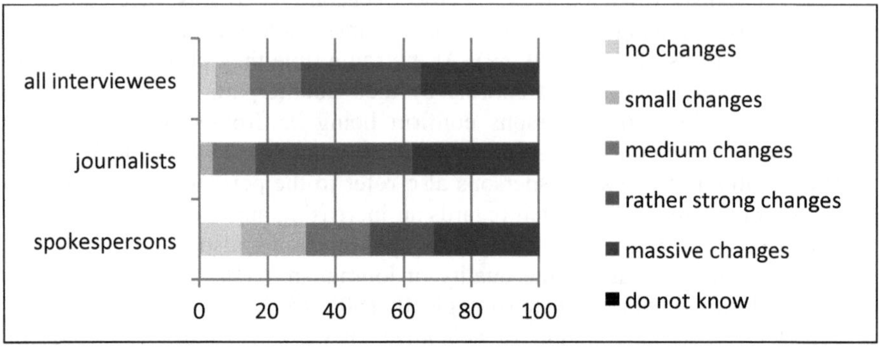

Fig. 13: Perceived strategic changes in interviewee's own organisation; (n(journalists)=24; n(spokespersons)=16; two further journalists did not answer, three gave invalid answers).

It emerges that the interviewees clearly perceive changes to their own organisations and the established routines of work due to digitisation. This is the case both for media outlets and political actors, although sometimes it concerns different areas and also to somewhat differing degrees.

Among the journalistic interviewees, 83.5% perceive changes to their organisations which they either classify as rather strong or even as massive. Given the fact that a further 12.5% describe perceived changes of a medium degree, it becomes apparent that there is hardly any journalistic interviewee who does not consider digitisation to be a process of influence for media organisations.

Asked specifically about the nature of these changes, they often refer to new internal structures reflecting media change. Media outlets employ community managers accounting for the interaction with audiences through social media channels (J18, §§44-46), online media designers for the adaptation of journalistic content to the demands of the online sphere (J15, §55) or promote the complete integration of their online editorial teams into the main departments (J21, §51; J29, §102; J17, §63). In the case of one leading newspaper, journalists even describe the establishment of an 'online first'-strategy (J05, §31; J06, §47).

Despite different degrees of off- and online linkages in various media outlets, there is a clear trend towards a greater emphasis on online content and on the integration of formerly excluded online editorial teams. As one journalist puts it:

> "It started with the online editorial teams being outsourced years ago — well not even that many years ago. These were usually subsidiary companies that paid less and to some extent had the reputation of being computer monsters. They are becoming more and more integrated and one can say (…). Basically, everything is merging together more and more." (J10, §28).[57]

Given the fact that in general the interviewees often perceive strong organisational changes and especially do so with regard to increasing linkages between off- and online editorial teams, it remains to be clarified what effect these changes have on some of their daily journalistic routines. In how far do the perceived linkages between off- and online reflect on the level of actual online content production and do they generally lead to higher levels of cooperation within editorial teams, thereby simultaneously moving away from an established model in which a reporter is often responsible for an article from the initial research through to final editing?

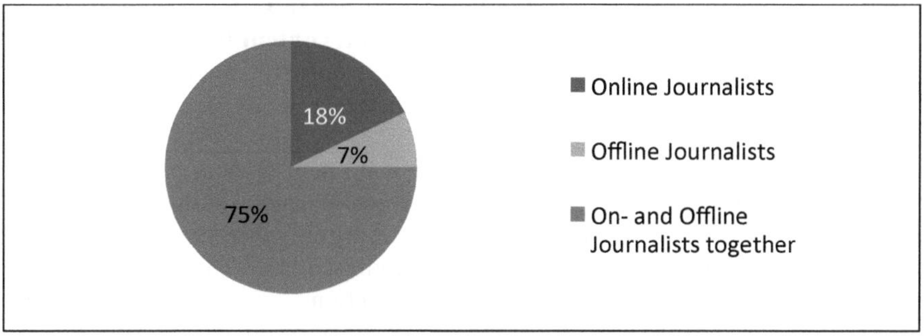

Fig. 14: 'Who provides content for your online-medium / the online-variant of your medium?'; journalistic interviewees only (n=28, one further interviewee did not answer).

According to the journalistic interviewees, most media outlets employ a model of cooperation between off- and online journalists for the production of online

57 Original quote: „Das fängt an, dass man früher ja auch noch, vor vielen Jahren - oder gar nicht so vielen Jahren, die Onliner ausgegliedert hat. Das waren in der Regel eigene Tochterfirmen, die auch schlechter bezahlt wurden, die auch ein bisschen den Ruch hatten nur so Computermonster zu sein. Und das wird mehr und mehr integriert, kann man sagen. (…) Also im Grunde, es wächst immer mehr zusammen."; [translation by the author (JNK)].

content. Nowadays, in many cases off- and online media outlets are separate entities or sometimes even legally independent companies (e.g. J09, §60), yet in the majority of cases content is produced together (e.g. J10, §28).[58]

The erosion of organisational boundaries has also affected daily work routines in terms of more collective content production, but to a smaller degree:

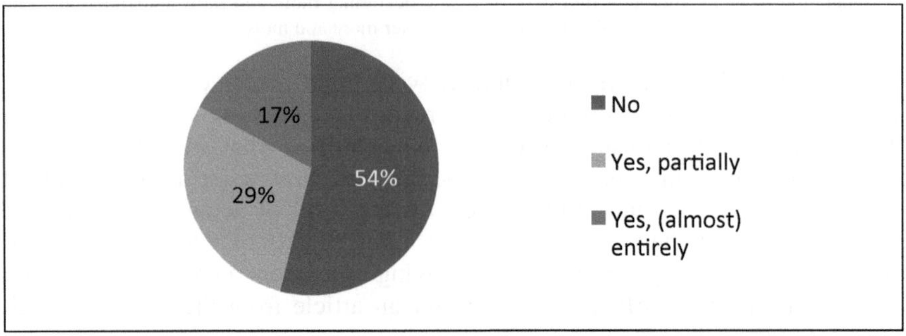

Fig. 15: Collective content production: 'Have organisational boundaries within your medium eroded so far that content is now produced collectively?'; journalistic interviewees only (n=25, one interviewee did not answer, three gave invalid answers).

Over half of the interviewees state that there is no new form of content production that could be described in terms of collectiveness and a further 29% refer to partial developments in this direction. So far, entirely collective production of content is – at least among the media outlets analysed here – hardly a mass phenomenon, despite some developments in this direction.

The interviewed spokespersons and communication managers also express perceptions of some form of organisational change due to digitisation, yet the degree to which they see this shows a greater variance than in the case of the interviewed journalists. While 50% of them perceive changes that could either be described as rather strong or even massive, a further 30% only perceive either small or no changes at all.

Interviewees often refer to the establishment of specialised (sub-) departments that deal with political online communication and the social media presences of their respective organisations; this goes both for political parties (S02, §§86-95; S03, §§85-88) and governmental bodies (e.g. S16 §41). Never-

[58] This even goes for the media outlet of the interviewee (J09) who clearly emphasised the legal separation of off- and online.

theless, the online departments are often seen as sub-departments subordinated to larger departments that account for (external) communication in general – especially in the case of governmental bodies (e.g. S15, §§65-69). According to the interviewees, political parties are putting greater emphasis on organisational adaptations of digitisation; some emphasise the autonomy of their online departments (as opposed to organisational subordination) (S02, §93), some even perceive themselves as pioneers in the implementation of online communication in their organisational structures (S04, §120).

However, not only do the interviewed spokespersons, communication managers and political journalists perceive changes to organisational structures of their own organisations: they also consider organisations on the other side of the field of political communication to be affected in their strategies by processes of digitisation. Political spokespersons and communication managers see media outlets changing their strategies due to digitisation and political journalists perceive changes affecting organisations and their strategies on the political side.

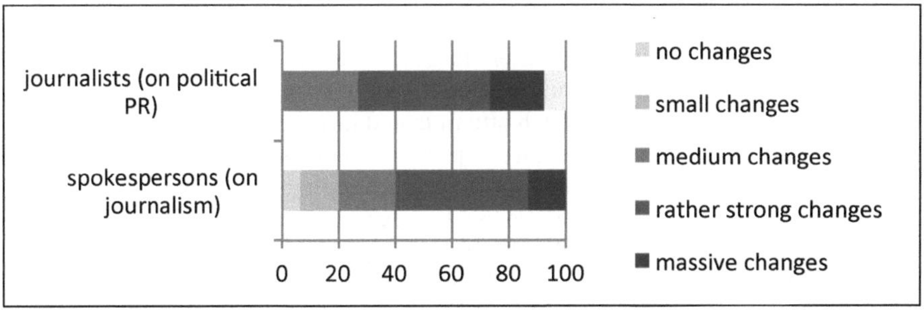

Fig. 16: Perceived strategic changes on the other side of political communication; (n(journalists)=26; n(spokespersons)=15; four interviewees did not answer).

The journalistic interviewees perceive strategic changes within political organisations that they mostly describe as rather strong (46.2%) or even massive (19.2%), a further 26.9% consider them to be on a medium level. The interviewed spokespersons and communication managers on the other hand again show a larger variance of perceptions; their accounts differ between no changes and massive changes, with a majority (46.7%) perceiving rather strong changes. Within the group of interviewees, political journalists appear to generally perceive stronger effects of digitisation, regardless of whether it is in their own field or another one.

Accordingly, they mostly perceive their own ability to set (political) agendas as being greater due to digitisation. They refer to new possibilities of online communication – often citing the micro-blogging platform *Twitter* as an example – and to the related increase in agenda-setting opportunities (e.g. J20, §17; J18, §17). The placement of hyperlinks and the implementation of dialogic possibilities, forums and social network connections are also named as contributing factors in this regard (J27, §15; J22, §9; J11, §9). Being able to reach new and wider audiences and a general increase in scope are perceived as advancing the possibilities for agenda-setting by a majority of journalistic interviewees. There are only a few exceptions here, namely one journalist insisting that agenda-setting was not part of the work description of his medium (J26, §13) and two others expressing scepticism about any increases in their ability to set (political) agendas (J17 §9; J14 §9).

Asked about attempts of political spokespersons to circumvent them and their gatekeeping-function, journalistic interviewees express a variety of different perceptions. Theoretically, new digital means of communication could enable political communication professionals to bypass established media outlets, communicating messages directly to their target audiences. In how far do political journalists – i.e. those that would eventually be circumvented under the conditions of digitisation – perceive such attempts and how do they evaluate these?

Nearly all journalistic interviewees perceive increasing attempts by political spokespersons to circumvent them in their gatekeeping-function. Only one journalist states explicitly that – based on his experience in the field of political communication – this does not hold true (J17, §§109-119): apart from that, there is a broad consensus in this regard. The interviewed political journalists feel that they are actually being bypassed to some extent by their counterparts within political organisations (e.g. J09, §79-84; J23, §§95-97). However, their evaluations of this phenomenon differ.

Some consider bypassing a strategy that is employed by political actors, yet (at least so far) without any great success. This is often attributed to the relatively small audiences that are potentially to be reached by social media, especially when compared to the far larger ones of established media outlets (e.g. J26, §81; J05, §53). Some journalists also refer to the actual employment of these channels by political actors, stating that inadequate ways of approaching audiences often undermine successful communication, thereby rendering attempts at bypassing unsuccessful (J24, §71; J25, §87). Others argue in a similar direction, pointing out that a large fraction of the recipients would actually identify bypassed content as mere public relations (J18, §74).

Another group of journalistic interviewees actually attributes success to attempts at bypassing by political communication professionals. They discuss the phenomenon with regard to the new possibilities for external communication political actors have due to digitisation and in some cases point out that they perceive an actual demand by citizens to be addressed by them directly (J21, §84; J15, §81). Some see the gatekeeping function of media outlets eroding under these circumstances (J03, §102) while others lament that classic media often fall for originally bypassed messages, subsequently transporting them to an even greater audience (J08, §99).

Among the interviewees, the circumvention of established media outlets is generally not considered a pure challenger-phenomenon (i.e. a strategy only applied by those that do not have access to the sphere of established media) but is often explicitly named in connection with high ranking established actors (J17, §87; J05, §49; J06, §75; J20, §150). Accordingly, some journalistic interviewees mainly discuss bypassing as a complementary phenomenon, as a strategy of political communication professionals to supplement their classic media work (J01, §76; J13, §65). They perceive new channels as ways by which political actors seek to become a topic of public debate – or to receive media attention. At the same time they emphasise that they still see these actors putting emphasis on media outlets when it comes to communicating their political views and actual policies (J22, §72).

As a matter of fact, bypassing could be regarded as a way for political actors to target new audiences with their external communication. So far they have largely concentrated on professional journalists, now – to varying extents – they also address civil society actors and individual citizens. The question, though, is whether or not these new actors are only to be regarded as targets of bypassed political information or if they are actually integrated into the field of political communication. According to the interviewees: Has digitisation led to an integration of new actors into established patterns? In how far do these actors play a role for political communication?

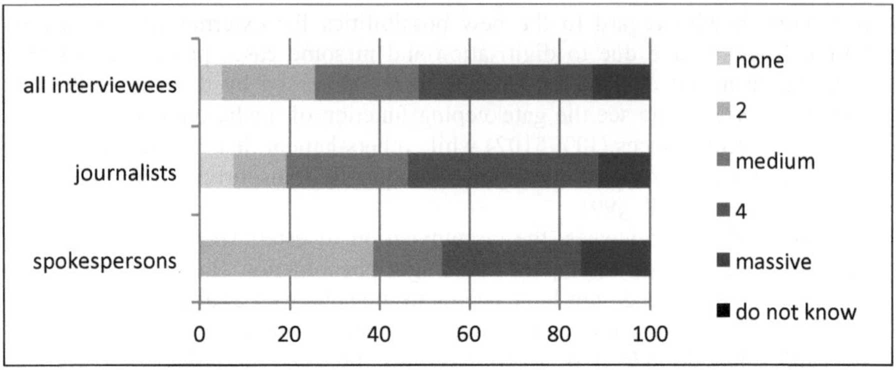

Fig. 17: Influence of new actors in the field of political communication; (percentage; n=39(all) /26 (j) /13 (s); two interviewees (one journalist, one spokesperson) gave invalid values (4.5 and 2.5), their answers are excluded here. Two members of each group did not answer).

Asked to rate the perceived influence of new actors in the field of political communication on a five point scale (ranging from 1: none to 5: massive), over 50% of the interviewed political journalists either opt for four (42.3%) or even five points (11.5%). A further 26.9% express perceptions of a medium influence of these actors, while only 19.2% perceive either small (11.5%) or no influence at all (7.7%). On average, journalistic interviewees perceive a level of influence of new actors that ranks above medium (M= 3.38), although their opinions do show some variance here (SD= 1.10).

The interviewed spokespersons and communication managers show a similar pattern of perceptions here, with over 45% of those answering rating the influence of new actors in the field of political communication with either four (30.8%) or even five points (15.4%). Yet at the same time the largest subgroup here is the one opting for a very small influence of these actors (with 38.5% opting for two points on the scale employed here); a further 15.4% opt for three points, i.e. a medium influence of new actors. The average level of influence these interviewees perceive is again slightly above medium (M= 3.23); their opinions also show some variance (SD= 1.17).

Asked which actors they perceived as having entered the field of political communication, the journalistic interviewees often name bloggers (e.g. J01, §18; J09, §§23-28), though repeatedly pointing out that these often come from backgrounds of professional journalism (e.g. J10, §17). Other bloggers can, according to some interviewees (J13, §38; J26, §69), become somewhat influential if they cover certain highly specified political fields. Additionally, some journalists refer to communities of individuals gathering and connecting on certain social media platforms such as *Twitter* or *Facebook* (J18, §37; J23, §49),[59] or to civic initiatives organising online (J19 & J28, §§41-48) as new influential actors.[60]

The interviewed spokespersons and communication managers also refer to bloggers (e.g. S10, §§55-57; S01, §33) and additionally name campaign-oriented platforms such as *Campact* in this regard (S03, §43; S10, §53; S08, §37). They furthermore also refer to civic pressure groups and NGOs (S15, §39; S10, §49; S07, §56).

Given the fact that they actually perceive new influential actors in the field of communication, both groups of interviewees are subsequently asked to prognosticate on the future role of these new actors: How will the influence of bloggers and other civil society actors named here beforehand develop in the future? Will there be a continuous growth in their importance in the field of political communication or have they achieved a status that will not undergo any further substantial changes? Might there even be developments leading in an opposite direction; developments causing these actors to actually lose some of their acquired influence in the field of political communication?

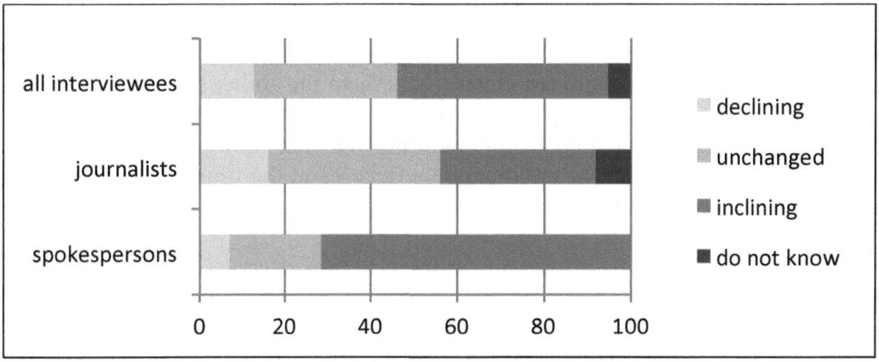

Fig. 18: Future influence of new actors in the field of political communication; (percentage; n=39(all) /25 (j) /14 (s); six interviewees did not answer this question).

59 In some cases the interviewees actually name these platforms as actors (e.g. J23, §49), emphasising the importance the platform per se has for the networking of new actors.

60 J19 and J28 were interviewed together; therefore there is one transcript for both of them in which their contributions are individually identified. The same also goes for J20 and J29.

The journalistic interviewees express diverging perceptions here: 40% of them do not foresee any future changes to the status of new actors in the field of political communication, while 36% predict a further increase. Yet at the same time 16% of them actually see the influence of new actors in decline. Among the interviewed spokespersons, the findings are somewhat more unanimous. 71.4% of them are convinced that the influence of new actors is about to grow further, while only 7.1% actually predict a decline here. 21.4% do not see any substantial changes to the importance of new actors in the near future.

While the findings emerging from the other questions often illustrate stronger perceptions of digitisation and its consequences among the journalistic interviewees, this does not hold true for the assessments of the future influence of new actors in the field of political communication. Here, they generally appear more sceptical than the interviewed spokespersons and communication managers which express relatively optimistic positions in this regard.

Given the fact that many interviewees perceive new actors entering the field of political communication under the conditions of digitisation, there is still a need to clarify the main beneficiaries of this process of digitisation. Does it primarily benefit new and formerly excluded actors or do those that already have their standing within the field of political communication make the larger gains? The perceptions of journalistic interviewees are divided on this matter. Some perceive new actors within the political field as the main beneficiaries of digitisation, pointing out that digitisation has given them the ability to reach larger and more dispersed audiences with their messages (e.g. J24, §55). Some of these interviewees then add a time factor, pointing out that they perceive new (and formerly excluded) actors as the main beneficiaries at the time of the interview, yet also expect established organisations to make up ground in this regard (e.g. J16, §43).

It is apparent that when journalistic interviewees describe new actors as the main beneficiaries of digitisation, they mostly do so with regard to the political side and generally not to the media; there is a clear differentiation in terms of gains between political actors and media outlets (J26, §§61-65; J02, §89).

Other journalists see both groups of actors benefiting equally from processes of digitisation. They point out that new actors could benefit, given their new ability to widen their scope and reach larger audiences, but that established players could also make considerable gains if they adapt to the new technological opportunities (e.g. J11, §59; J09, §68). Some emphasise that the beneficiaries of digitisation might differ depending on the actual topic in question, stating that there could be policy fields in which new actors might gain importance while other fields would favour the already established ones (J25, §§73-79). Interviewees perceiving beneficiaries both among new and established actors often emphasise that the professional adoption of new technological possibilities would determine gains, regardless of the former standing of an actor within the field of political communication (J23, §§73-77; J17, §91; J12, §72).

Then there are journalistic interviewees who primarily regard already established actors as beneficiaries of digitisation. As indicated, a large majority of the interviewed journalists express such perceptions with regard to media outlets, where they clearly see the already established ones as the main beneficiaries of digitisation (J06, §62; J26, §§61-65; J02, §89; J15, §§59-61). This is often related to the resources journalists deem necessary for media outlets to successfully adapt to new technological opportunities. As one journalist puts it:

> "Well, you have to have manpower to be able to afford a neat online presence, to be able to afford a nice *Facebook* community; you have to have a large publisher in the background. And these actors are usually newspapers and organisations that were big in the first place. I do not see shifts comparable to those in the political field there" (J18, §62).[61]

Here one again finds a differentiation between political actors and media outlets in terms of potential profits from digitisation; while the process is deemed to strengthen the position of already strong actors in the latter field, it is also attributed with chances for new ones in the political field. There are also journalistic interviewees who generally perceive established actors in both fields as the main beneficiaries of digitisation (J10, §34; J08, §71; J13, §61; J14, §44; J27, §73). According to these interviewees, digitisation benefits established media outlets and political actors who are already influential without having hardly any larger effect on the standing and representation of new and marginal actors within the field of political communication. As indicated, this is often attributed to a lack of necessary resources these actors face, yet one journalistic interviewee also explains that he perceives some form of communicative abstention among these actors, indicating a state in which many marginal actors refrain from taking part in digitised debates and rather utilise the Internet for other less serious and politically efficient activities (J14, §44).

Among the interviewed spokespersons and communication managers, one also finds some that perceive digitisation as a process primarily benefiting those actors that are already established. Here, two party spokespersons express such

61 Original quote: „Also wer sozusagen sich einen ordentlichen Internet-Auftritt leisten kann, wer sich eine schöne Facebook-Community leisten kann, der braucht Manpower, der braucht einen großen Verlag. Und das sind meistens die Zeitungen und Organisationen, die ohnehin schon groß waren vorher. Ich glaube, da hat sich nicht so viel verschoben wie im politischen Bereich."; [translation by the author (JNK)].

perceptions (S02, §§123-125; S06, §§121-127).[62] Again, reasons given for this are primarily related to the amount of resources interviewees deem necessary to maintain a continuous and professional presence in the online sphere.

Other interviewees from this field see the gains actors make due to digitisation change divided equally between established and new and often formerly marginal actors (S04, §§111-117; S14, §45-48; S07, §§87-94). Interviewees point out that active participation in the online sphere would benefit both types of actors, new ones by enabling them to have their say and established ones by further strengthening their position within the field of political communication. They often name the professional and strategic management of digitised communications as a necessary precondition for benefiting from digitisation; according to them this holds true for both types of actors regardless of their former standing (e.g. S07, §94).

Then there are spokespersons and communication managers who perceive digitisation as (predominantly) benefiting new and formerly marginal actors. According to them, it has the potential to alter patterns of political communication in so far as it enables new actors to communicate quickly and directly with their target audiences and relevant media outlets, often circumventing obstacles such as established gatekeepers and their threshold of relevance (e.g. S11, §§105-111; S12, §§148-150; S13, §§88-94). Some of these interviewees even perceive the organisational nature of new actors as an advantage under the conditions of digitisation, pointing out that adaptations of new communicative practices and accelerated routines would be easier for them (S15, §85). Digitisation is described as a process by which new and marginal actors get the chance to communicate in equal ways (and often equally professional) as established actors that are generally richer in resources (S08, §83).

In sum, the interviewed spokespersons and communication managers put a stronger emphasis on the potential digitisation might have for new and marginal actors in the field of political communication. While political journalists often describe already established actors (especially media outlets) as the main beneficiaries or see benefits for both sides, a large share of the other interviewees (especially those working for governmental bodies) have a different perception, as a categorisation of the main tenor found in the specific answers clearly illustrates:[63]

---

62 Interestingly, these interviewees come from very diverse party backgrounds; one is working for the relatively far-left party Die Linke, the other one for the conservative CSU.

63 Especially journalistic interviewees often gave complex answers when asked about their perceptions regarding digitisation's main beneficiaries. In order to enable a categorisation here, these answers have been analysed to identify their main tenor. This procedure admittedly leads to a re-

Digitisation primarily benefits→	*Established actors*	*Both established and new actors*	*New political actors, established media outlets*	*New actors*	*n/a*
according to **Journalists**	J01; J08; J10; J13; J14; J15; J27	J04; J09; J11; J12; J17; J20 & J29; J23; J25	J06; J18; J19 & J28; J21; J26	J02; J16; J22; J24	J03; J05; J07
according to **Spokespersons**	S02; S06	S04; S07; S14	-	S01; S03; S05; S08; S09; S10; S11; S12; S13; S16; S15	-

Tab. 4: Perceived main beneficiaries of digitisation; [main tenor of answer to open question about main beneficiaries of digitisation].

4.3.3 Summary and Interim Conclusion

The preceding analyses seek to enquire into the ways in which elite actors from the field of political communication in Germany perceive the process of digitisation and its implications and consequences (RQ1).

This question considers aspects of technological change, organisational political change, changing patterns of interaction and network integration. The first sub-question (RQ1a) focuses on technological change: *How do elite actors from the field of political communication in Germany perceive technological change under the conditions of digitisation?*

All interviewees perceive digitisation as an important process, regardless of their organisational background, position or age. This also reflects in the degrees of agreement they show with regard to certain assumptions concerning the effects of technologically induced media change: Both groups of interviewees show high degrees of agreement concerning the assumption that the Internet could replace established forms of mass media in the long run; among the journalistic interviewees the percentage is even higher. Similar observations can be

duction in complexity, yet it allows for a more concise visualisation of patterns of perceptions among the different group of interviewees.

made for agreements on the assumption that ICTs would increasingly blur the boundary between producers and consumers of information.

Technological change then has the potential to induce organisational change in the fields it affects. The second sub-question (RQ1b) focuses on that form of organisational political change: *How do elite actors from the field of political communication in Germany perceive organisational change under the conditions of digitisation?*

Both groups of interviewees perceive strategic changes related to technologically induced media change within their own organisations. However, there are differences between journalists on the one side and political spokespersons and communication managers on the other. The journalists interviewed overwhelmingly express perceptions of rather strong or even massive changes within their organisations, often referring to (strongly) altered internal structures in this regard. This inter alia regards the integration of online journalists into their editorial teams and new forms of collaboration between off- and online teams and even media outlets. The interviewed spokespersons and communication managers express perceptions that are on average less strong and they again show a greater variance between their individual answers. Asked specifically about the character of perceived strategic changes, they often refer to the establishment of sub-departments taking care of external online communication for their specific political organisations. Yet the evaluation of their actual importance differs between the two groups of interviewed spokespersons, those from a background of political parties generally consider them more important than their colleagues from a background of governmental bodies.

Subsequently questioned about the changes affecting organisations on the other side of the field of political communication, many journalists express perceptions of rather strong or even massive strategic changes within political organisations, a further third considers them to be on a medium level. The interviewed spokespersons and communication managers again show a larger variance of perceptions; their accounts differ between no changes and massive changes, with a majority perceiving rather strong changes.

In general, political journalists appear to have perceptions of stronger effects of digitisation, whether it regards the phenomenon as such and its consequences for their own field or for another one. The perceptions expressed by political spokespersons and communication managers are slightly weaker and show a considerably greater variance; opinions among these interviewees are far from unanimous.

Technological change can then also affect actual interactions between actors from the fields of politics and the media. The third sub-question (RQ1c) focuses on that potential consequence of technological change: *How do elite actors from the field of political communication in Germany perceive changing patterns of interaction in their field under the conditions of digitisation?*

Asked in how far digitisation had altered inter-organisational relations and the related exchange of information, most journalistic interviewees say they perceive rather strong or even massive changes. The answers from political spokespersons and communication managers answers have a similar tendency here, yet they show a slightly greater variance. The consequences of this process are often described in terms of general acceleration and changes to scale, scope and timing of political communication. Especially journalistic interviewees feel that their daily work is to some extent simplified through these developments, yet at the same time they also point out the perils of increasing superficiality in accelerated political communication.

The journalistic interviewees also widely agree on a perceived increase in attempts by political spokespersons to circumvent them in their gatekeeping function by digital means, even though their evaluation of the actual success of this strategy differs widely.

Last but not least, technological changes are also regarded as having the potential to affect patterns of influence and the overall construction of communication networks in the field of political communication. The fourth sub-question (RQ1d) focuses on these aspects: *Which changes do elite actors from the field of political communication in Germany perceive regarding the set of actors present and the patterns of influence prevalent in the field of political media relations?*

When it comes to the perceived influence of new actors in the field of political communication in Germany, the differences between the groups of interviewees are comparatively small. On average, both groups of interviewees see a medium influence of these (formerly excluded) actors in their field; the variances are quite similar as well. Asked specifically about these new actors, both groups mostly refer to bloggers. Journalistic interviewees often emphasise that these tend to be from backgrounds of professional journalism. Apart from that, journalistic interviewees additionally name communities of individuals gathering on social media platforms and civic initiatives organising online as new influential actors. The interviewed spokespersons also refer to campaign-oriented platforms, civic pressure groups and NGOs.

Regarding the future influence of new actors, the journalistic interviewees are more pessimistic in their prognoses than their counterparts; often expressing the view that there will not be any further increases in this regard or even predicting a decrease here. Spokespersons and communication managers on the other hand overwhelmingly predict an increasing influence of these new actors.

This also reflects in the perceptions interviewees express with regard to the main beneficiaries of digitisation. While political journalists show divided opinions here, the perceptions of the interviewed spokespersons and communication managers appear more unanimous. Most of them agree on an understanding in which digitisation would primarily benefit new and formerly marginal actors, this applies especially to interviewees from a background of governmental bodies. The majority of the interviewed political journalists on the other hand either perceives already established actors, both new and established actors, new political actors and established media outlets as the main beneficiaries of digitisation; the notion of digitisation as a process primarily benefiting new and formerly marginal actors is less common among them.

Interim conclusion

Both groups perceive digitisation as an important process and emphasise its strong effects on political communication, patterns of interaction and organisational bodies within the field. It is apparent that journalistic interviewees generally tend to perceive even stronger effects here. They feel that political communication is highly affected by digitisation and see considerable changes within organisations and general patterns of interaction. Yet at the same time their perspective on future developments is sometimes ambiguous, they critically reflect on perceived effects and often describe processes of change primarily benefiting already established actors.

The interviewed spokespersons and communication managers on the other hand are often less critical about the effects of digitisation and predominantly frame it as a process benefiting new and formerly marginal actors here. Even though they perceive comparatively less strong effects in the first place, the overall picture they draw is a comparatively more cyber-optimistic one.

Given the fact that digitisation is generally considered a process of tremendous technological changes, it is hardly surprising that the interviewees perceive strong effects in this regard. Technologically induced media change now seems ubiquitous and changes established technological environments, especially in the field of political communication (cf. Kocks & Raupp, 2015). The interviewees occupy important positions in this field and accordingly directly perceive these changes. The strong perceptions they express in this regard are explicable.

This also holds true for their strong perceptions of organisational change. Again, the organisations for which they work (and in which they occupy focal positions) are directly affected by strong technological change in the field of political communication (cf. Pöttker, 2013; Waters, Tindall, & Morton, 2010). In particular this concerns media outlets which face drastically changing patterns of reception by their relevant audiences. Therefore it is again explicable that both groups perceive organisational changes, with the journalistic interviewees expressing a stronger perceived degree of change.

Perceptions regarding the inclusion of new actors into established patterns of communication and the main beneficiaries of digitisation are a central area of interest here. Members of both groups of interviewees see new actors entering their field. The interviewed spokespersons and communication managers even describe digitisation as a process benefiting new and formerly marginal actors. Given the fact that empirical studies on political media relations under online conditions generally tend to describe them as largely exclusive phenomena, this appears somewhat surprising. Additionally, the general debate on digitisation also clearly goes in a different direction, often discussing the process in increasingly sceptical terms.

However, cyber-optimism has always been a practitioners' domain. The rather optimistic perceptions expressed, especially by the interviewed spokespersons and communication managers, might just be an example of persistent cyber-optimism. On the other hand, the actual situation the interviewees face could indeed be different to the one described in the analysed empirical studies. To clarify that, empirical analyses of the ways in which the interviewees and their specific organisations actually adapt to digitisation are necessary. These are provided in the following.

4.4 Adaptations of Digitisation

Adaptations can be defined as the processes by which actors strive to become fitted to their environment, often in order to conserve or even ameliorate their specific position. As Wells (1945, p. 19) puts it: "Adapt or perish, now as ever, is nature's inexorable imperative.“ This part of the analyses investigates the ways in which elite actors from the communication network between politics and the media and their specific organisations adapt new means of communication and about how they construct their communication networks under the conditions of digitisation, both assumingly in the very interest of conserving or ameliorating their position.

It focuses on the extent to which new means of communication and technological innovations are included in the strategic communicative portfolio of the actors in question, in political online presences and the daily communicative routines of political spokespersons, communication managers and journalists. It also concentrates on the communication networks surrounding these actors, enquiring into their structures and their in- or exclusiveness.

Adaptations should not be regarded here in a strictly biological sense; as theoretical reflections indicate, they are about processes fostering the conservation or amelioration of one's position in general. Yet the question remains: If 'adapt or perish' is not only an inexorable imperative in nature but also – at least to some extent – in processes of human interaction such as political communication, shouldn't one then expect some forms of actual adaption here? The next question is what these might actually look like.

The following analyses concentrate both on individual and organisational actors. They measure the adaptations of digital means by political organisations, i.e. the integration of certain means into their external communication. They evaluate the channels through which political organisations distribute their messages to the media and through which journalists engage in communicative interaction with political organisations. Then they focus on the (organisational) networks between politics and the media, on processes of interaction and patterns of influence within them.

Specifically, they seek to answer the second complex of research questions postulated here. These surround one central question:

> *RQ2: How do elite actors from the field of political communication in Germany and their specific organisations actually adapt to the process of digitisation?*

Again, this central research question is divided into a set of four sub-questions. Since adaptations have to be considered a multi-level phenomenon, one might find examples of actual adaptations on the level of organisational online presences, within communicative exchanges between individual actors and of course also in the actual construction of communication networks within the field of political media relations in Germany. In particular, the following aspects are of special interest for the analysis of actual adaptations here:

> *RQ2a: How do organisational political actors construct their online presences? Which communication options do they maintain and in how far do they integrate reciprocal elements?*
>
> *RQ2b: Through which channels do individual actors from the field of political communication (i.e. political spokespersons and journalists) engage in communicative exchange in the online age?*
>
> *RQ2c: How are communication networks between politics and the media constructed under the conditions of digitisation?*
>
> *RQ2d: Which role do new or formerly marginal actors play in political media relations under online conditions?*

As indicated, a combination of empirical methods is employed here. It consists of content analysis, semi-structured interviews and social network analysis. The online presences of organisational political actors are subjected to content analysis; this considers both websites and social media sites. Analysis inter alia enquires into the channels maintained, the predominant form of communication, its addressees and the amount of possible dialogue. The aim is to analyse in how far the political actors in question have adopted new means in their external (organisational) communication.

Data deriving from semi-structured interviews with political spokespersons, communication managers and journalists then grounds an enquiry into the channels utilised for personal communicative exchange and journalistic research. It also grounds a subsequent social network analysis which focuses on communication networks in the field of political media relations and on the actors forming these.

In accordance with research questions 2a – 2d, there are three subchapters following here. The first one concentrates on the online presences of organisational political actors and analyses them with regard to their actual employment (RQ2a). The second one focuses on the employment of technical means in communicative exchanges between politics and the media, analysing the ways in which political actors distribute their messages to the media and in which individual journalists interact with them (RQ2b). The third subchapter focuses on the communication networks between politics and the media (RQ2c & RQ2d).

4.4.1 New Means of Communication: Organisational Presences

In an era of digitisation, one might assume that all organisational political actors of importance and standing would maintain some form of online presence. The question is though: What do these online presences actually look like? In how far are the external communications of political actors digitised, which communicative channels are maintained and to what extent are they used? The following analysis focuses on the utilisation of new means of communication by central political actors in Germany. The analysed data derives from two waves of content analyses conducted within 'Media Relations Online' in 2011 and 2013 and from an additional content analysis focusing on the employment of social media by governmental bodies conducted in 2013.[64]

[64] An additional overview of the empirical analyses utilised here is to be found in the empirical fact sheet in the appendix to this thesis.

Findings

Analyses show that the digitisation of political communication in Germany is advanced in so far as every organisational actor in question here maintains an online presence in the form of a website; there is neither a ministry nor a party without such a presence. These websites are well maintained and kept up to date by regular updates with new content, as the following figures show:

	Average days since last update (Analysis 2011)	**Average days since last update** (Analysis 2013)
Governmental Bodies (n=18)	**2.13** (SD= 2.58)	**0.85** (SD= 1.07)
Political Parties (n=6)	**1.50** (SD= 1.38)	**1.83** (SD= 3.13)

Tab. 5: Average days since the last update of website content.

Online presences are not maintained as mere 'cyber-safety-valves' (cf. Jackson & Lilleker, 2009, p. 247), as presences that just exist to secure a claim (i.e. to make sure that no one steals them or their actual address), they rather constitute communication channels. These channels are maintained professionally, it is ensured that audiences can easily reach and utilise them. Employing an additive index focusing on four dimensions (menu navigation, search-and print functions and accessibility),[65] the analyses focus on the actual usability of political online presences:

65 The availability of the former three features is analysed on a dichotomous 'yes/no'basis, the accessibility is rated on a three-point scale (see also: Kocks et al., 2014).

	Un-usable	Hardly usable	Some-what usable	Usable	Readily usable	Perfect-ly usa-ble
Governmental Bodies (2011) (n=18)	0	0	0	**1**	**10**	**7**
Political Parties (2011) (n=6)	0	0	0	**1**	**4**	**1**
Governmental Bodies (2013) (n=18)	0	0	0	0	0	**18**
Political Parties (2013) (n=6)	0	0	0	0	**1**	**5**

Tab. 6: Usability of political websites (ranked on an additive index); absolute numbers.

Findings clearly confirm the picture of well-maintained political websites. All are highly usable, smaller problems ascertainable in 2011 had vanished completely in 2013 when all websites were easy to navigate and access, allowing information to be found and saved without any major obstacles.

But which audiences do these presences actually target? Are the websites of the governmental bodies and political parties in question aiming at the general public (thereby possibly serving as a means for reaching new audiences or even as tools for the circumvention of established media outlets) or should they be considered more as digital means of otherwise 'classical' media relations, predominantly targeting political journalists?

Analysis (2013) shows that a large majority of actors (n=22) target both professional journalists as well as the general public and, in the case of political parties, also current and potential party members. Press releases are sometimes directly offered on the 'general' websites (n=13), yet all actors in question additionally maintain a specialised press section within their websites, reserving parts of their online presences especially for online media relations. However, in most cases these sections are accessible to the general public; only one actor secures his online press section with a password. In these sections, journalists are provided with contact data of spokespersons; in some cases (n=8) these contacts are even sorted according to different fields of interest, i.e. journalists can directly identify specialist contact persons within the respective press department.

Furthermore online press sections are employed to distribute information and additional content to political journalists. They generally feature the latest press releases of the respective political actor, in many cases (n=11) even allowing for a selection of these according to different subjects or political fields. The amount of available press releases (here measured as press releases brought forward in a one-month period) does however vary widely.

On average, governmental bodies distributed 22.81 press releases per month in 2011 and 15.67 in 2013. The values for political parties here are slightly higher, with 29.83 in 2011 and 22.67 in 2013, yet Student's t-test shows no significant difference between arithmetic means.[66] As indicated, one does see relatively high standard deviations here, i.e. larger in-group differences regarding the amount of press releases that are distributed online.[67] There are some actors that appear especially active in this regard (such as for example the *SPD* and the *FDP* or, among governmental bodies, the *Federal Ministry for Economics and Technology,* which are among the most active distributors in both waves), but apart from this, there is no clear pattern of activity ascertainable here.

Apart from the mere distribution of press releases, political actors also often opt for the provision of professional audio, video and photo material online; in total, 17 of them offer such options within the press sections of their web presences in 2013.[68] The online-accreditation of journalists for press conferences and other events, which was only provided by five actors in 2011, was possible in eight cases in 2013.

The analysis of the press sections of political online presences shows that these are indeed employed as a means of media relations, offering a variety of features to support political journalists in their coverage on the respective political actors.

66 The difference between 2011 and 2013 is not significant either.

67 Governmental bodies: 2011: SD= 18.09, 2013: SD= 13.27; Parties: 2011: SD= 25.03, 2013: SD= 20.01.

68 As indicated, data is missing for one governmental body whose online press section was password-secured in 2013, thereby rendering it unavailable to analysis here.

Communication option	Analysis 2011 (option available in n cases)	Analysis 2013 (option available in n cases)
press contacts	**21**	**21**
specialised press contacts	**11**	**8**
press releases	**22**	**21**
press releases (sortable)	**8**	**11**
audio/video/photo	**18**	**17**
accreditation	**5**	**8**

Tab. 7: Availability of communication options in online press sections; n(actors)=24, n(online press sections)=22, as indicated, one was password protected during the 2013 analysis; absolute numbers.

But apart from offering a variety of functions for journalistic audiences, the political web presences analysed here are also targeting the general public. Which communication options are included in this regard, what can recipients do and see on the websites of governmental bodies and political parties? Furthermore: How are they actually addressed?

As indicated, the websites of political actors (both governmental bodies and political parties) in Germany are well maintained and highly usable. This means that they regularly offer a variety of up-to-date information, not only to professional journalists but also to the general public, inter alia in the form of news about the organisation in question and about its current activities and policies.

It is quite common to distribute this news not only via the website as such but to additionally offer RSS feeds (n=24; 2013 analysis) and newsletters distributed via e-mail (n=21; 2013 analysis). Pulling content (i.e. actual information) from the web presence of a specific political actor is largely facilitated by these means; staying informed about its activities and actual policies becomes an automatised process once the recipient has subscribed to one of these services.

Sections with frequently asked questions (n=14; 2013 analysis) and calendars (n=19; 2013 analysis) featuring important dates (e.g. political summits, international conferences or official visits) often complement the informational content of these websites. Between a third and half of the actors in question additionally distribute audio and video material addressed at the general public via their website, though there appears to be a slight decline in the communication options between the two waves of analysis (n=9 & n=11 (2011) and n=6 & n=9 (2013)).

The communication options discussed above can best be categorised as unidirectional ones since they represent a form of online communication without reciprocity, i.e. one in which the recipient is addressed by the political communicator, equipped with information and news but not asked for his feedback or interaction. A large variety of textual content is distributed here, the question is though, how this can be characterised: Do the communicators in question actually seek to inform their audiences or rather to mobilise them with the content offered? Do they seek to distribute pure facts to them or is it their goal to actually trigger some form of action, to get recipients to do or to refrain from something?

In order to clarify on this, textual website content is analysed according to a five point scale ranging between pure information and pure mobilisation:

1	2	3	4	5

pure information **balanced** **pure mobilisation**

Fig. 19: Five point scale: information vs. mobilisation.

Factual information regarding a political organisation, its policies or its members and officeholders is categorised as '1 – pure information'; this category grasps content that provides the recipient with factual knowledge. On the other side of the spectrum one finds '5 – pure mobilisation', a category that grasps content that seeks to get recipients to engage in some form of action, to either do something or to refrain from doing it. In this case, no factual information is distributed, the content purely seeks to mobilise. In between are categories grasping content that is either predominantly informational ('2'), predominantly mobilising ('4') or regarded as balanced between these poles ('3').

Analysis of textual (unidirectional) website content clearly indicates a predominance of informational content, this goes for both waves of analysis:

	Information vs. mobilisation(2011 analysis; arithmetic mean)	**Information vs. mobilisation** (2013 analysis; arithmetic mean)
Governmental Bodies (n=18)	**1.53** (SD= 0.63)	**1.11** (SD= 0.32)
Political Parties (n=6)	**2.33** (SD= 1.03)	**1.50** (SD= 0.55)

Tab. 8: Information vs. mobilisation: arithmetic means (and standard deviations) per group.

Governmental bodies and political parties both rank between purely and predominantly informational textual website content, furthermore there is no large variance within the two groups of actors. However it emerges that governmental bodies now restrict themselves even more strongly to informational content. As Student's t-test (with a level of significance of $p<.05$) shows, this difference is even to be assumed beyond the sample of textual website content analysed here.[69]

Apart from unidirectional content, websites also have the potential to provide functions that allow for some form of exchange between communicator and recipient, functions that equip the latter group with the possibility to give their opinion, to provide feedback and to interact. This form of online-communication appears quite popular among certain groups of actors, especially among those that have some form of challenger-status (e.g. NGOs, political intermediaries and citizen's initiatives), yet they are (to some degree) also employed by more established actors.

The political parties and governmental bodies analysed do not generally refrain from the employment of such bidirectional functions, even though numbers here are remarkably lower compared with those for unidirectional content on their websites. Seven actors allow commenting of website-content (2011 and 2013 analysis), this is mostly done in the form of a web forum. Five of them require registration and two allow for anonymous unregistered commentators. While parties (with the exception of *Die Linke*) all provide tools that allow

69 It is noteworthy that connections between organisational factors and the degree of mobilisation ascertainable in textual online communication have also emerged from other shares of the 'Media Relations Online'-data; see for example Schink, Raupp and Kocks (2013).

comments to be made via a forum-like exchange, only two governmental bodies in the sample do so.

Another way to enable interaction and allow recipients to become active could be the provision of some form of chat or video-chat on a website. However, this is extremely rare here: only two parties (*SPD* and *FDP*) offer such options (2013 analysis). Furthermore, in both cases chats are not provided constantly but only at certain times, functioning as a kind of digitised consultation hour. The political parties analysed here also allow and sometimes even advertise for donations on their websites, a measure which could indeed be understood as a form of monetary feedback. Naturally, governmental bodies do not engage in such activities.

In sum, the websites of political parties and governmental bodies analysed here only offer a limited amount of bidirectional functions, many actors entirely refrain from making such offers to their online-audiences. This contrasts some extent with the extent of unidirectional, textual and predominantly informational content that they otherwise provide on their websites.

In the age of the so-called Web 2.0 there are of course other possibilities besides websites to become active online. A variety of social networks is not only open to individual users but also allows companies, organisations and political bodies to become active. The analysis here focuses on the ways in which political parties and governmental bodies employ social networks (*Facebook* and *Google+*),[70] the micro-blogging service *Twitter* and the video-hosting service *YouTube*.

[70] The original analysis conducted within 'Media Relations Online' also focused on the German social network 'StudiVZ' (part of VZ-Netzwerke); yet this network does in many regards not work like Facebook and Google+ (limiting its political usability and thereby also its value for the analysis here) and it furthermore largely became defunct during the course of the analysis; it is therefore not included here.

	Facebook[71]	*Google+*	*Twitter*[72]	*YouTube*[73]
Governmental Bodies (2011) (n=18)	**2** (3)	**0**	**5** (6)	**10** (12)
Political Parties (2011) (n=6)	**6**	**3**	**6**	**6**
Governmental Bodies (2013) (n=18)	**4** (5)	**2**	**9** (13)	**10** (12)
Political Parties (2013) (n=6)	**6**	**6**	**6**	**6**

Tab. 9: Employment of Web 2.0 tools by political actors (absolute numbers).

It is apparent that political parties are active in all areas here, engaging in social networks as well as in micro-blogging and the distribution of videos via

71 The Federal Ministry of Justice used to link to the personal Facebook page of the office holder during the two waves of analysis. Despite being somewhat problematic under legal aspects (cf. Holtz-Bacha, 2013; Kocks & Raupp, 2014b), this form of social media activity is not to be considered as organisational Web 2.0-representation and therefore excluded from the analysis here.

72 The Federal Ministry of Justice used to link to the personal Twitter-account of the office-holder during the two waves of analysis; again, this form of social media activity is (despite being potentially problematic) not to be considered as organisational Web 2.0-representation and therefore excluded from the analysis here. In 2013, three other governmental bodies linked to Twitter accounts of neighbouring actors and organisations (e.g. to the account of the governmental spokesperson or, in the case of the Federal Ministry of Defence, to the account of the German Defence Forces); these are excluded from analysis here at first but will be, in selected cases, briefly discussed individually later on. The Federal Information Office did not independently link to the Twitter-account of the governmental spokesperson in 2011, thereby not treating it as an organisational Web 2.0-representation; it was therefore excluded from analysis in 2011. By 2013 the account was clearly marked and advertised as an organisational account (and furthermore also used by BPA employees), then leading to its inclusion into analysis here.

73 Two governmental bodies link to YouTube channels that are not theirs (but belong to neighbouring actors); again, these are excluded from analysis here.

YouTube. Governmental bodies on the other hand show a different pattern of employment of such digital tools: While the distribution of videos via *YouTube* is quite popular (with about two thirds of the actors engaging in this form of communication), social networks (which require comparatively less effort for individual postings) are only of minor importance. This finding not only distinguishes them from the political parties analysed here, but also from many other political organisations active online (cf. Kocks et al., 2014). The micro-blogging service *Twitter* has seen a rise in importance between the two waves of analysis, the number of governmental bodies that employ it almost doubled between 2011 and 2013. Analysis of Web 2.0 presences shows general adoption by political parties (i.e. the employment of all available tools) on the one hand and distinct governmental patterns on the other:

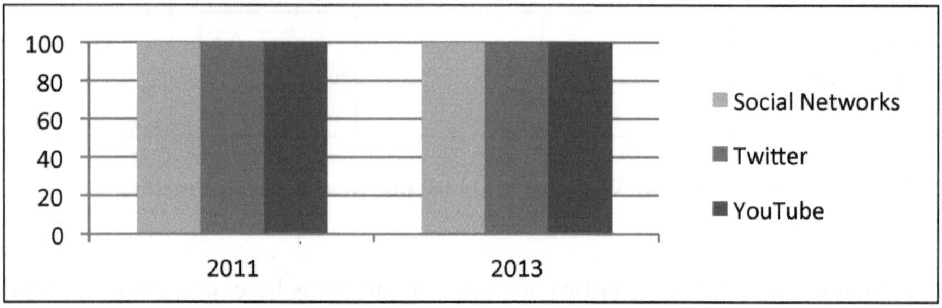

Fig. 20: Employment of Web 2.0 tools by political parties (percentage of users).

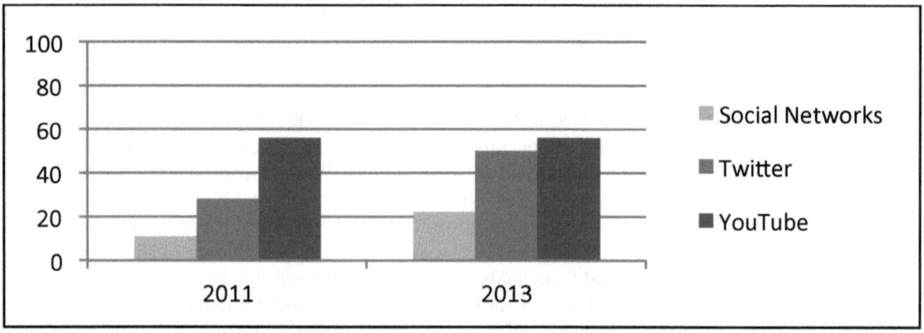

Fig. 21: Employment of Web 2.0 tools by governmental bodies (percentage of users).

Social networks (e.g. *Facebook* & *Google+*) inter alia allow the sharing of content, dialogue and networking. As indicated, all political parties analysed employ them in their external communication while governmental bodies do so to a considerably lower extent. But how do these actors actually use their social network presences? Are social network sites regularly equipped with new content or (unlike the websites analysed here) used rather as 'cyber safety valves' (cf. Jackson & Lilleker, 2009)? To what extent is dialogue enabled and fostered?

Analysis of *Facebook* postings shows divergent patterns of usage: the amount of monthly postings varies between 15 and 89 (2011 analysis) and between 5 and 77 (2013 analysis). High standard deviations of 28.16 (2011; M= 48.13) and of 20.78 (2013; M= 35.6) support this picture of a division between irregular and regular users. Statistical testing however shows that there is no significant difference between 2011 and 2013; despite the slightly lower usage-numbers in the second sample utilised here, one cannot postulate a general decline in *Facebook* activity among political actors.

Generally, *Facebook* postings can be commented on by other users (to some extent depending on the privacy settings of the account holder). The account holder then has the possibility to answer these comments, to engage in dialogue with those recipients that have provided their feedback on postings. Here, users can comment on the postings made by all political actors maintaining a *Facebook* presence (2011: n=9; 2013: n=10), yet not all of them provided answers to these comments during the analysed periods (2011: 7/9; 2013: 7/10). In both waves, this was the case with both the *CSU* and the *Federal Ministry of Labour and Social Affairs*, in the latter wave the *CDU* refrained from providing feedback as well.

Analogue to the analyses of textual website content, *Facebook* postings are analysed regarding their actual employment by the communicators in charge: Do they serve informational purposes or are they utilised rather to mobilise recipients? Again, textual (and partially graphic) postings are subjected to content analysis with reference to a five point scale ranging from '1 – pure information' to '5 – pure mobilisation'.

Facebook *postings of:*	**Information vs. mobilisation** (2011 analysis; arithmetic mean)	**Information vs. mobilisation** (2013 analysis; arithmetic mean)
Governmental Bodies (n=2 (2011) and 4 (2013) accounts)	**1.50** (SD= 0.71)	**2.00** (SD= 0.82)
Political Parties (n=6 accounts)	**2.33** (SD= 1.03)	**2.50** (SD= 0.55)

Tab. 10: Facebook postings: Information vs. mobilisation.

Again, governmental bodies show a stronger restraint to informational content.[74] Here, *Facebook* is utilised as a means to distribute information to the audiences. But which kind of information do governmental communicators distribute through this channel? An additional dataset retrieved on (inter alia) *Facebook* postings made by these governmental bodies in autumn 2013 provides clarification on this matter:[75]

74 Unfortunately it is not possible to postulate statistical significance beyond the analysed sample here; a small sample in combination with rather small differences leads to non-significant results. Yet at least the tendency corresponds to the significant difference found in the analysis of textual website content.

75 The data was retrieved by 17 student coders in the context of a seminar taught by the author at Freie Universität Berlin in 2013/14; tweets and Facebook postings made by governmental bodies in the 37th& 38th and the 45th& 46th calendar week 2013 were subjected to in-depth content analysis.

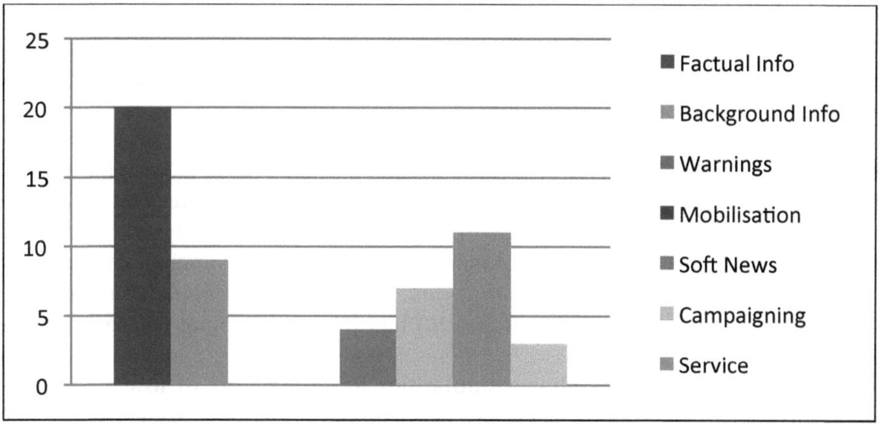

Fig. 22: Facebook postings by governmental bodies: type of content (absolute numbers; multiple answers (up to two) possible; n(Postings)=39).

A large proportion of the *Facebook* postings made by governmental bodies can best be qualified as 'factual information'. The recipient is provided with facts about the respective governmental body and its actual work. Another important type of content can be subsumed under the notion of 'service'; here governmental bodies provide recipients with information of a clear service character; in this case, public administration acts as a service provider, informing citizens about their offers via this channel.

Furthermore, governmental bodies utilise *Facebook* to provide background information; in these cases, they explain the background of legislative and administrative measures to their audiences. Other – not predominantly informational – usages of this platform are relatively scarce. One does sometimes find content that is of a more entertaining nature (often in combination with forms of soft news about the office holder) or that has a campaign component attached to it.

Given the fact that this additional analysis focuses on four weeks of *Facebook* activities, the relatively low number of postings becomes apparent. Four governmental bodies have made a total of just 39 postings within four weeks. At first sight, one might attribute this to (legally demanded) communicative restraints in pre-election periods (cf. Holtz-Bacha, 2013; Kocks & Raupp, 2014b), yet closer inspection shows no real difference between the pre- (n=18) and post-election period (n=21). Governmental bodies generally appear to be very modest *Facebook* posters.

The second social network of importance for the analysis here is *Google+*. Founded in 2011, shortly before the beginning of the first wave of analysis, it has continuously gained importance (and users) since then, even though it still is considerably smaller than *Facebook.*

The political parties analysed here began adopting this new social network early on; in the first wave of analysis conducted at the end of 2011, and already three of them (*CDU, CSU and SPD*) maintained a presence there. Governmental bodies had not then joined this network. By 2013, all parties analysed maintained a presence within *Google+*; additionally, two of the governmental bodies analysed (*Federal Ministry of Economics and Technology* and *Federal Ministry of Economic Cooperation and Development*) had joined the social network by this time.

The usage of *Google+* shows similarities to the patterns of usage of *Facebook.* In 2011, there was great variety in terms of regularity of usage; while one party (*SPD*) did not post at all (within the month of analysis), the others were quite active, making 28 (*CSU*) and 33 (*CDU*) postings within this one-month period. By 2013, the average number of posts (for all actors maintaining a presence) was 19.25, but a comparatively high standard deviation of 13.31 again indicates a large variance between moderate and highly active posters.[76]

The content distributed by political parties and governmental bodies via *Google+* is again analysed with regard to a five point scale differentiating between pure information and pure mobilisation. However, these results have to be interpreted with caution; a considerably low number of cases and the novelty of the medium in 2011 (when additionally only two actors made active use of it) render the validity of the calculated values potentially dubious. The mean value for parties for 2011 would then be 1.00 (SD= 0.00), indicating a purely informational usage in the early stages. By 2013, the arithmetic mean is 2.60 (SD= 0.55), indicating an informational usage with strong mobilising components. Finally, the value for (two) governmental bodies in 2013 is 2.00 (SD= 1.42), indicating an informational employment of *Google+* with a small mobilising component. Again, due to the reasons discussed, these values have to be considered cum grano salis, even though they do to some extent support tendencies observed before.

Apart from social networks like *Facebook* and *Google+*, the micro-blogging service *Twitter* has become increasingly important since its foundation in 2006.

---

[76] Due to the very small number of governmental bodies (n=2) further differentiation does not seem exactly adequate here. However, these did in fact post 17 & 23 postings in the one-month period analysed; greater variance is to be found among parties. Again, the postulation of statistical significance beyond the analysed sample is impossible here, a small sample in combination with rather small differences leads to non-significant results.

Allowing users to distribute short messages of under 140 characters to widespread audiences, *Twitter* is employed nowadays inter alia by private citizens, companies, political organisations and governmental actors. But do governmental bodies and political parties in Germany make recourse to this means of communication? If so, how do they actually use the micro-blogging service? What kind of content is distributed and with what frequency?

As the figures discussed beforehand demonstrate, *Twitter* is a very popular tool among political actors in Germany. In 2011, all political parties analysed were employing it in their digital external communication; five governmental bodies maintained *Twitter* accounts as well. By 2013, nine out of 18 governmental bodies had joined the micro-blogging service. Four did not maintain an account of their own but instead linked to those of neighbouring actors and organisations.

Again, the first question of interest concerns the actual employment of this platform: Is it regularly equipped with new content or used more as a form of 'cyber safety valve'? How much do the political actors in question actually tweet within a two-week period?

	2011 analysis[77]	**2013 analysis**	**Add. 2013 analysis (pre-election)**	**Add. 2013 analysis (post-election)**
Governmental Bodies	40.80 (SD= 39.23) n=5	20.11 (SD=13.77) n=9	36.63 (SD=28.29) n=9	39.86 (SD=28.93) n=9
Political Parties	49.50 (SD= 57.87) n=6	27.33 (SD= 14.58) n=6		

Tab. 11: Average number of tweets in a two-week period.

The arithmetic means displayed here show a great variance and the standard deviations given for the individual values are also quite high. In fact, the large

77 The very high deviation measured for political parties here is caused by one extreme value of 167 tweets in a two-week period (account of the SPD).

in-group variance here is caused by strongly divergent usage patterns. There are actors that make high usage of *Twitter*, regularly sending out several *tweets* per day (e.g. the *SPD* as the most active party on this platform in both the 2011 and 2013 analyses and the *Federal Ministry for Economic Cooperation and Development* as the most active governmental body in both waves). Others maintain a presence but seldom employ it (e.g. the *Federal Ministry of Family Affairs, Senior Citizens, Women and Youth* which began to use *Twitter* between the two waves and had 9/9/3 *tweets* in the three two-week periods analysed in 2013). Even though one cannot exactly identify 'cyber safety valve' usages, the political parties and governmental bodies analysed here do in fact show patterns ranging between hardly and heavily using the micro-blogging service.

Against a background of strong legal constraints calling for communicative restraints in pre-election periods (cf. Holtz-Bacha, 2013; Kocks & Raupp, 2014b), one could again expect differences between the *Twitter* activities shown by governmental bodies in these periods. Yet the difference between the arithmetic means measured here is only marginal and of no statistical significance.

The content distributed by political parties and governmental bodies via *Twitter* is again analysed with regard to a five point scale differentiating between pure information and pure mobilisation.

Tweets of:	**information vs. mobilisation** (2011 Analysis; arithmetic mean)	**information vs. mobilisation** (2013 Analysis; arithmetic mean)
Governmental Bodies (n=5 (2011) and 9 (2013) accounts)	**1.00**(SD= 0.00)	**1.67**(SD= 0.50)
Political Parties (n=6 accounts)	**2.17**(SD= 1.17)	**2.17**(SD= 0.75)

Tab. 12: Tweets: information vs. mobilisation.

Again, both groups of actors employ a digital means of communication (i.e. *Twitter*) in a predominantly informational way. Yet while governmental bodies clearly communicate in ways that can best be described as overwhelmingly or even purely informational, political parties show slightly higher tendencies towards mobilisation on this platform. The difference between the two groups of actors is statistically significant (p<.05), it goes beyond the analysed sample of *tweets*.

Given the fact that governmental bodies again show clear patterns of informational communication on a digital platform, it remains to be clarified which type of (informational) content they distribute through these channels. Again, recourse is made to the additional dataset focusing on the social media activities of governmental bodies surrounding the federal elections in autumn 2013:

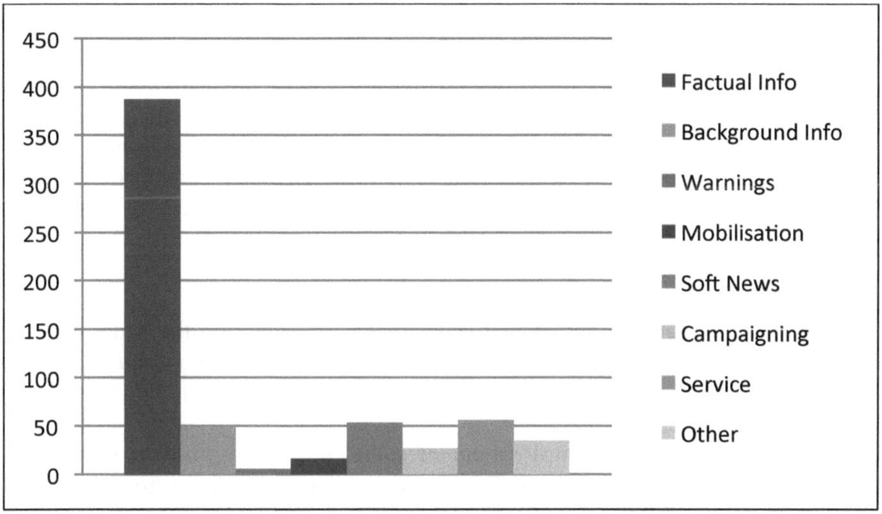

Fig. 23: Tweets by governmental bodies: type of content (absolute numbers; multiple answers (up to two) possible; n(tweets)=537).

The findings show large similarities to those made with regard to the *Facebook* postings made by the very same actors. Factual information is by far the most important category; the distribution of background information, entertaining soft news and service-oriented *tweets* are a considerable distance behind.

As a platform, *Twitter* does also allow some form of digitised dialogue, but in a different form than 'classic' social networks do. It is not possible to comment on postings and subsequently engage in dialogue, but to *re-tweet* content (i.e. to distribute a message originally created by another author through one's own *Twitter* account) or to answer to *tweets* made by other authors, directly addressing them and then subsequently potentially engaging in mutual communicative exchange with them. Dialogue functions differently on *Twitter*, yet it is possible.

The governmental bodies analysed here seldom if ever make use of these dialogic possibilities. Of 537 *tweets* analysed, 398 were original *tweets* made by the respective governmental body. In 130 cases they *re-tweeted* content posted by other actors.[78] In only eight cases *tweets* made by other actors actually answered in a way that allows for communicative exchange (i.e. by addressing them with an '@' followed by the actual username). *Twitter* is used predominantly in a unidirectional way here.

A particularity regarding the employment of this micro-blogging platform is the fact that several governmental bodies link to *Twitter* accounts that are not organisational accounts or not their accounts at all. In one case (*Federal Ministry of Justice*), this meant linking to the Twitter account of the actual office-holder, in two other cases the websites of leading governmental bodies (the *Chancellery* and the *Federal Government*) linked to the account of the governmental spokesperson (which, since 2013, was utilised as an organisational account by the *Federal Information Office*) and in the case of the *Federal Ministry of Defence*, a link was made to the *Twitter* account of the German Defence Forces. Apparently, governmental bodies strive to demonstrate presence within this platform without necessarily maintaining an actual presence of their own.

The last category of social media analysed here regards the video-hosting service *YouTube*. This platform allows users to distribute video content to large audiences; these audiences do not have to maintain accounts on *YouTube* themselves.

As the figures on the employment of social media by political parties and governmental bodies show, *YouTube* is very popular within these groups, despite the comparatively high effort necessary to distribute content here. All political parties analysed maintain a presence on *YouTube*, it is also the leading form of social media among governmental bodies with almost two-thirds of them maintaining a presence.

The amount of content that is distributed through this channel varies. In the 2011 analysis, governmental bodies posted an average of 8.3 videos per month (SD= 9.96) while political parties distributed an average of 20 videos (SD= 14.52) in the same period. In 2013, governmental bodies provided an average of 5.6 videos for their online audiences (SD= 6.48) while on average political parties put 14 videos on their *YouTube* channels (SD= 9.82).[79]

---

78 This was mostly content by other governmental bodies or by federal agencies.

79 The difference between the groups of actors appears quite strong in both waves. It is – by a rather slight margin – not statistically significant (p= 0.57(2013) and p= 0.75 (2011), yet a tendency which is in accordance with the other findings made here clearly emerges.

As a platform within the so-called Web 2.0, *YouTube* also (principally) allows dialogic exchange between those that provide some form of content and their recipients; users have the opportunity to post comments on the channel sites of those maintaining a presence, and these can then react to these comments and engage in communicative exchange. *YouTube* allows this function to be deactivated but channel owners do not have to accept comments.[80] This leaves three possibilities: channels that do not allow comments, those that allow comments but do not provide any response and finally those that allow comments and answer these.

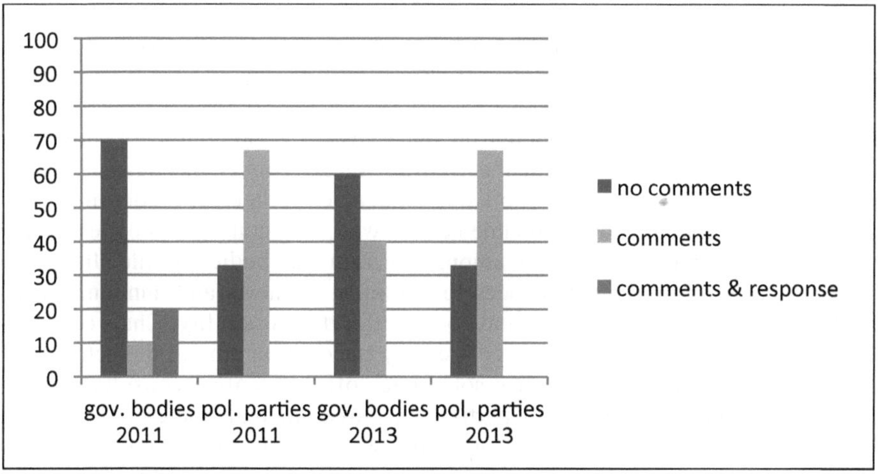

Fig. 24: Dialogic functions on YouTube; (percentage; n(parties): 6, n(gov. bodies): 10).

While governmental bodies often opt for the employment of *YouTube*, it is also apparent that they predominantly utilise it as a means for the unidirectional distribution of information; responsive functions – which are conceptually linked to the so-called Web 2.0 – are very often deactivated here. Political parties on the other hand often allow recipients to provide feedback on the content they distribute on this platform. Actual response to user comments (i.e. actual dialogue) is extremely rare; only two governmental bodies did – during the 2011 analysis –

80 The analyses were both conducted before YouTube became linked to Google+ in its comment-function in November 2013.

actually provide answers to comments posted by their recipients. Political parties did not do so at all.

Summary

In sum, the online presences of political actors in Germany appear very professional and well maintained. All actors here maintain a website; these are regularly updated with new and predominantly informational content. These websites target both professional journalists (often in the form of an online press section) and the general public. Their usability is very good.

Professional journalists are provided with regular press releases and additional (audio-visual) material for their coverage; political actors ensure that their press departments can be reached easily by journalists, often naming a variety of press contacts on their websites.

The general content distributed on the websites is predominantly informational; this is especially true for the websites of governmental bodies. Political parties show slightly stronger mobilising tendencies yet a clear predominance of informational content is ascertainable here as well. Engaging in dialogue through websites is a scarcer phenomenon among governmental bodies. While all but one political party allow their audiences to comment on news and announcements made online, only two governmental bodies offer this possibility. Chats or videochats as a means of direct exchange are very uncommon among the actors analysed here, apart from two parties sometimes offering online consultation sessions. The websites of political parties and governmental bodies only offer a limited number of bidirectional functions, which is in contrast to the large amount of textual and predominantly informational content that they otherwise provide on their websites.

Political actors also maintain presences in the so-called Web 2.0. Political parties are active within social networks; they distribute visual content via *YouTube* and engage in micro-blogging on *Twitter*. Governmental bodies show another pattern of communication here: they are barely active in social networks, yet very often opt for the distribution of video material via *YouTube*. *Twitter* also gained in popularity with them between the two waves of analysis.

Social networks are generally used in an informational way by those governmental bodies that employ them, mostly to distribute factual information. Again, parties show greater tendencies towards mobilisation, yet a (slight) predominance of informational content prevails among them. The micro-blogging platform *Twitter* is a popular tool with both groups of actors and mostly employed as an informational tool; again there is a slight yet statistically significant difference between governmental bodies and political parties confirming the tendency observed before. *YouTube* is – despite the comparatively high effort necessary to provide content – very popular among governmental bodies; it is in fact the most popular Web 2.0 tool for them. However, many governmental bodies disable dialogic functions, using it exclusively as a means of unidirectional distribution and not allowing any response at all.

A comparison of the analysed online presences of political actors shows several similarities but also distinct differences between those maintained by governmental bodies and political parties. Both groups of actors are active online and maintain professional presences. Both utilise these to distribute information to their audiences, i.e. to professional journalists and the general public. Yet offering dialogic functions – allowing for some form of feedback – is not common among governmental bodies at all. Political parties do – at least to some extent – allow for such forms of communicative interaction. Social media are employed by both groups of actors, but again distinct patterns emerge. While parties maintain all possible channels, allowing for interaction in social networks, sending out short bites of information on *Twitter* and distributing videos via *YouTube*, governmental bodies act differently. They clearly opt for means that allow them distribute informational content unidirectionally and even deactivate dialogic functions in some cases.

The online presences of the political actors analysed here serve as a means of informing journalists and the general public. Interactive potential are utilised to some extent by political parties and only to a considerably lesser extent by governmental bodies. Governmental online communication appears as distributive communication executed through professional and well maintained modern channels, the online communication of political parties as distributive communication enriched with (some) dialogic options, executed through similarly professional and well maintained modern channels.

4.4.2 New Means of Communication: Communicative Exchange

Informing the media and thereby also the public about actual policies and actions of their specific organisation is part of the job description of political spokespersons and communication managers. They need to get information to relevant audiences on a regular basis. This can be facilitated through a variety of channels, from 'classic' face-to-face exchange up to modern digitised means. The preceding analyses have shown that organisational political actors are well equipped with such means, often maintaining presences not only in the form of websites but also within the so-called Web 2.0. But which channels do they actually employ when it comes to their work with the media, by which means do their spokespersons engage in communicative exchange with professional journalists?

Vice versa, professional political journalists need to be in contact with the political actors they cover. They need to be informed about their policies and actions and need to get in touch with them to gather background information, comment or statements. The question is what channels do they employ in their daily work? By which means do they research their political coverage? Do they actually make use of modern ICT or rather stick to established channels?

The communicative exchange between political spokespersons and communication managers on the one side and political journalists on the other is elementary to political media relations; the following analysis enquires into its patterns and routines in Germany in order to arrive at an insight into political media relations under the conditions of digitisation.

As indicated beforehand, the data derives from 45 personal interviews. Six of the interviewees are party communicators (one from each party in the sample) and ten are responsible for the communication of governmental bodies. 29 of the interviewees come from a journalistic background, 20 work for offline-, nine for online media.

Findings

Since getting information about their specific organisation and its actions and policies to relevant journalists is vital for political spokespersons and communication managers, the selection of communication channels to address these is of utmost importance for their work. Reaching professional journalists is necessary to secure coverage and to influence public agendas and the news. The question is: Through which channels do political spokespersons and communication managers now address professional journalists, which (modern) means of communication do they employ in media relations and in the communicative exchange with their journalistic counterparts? Which channels actually dominate media relations under the conditions of digitisation?

Political spokespersons and communication managers were therefore asked to name those channels that they actually employ in their daily work. A wide understanding of 'channel' was utilised here; e.g. holding a press conference counts as does using the telephone or becoming active on *Twitter*. The first group to consider here is made up of six party spokespersons and communication managers:

Channel	Named by:
1. E-mail	6/6 interviewees
2. Telephone	5/6 interviewees
3. Social Networks	4/6 interviewees
4. Face-to-Face Conversation	3/6 interviewees
5. Press Conferences ***Twitter***	2/6 interviewees

Tab. 13: Media relations and communicative exchange: communication channels employed by party spokespersons and communication managers (n=6).

All of them name e-mails as an important channel of communication for their daily work, closely followed by telephone conversations with relevant journalists. The employment of social networks is considered a relevant channel for daily media relations by four out of six interviewed party spokespersons. Within the top five (here made up of six items due to equal figures for press conferences and *Twitter*) one finds three digital options, two of these (*Twitter* and social networks) could be considered quite modern, one (e-mail) has been established for a longer time. It is noteworthy that Twitter is named as an important tool within daily media relations by the communicators of those two parties (*SPD* and *FDP*) that have shown a comparatively widespread adoption of new means in the analyses of their web presences here. Communicators not naming social networks as an important tool in daily media relations came from the *CSU* and the *Green Party*; there is however no apparent connection between that and the actual employment of digital means by these parties.[81]

The second group of interviewed spokespersons and communication managers accounts for the communication of ten governmental bodies in Germany. Which channels do they utilise in for communicative exchange with political journalists?

[81] Admittedly, the CSU was the only party not to offer any dialogue within Facebook in both waves of analysis, yet it was among the earliest adopters of new social networks and generally showed a high degree of online-activity.

Channel	Named by:
1. E-mail	9/10 interviewees
2. Face-to-Face Conversation	8/10 interviewees
3. Telephone	6/10 interviewees
4. Background Circles **Press Conferences**	5/10 interviewees

Tab. 14: Media relations and communicative exchange: communication channels employed by governmental spokespersons and communication managers (n=10).

Again, communicative exchange via e-mail is named most often here. This is closely followed by private face-to-face and telephone conversations. Background circles, which are an established form of confidential personal exchange, and press conferences, which are a relatively well established public variant, are also cited as important tools of daily media relations here. The list of channels governmental spokespersons and communication managers regularly name appears relatively 'non-technical'; they do of course name e-mails as the most important tool but apart from that they largely conduct their media relations using traditional means of communication.

Means that are normally often associated with contemporary processes of the digitisation of political communication are not to be found in this list. This largely confirms a tendency observed in the preceding analyses of governmental online presences where one could in fact ascertain a comparatively higher degree of structural conservatism, a more cautious employment of new means. The tendency observed with regard to the ways in which governmental bodies communicate online (with both professional journalists as well as the general public as target audiences) is apparently confirmed here.

But how do political journalists – which constitute the other side in the communicative exchanges analysed here – communicate? Which channels do they employ when doing research for their coverage of political topics? How do they get political information?

Channel	Named by:
1. E-mail	29/29 interviewees
2. Telephone	27/29 interviewees
3. Face-to-Face Conversation	26/29 interviewees
4. Background Circles	23/29 interviewees
5. News Agencies	22/29 interviewees

Tab. 15: Media relations and communicative exchange: channels employed by leading political journalists when researching political coverage (n=29).

Again, e-mails are named as the most important channel here. All interviewed journalists emphasise their importance in their daily work and for the exchanges on which their coverage is based. This is closely followed by telephone and face-to-face conversations with representatives of the political field and, in fourth place in this table, by political background circles that bring together politicians, political communication professionals and journalists. News agencies, here in fifth place, are of course not to be regarded as direct channels of communication between politics and the media, yet they aggregate information distributed by political actors and provide it to journalists as a foundation for their individual coverage. Some 22 of the 29 interviewees name these agencies as important sources of their political coverage.

The channels of information named by the journalists interviewed again appear fairly traditional: apart from e-mails they do not include any digital means. Yet given the fact that interviewees come from both traditional and online media outlets, the question is whether this finding holds for the individual groups or whether there are actual difference between them. Again the interviewees were asked to name their channels of research and then to recall recent communicative exchanges and name the means utilised in these.

Channel	Named by:
1. E-mail	20/20 interviewees
Face-to-Face Conversation **Telephone**	19/20 interviewees
4. Background Circles	18/20 interviewees
5. News Agencies **Newspaper Archives** **Social Networks**	15/20 interviewees

Tab. 16: Media relations and communicative exchange: channels employed by leading political offline journalists when researching political coverage (n=20).

According to these figures, journalists working for offline media outlets largely rely on those channels of information that have been named by the entire journalistic sample here; apart from smaller differences in ranking, the top five channels correspond to that. A further non-digital source named by this subgroup of interviewees is newspaper archives; researching past newspaper coverage when producing new coverage is considered important by 15 of the 20 interviewees. An equal number names social networks here, thereby underlining the importance of a digital means for their coverage. The channels offline journalists name as means for the research necessary for their political coverage again appear fairly traditional, with the notable exception of social networks.

But how about those journalists that work for online media outlets? Does this subgroup employ a selection of channels that is more digitised, dominated to a greater extent by digital means or is their selection as traditional as that of their offline colleagues? Which channels do they name?

Channel	Named by:
1. E-mail	9/9
2. Telephone	8/9
3. Face-to-Face Conversation **News Agencies** ***Twitter***	7/9
6. Newspaper Archives **Press Conferences**	6/9

Tab. 17: Media relations and communicative exchange: channels employed by leading political online journalists when researching for political coverage (n=9).[82]

Once again, the most popular way to research political coverage named by the interviewees is e-mail, closely followed by telephone conversation. The third place is shared by face-to-face conversation, the employment of news agency coverage and a digital tool: the micro-blogging service *Twitter*. Leading online journalists name this form of digitised communicative exchange as being as equally important as established forms of research. Furthermore they indicate that they regularly employ newspaper archives and attend press conferences. The ranking of channels made by this subgroup again appears fairly traditional with the notable exception of *Twitter*, a quite modern tool (first established in 2006) that is regarded as an important means by a large majority of the interviewed leading online journalists.

In sum, all subgroups analysed here often opt for fairly traditional channels for communicative exchange and coverage-related research. Looking at these tables, political media relations under online conditions appear – at least at first sight – to be rather dominated by means established long before the beginning of digitisation.

But which role do the various digital means actually play? Are they employed in these exchanges at all, is there some form of digitisation ascertainable? How often do the interviewees cite them as being important and which share of

82 Due to the fact that three channels share the third place in this ranking, the table features an additional sixth place in order to provide a more comprehensive visualisation of the spectrum here.

analysed communicative exchanges is undertaken through them? The first table concentrates on channel-related statements made by the interviewees:

	Spokespeople (pol. parties) *n=6*	**Spokespeople (gov. bodies)** *n=10*	**Journalists (offline)** *n=20*	**Journalists (online)** *n=9*
Blogs	0 %	20 %	45 %	33 %
Chats	0 %	10 %	25 %	0 %
E-mail	**100 %**	**90 %**	**100 %**	**100 %**
Online Press Conf. *(streaming)*	0 %	10 %	35 %	33 %
Skype	0 %	10 %	10 %	11 %
Social Networks	**66 %**	20 %	**75 %**	**56 %**
Twitter	33 %	40 %	**60 %**	**78 %**

Tab. 18: Digital means of communication and the degree of their proliferation among political communication professionals; (values over 50% are in bold).

Again, one trend is confirmed: e-mails are of utmost importance among all actors. According to their statements, social networks play a viable role for party communicators as well as for both groups of journalists. Only governmental spokespersons and communication managers are reluctant to employ these, a finding confirming a tendency observed in the preceding analyses of political online presences. *Twitter* is regarded as an important tool by both groups of journalists but especially by those that work for online media outlets. Their counterparts responsible for the communication of political actors do not assign such importance to the micro-blogging service.[83]

While utilising the 'classic' telephone to engage in communicative exchange is very popular among all groups of actors, its modern variant, the VoIP service

[83] This tendency is confirmed by the data regarding the interviewees' perceptions of potential increases in the importance of individual channels: while 62% of the interviewed journalists see an increase with regard to the micro-blogging service Twitter, only 32% of the spokespersons and communication managers do so.

Skype is hardly ever named. The same goes for digitised conversations in the form of online chats; these do not play any substantial role at all among the leading communicators interviewed here. A similar difference can be observed with regard to press conferences: the 'classic' variant is fairly popular while the digitised online-variant (inter alia in the form of a livestream distributed via political online presences) is hardly common or requested. Communicative exchange on weblogs is sought by some journalists yet the interviewed spokespersons and communication managers very seldom name it as part of their communicative portfolio.

The communicative exchanges subsumed under the notion of media relations are to a large extent dominated by 'classical' means, yet there are a few digital channels of importance, as the preceding analysis shows. There are some differences between the groups of actors analysed here – with for example those from a background of governmental bodies being more reluctant than others to integrate digital means in their communicative portfolio. Nevertheless most of the interviewees say they employ some form of digital media in organisational media relations or journalistic research. But why do they do that at all? What reasons do the interviewed spokespersons, communication managers and leading journalists give for their selection of digital means?

It emerges that the main reason for the employment of new (digital) means is in fact the time factor, i.e. the potentially faster speed of communicative exchanges undertaken by digital means. By using them, spokespersons and communication managers are able to get their messages distributed faster and vice versa, journalists can do their research much more quickly. As a matter of fact, 47% of the interviewees name this as the main reason for their selection. Financial reasons are on the other hand of no considerable importance here, the same goes for the communicative choices colleagues make. Some interviewees (mainly journalists) do however name compliance with the preferences of their contacts as an important reason; they opt for those channels that persons of interest already employ.

Summary

As the analyses of political web presences discussed in a preceding sub-chapter have shown, political parties and governmental bodies provide not only the general public with information online but also address relevant journalists. But this is of course only one element of their work with the media.

The direct communicative exchanges between political spokespersons and communication managers and professional political journalists analysed here are in fact another, and arguably even a key element of political media relations.

Representatives of political organisations seek to communicate organisational policies and information regarding current events and actions to their audiences through the mass media and vice versa, professional journalists seek to acquire information to allow comprehensive political coverage.

This subchapter has aimed to analyse these communicative exchanges with regards to the means employed in them; it has sought to measure the actual state of digitisation in these exchanges by analysing communicative preferences of both professional journalists and political communicators working for political parties and governmental bodies and then taking actual communicative exchanges into consideration.

Findings illustrate that e-mails are (momentarily) by far the most popular medium among those professionally involved in political communication. However, this is then closely followed by means that are rather traditional: spokespersons and communication managers often rely on direct conversations with their journalistic counterparts, either by telephone or face to face. Party spokespersons and communication managers also name social networks as an important tool in this regard, a finding which corresponds to the tendencies observed in the preceding analyses of party online presences.

Personal encounters between organisational representatives and political journalists are also established in the form of political background circles (which are a popular choice among the interviewed governmental communicators) and press conferences, which are often named as important by those that account for the external communication of political parties here.

Political journalists conduct a large proportion of their research via e-mail but also rely heavily on more traditional means, namely face-to-face and telephone conversations. When it comes to digital means, they either say they employ *Twitter*, which is especially popular among online journalists, or social networks. If press conferences are attended, this is generally done in person; the online variant is hardly popular among political journalists.

Apart from relying on direct communicative exchanges, the interviewed journalists also utilise previous coverage for their research (i.e. they make recourse to newspaper archives) or employ information that has already been aggregated by news agencies, thereby employing an intermediary instance between them and the organisational communicators of relevant political actors.

Communicative exchanges are to some extent digitised, yet one still finds a dominance of traditional means. New complementary channels such as *Twitter* and social networks are established, though their popularity among journalists exceeds their degree of proliferation among organisational communicators. Those that account for the external communication of governmental bodies show a relatively high degree of structural conservatism. In general, channels that might be regarded as digitised versions of traditional means, such as *Skype* (fulfilling functions of the telephone) or online press conferences (being streamed versions of the live variant), are not popular at all.

While the analyses of political online presences generally showed a high state of digitisation in this sphere despite the differences between the groups, the findings are somewhat different for the communicative exchanges that shape political media relations. One finds a cautious employment of digital tools here, yet traditional means are still largely popular and often dominate the field. According to those active in political media relations, social networks and *Twitter* complement traditional forms of communicative exchange, while other means are of no importance at all.

In general, political spokespersons and communication managers even appear more cautious than their journalistic counterparts, although the latter group also often relies on telephone or face-to-face conversations or even makes recourse to forms of existing or aggregated coverage. The communicative exchanges taken into consideration here are only partially digitised and in many cases hardly an example of online media relations.

4.4.3 Communication Networks Between Politics and Media

Political media relations are largely shaped by those that communicate for political actors such as parties and governmental bodies and by political journalists providing coverage within leading media outlets. On an organisational level, one finds these parties, governmental bodies and media outlets as the central players in the field of political communication.

Knowing about the ways in which political actors communicate online and about the channels through which political spokespersons, communication managers and journalists interact, the question remains as to how focal actors are interconnected in communicative regards. Which communication networks exist between politics and the media? How is information distributed and which patterns of influence exist?

The following findings derive from a social network analysis conducted within the aforementioned personal interviews with leading political journalists and political spokespersons and communication managers. The interviewees were asked to name organisational contacts recently utilised for the exchange of information. Which political parties and governmental bodies did journalists contact when researching for their political coverage? Which media outlets did those accounting for the communication of political actors supply with information?

As indicated, networks are analysed here on an organisational level; the focus is on informational ties between political actors and media outlets. Thereafter the analysis concentrates on patterns of influence: Which actors are perceived as influential and how does this relate to their centrality within the informational network? The subchapter concludes with selected analyses concerning some actors and subsets of actors.

Findings

How do political actors – both governmental bodies and political parties – and media outlets interact in the field of political media relations? Which patterns of informational exchanges can one actually find between them?

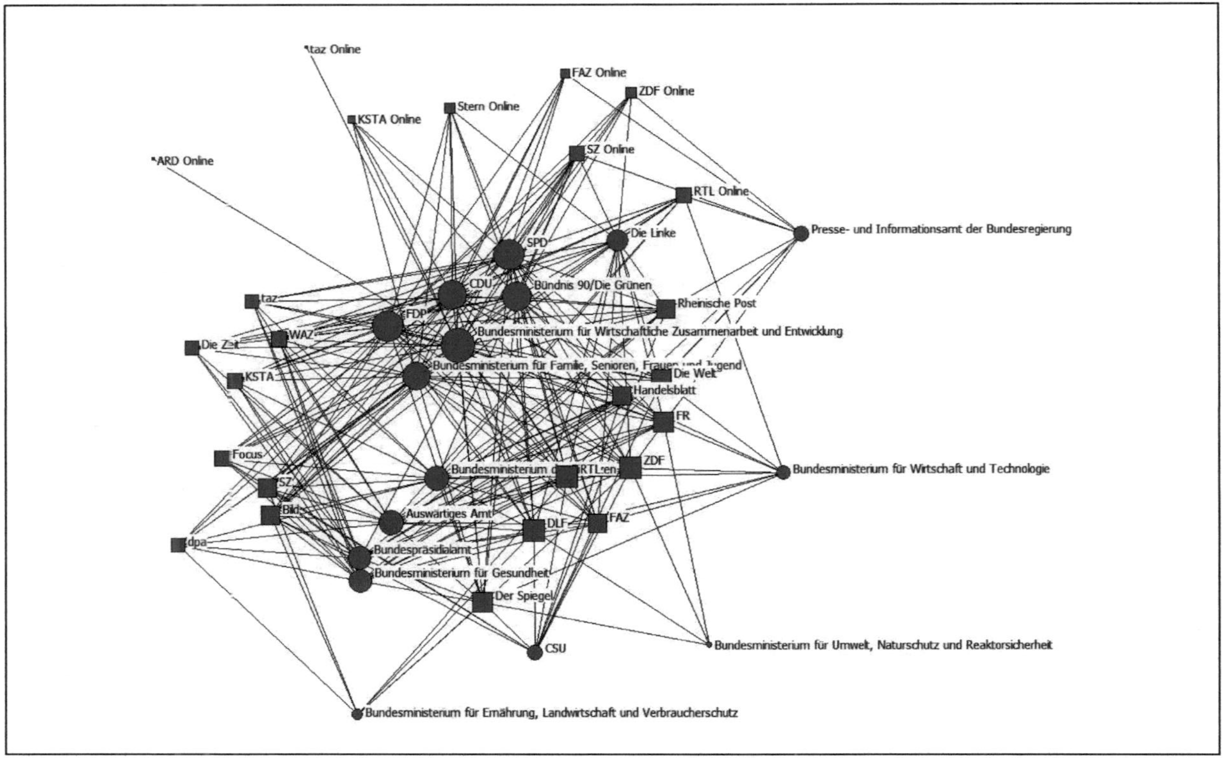

Fig. 25: Information network between politics and the media; [node size adjusted according to degree based centrality (n=41); circles: political actors, squares: media outlets; 2 mode network; visualisation composed according to geodesic distance].

The first network analysed here is constructed from those actors that actually participated actively in the interview study (n=41 organisations). The visualisation shows actors as nodes, the ties between them indicate informational exchanges. Node size here is adjusted according to degree-based centrality, i.e. the more informational ties an actor has, the bigger its node appears.

Central positions are often occupied by political parties; these appear strongly involved in informational exchanges. The nodes representing the socialist party *Die Linke* and the (mostly regionally active) conservative *CSU* however appear smaller than those representing the other parties. Between governmental bodies one finds greater variety: they are to be found both on very central and rather fringe positions in this network. On the media side, one often sees established offline media outlets as well-connected nodes; however, some online media outlets also show a variety of informational ties here.

Given these observations, which actors are then actually regarded as being central in terms of their informational connections?

Political actors: degree based centrality	
1. BMZ	0.595
2. FDP **SPD**	0.524
4. Bündnis 90 / Die Grünen **CDU**	0.500
6. BMFSFJ	0.476
7. AA **BMF**	0.429
9. BMG **Bundespräsidialamt**	0.405

Media outlets: degree based centrality	
1. DLF **RTL (aktuell)**	0.381
3. Die Welt **ZDF (heute)**	0.357
5. Frankfurter Rundschau **Der Spiegel**	0.333
7. Bild **Frankfurter Allgemeine Zeitung** **Handelsblatt** **Süddeutsche Zeitung** **Rheinische Post**	0.310

Tab. 19: Network-centrality of political actors and media outlets: top 10 ranking (based on degree-based centrality; only organisations interviewed are included).

The ranking of political actors according to their degree-based centrality confirms the tendencies visible in the network visualisation discussed above. Four major political parties occupy high ranks, with two (*FDP* and *SPD*) sharing second and two (*CDU* and *Bündnis 90 / Die Grünen*) sharing fourth place; the more regionally oriented *CSU* (which is only active in the federal state of Bavaria) and the relatively far-left party *Die Linke* are not among the most central actors. There are, in fact, some very well-connected governmental bodies, this is especially true for the *Federal Ministry of Economic Cooperation and Development* and the *Federal Ministry of Family Affairs, Senior Citizens, Women and Youth*.

One only finds offline media outlets among the media in this ranking; the top position is occupied by a nationwide public service radio station (*DLF*) and the newscast of a private TV station (*RTL aktuell*). Leading quality newspapers and a weekly political magazine (*Der Spiegel*) follow, together with a public service broadcaster and its TV news programme (*ZDF heute*). The outlets sharing seventh place include the major German tabloid *Bild* and a leading regional newspaper (*Rheinische Post*).

As indicated, degree-based centrality measures the actual number of ties a node has, i.e. in this case the number of informational ties an actor has with others. So the question is: In how far does this ranking change when another measure of network centrality is employed?

The eigenvector centrality measure can be regarded as a measure of popularity: nodes with connections to well-connected nodes score highly here. An actor with a comparatively small degree centrality could in fact have high values for eigenvector centrality if its contacts were well connected while another with a relatively high degree could score lower in terms of eigenvector if its contacts were rather isolated and unpopular (cf. Borgatti et al., 2013, p. 168).

Adapted to the present context of political media relations, high degree centrality would mean that an actor was simply connected (in terms of informational exchange) to a high number of other actors; e.g. in the case of a political actor being in exchange with many media outlets. A high eigenvector centrality on the other hand would imply that an actor would have informational exchanges with others that are well connected themselves, e.g. in the case of a political actor that exchanges with media outlets that are regularly in contact with a high number of other political actors. The question is whether there are actually different outcomes in the centrality ranking here depending on the measure employed. Is there a difference between actors with many connections and those with popular connections?

Political actors: Eigenvector based centrality		**Media outlets: Eigenvector based centrality**	
1. BMZ	0.324	**1. RTL (aktuell)**	0.261
2. FDP	0.314	**2. DLF**	0.256
3. SPD	0.310	**3. Die Welt**	0.253
4. Bündnis 90 / Die Grünen	0.302	**4. ZDF (heute)**	0.242
5. CDU	0.296	**5. Frankfurter Rundschau**	0.239
6. BMFSFJ	0.287	**6. Frankfurter Allgemeine Zeitung**	0.237
7. AA	0.274	**Rheinische Post**	
BMF		**8. Bild**	0.235
9. BMG	0.261	**Süddeutsche Zeitung**	
10. Bundespräsidialamt	0.257	**10. Der Spiegel**	0.233

Tab. 20: Network-centrality of political actors and media outlets: top 10 ranking (based on eigenvector based centrality; only interviewed organisations integrated).

As the table shows, the ranking of actors according to their centrality largely remains the same; as a matter of fact there aren't any changes in their order. One does however see minor differences: actors previously sharing a rank are now separated by a small margin. In terms of popularity one finds very small differences between the four political parties previously sharing two ranks, inter alia the same goes for the most central media outlets. But as indicated, there is no spectacular difference between the two rankings of central actors.

This also means of course that the list of media outlets is again purely dominated by offline media outlets. The online media outlets that are part of this sample of interviewed organisations have a comparatively low ranking with regard to both centrality measures. Even those with relatively high values (such as the online variant of *Süddeutsche Zeitung*, *süddeutsche.de,* which has a degree value of 0.238 and an eigenvector value of 0.188) do not even come close to the top 10 here.

The findings of preceding analyses are somewhat problematic despite their methodological accuracy: the network analysed is an undirected network of informational ties between nodes representing actors that have participated in the interviews substantiating the social network analysis here. This leads to the exclusion of actors that have refused to take part, yet have been named as contacts repeatedly by other interviewees. This applies particularly to the media outlets; political spokespersons and communication managers have often reported informational exchanges with media outlets that are not integrated into this analytical step due to their (repeated) refusal to participate.

In order to find out about those media outlets that are actually central for those accounting for the communication of political actors, it is now necessary to integrate the entirety of them into the analysis. Naturally, the fact that parts of the media sample have now been interviewed while others have not means that it is only admissible to measure incoming informational ties. Utilising an undirected network in which both incoming and outgoing ties would be treated equally would potentially privilege participating organisations which had the chance to name contacts themselves.

Taking into account only incoming informational ties, which role do individual media outlets play for the media relations network in Germany? How often are they actually named as partners of informational exchange by those accounting for the external communication of political actors? Is there any substantial difference between off- and online media outlets?

	Media outlets: degree-based centrality (incoming informational ties)	
1.	**ARD (tagesschau)**	0.875
2.	**Bild** **Süddeutsche Zeitung** **RTL (aktuell)**	0.813
5.	**Die Welt** **Rheinische Post** **Der Spiegel** **n-tv** **ZDF (heute)** **DLF**	0.750
11.	**Focus** **Frankfurter Allgemeine Zeitung** **Handelsblatt** **Westdeutsche Allgemeine Zeitung** **N24**	0.688

Tab. 21: Media outlets as approached by political actors (based on degree-based centrality; all media outlets integrated, only incoming ties from interviewed political actors integrated).

The table illustrates the choices the interviewed political spokespeople and communication managers make when engaging in communicative exchange with media outlets: they clearly opt for established offline outlets; one finds major quality newspapers, news programmes and two large regional newspapers from Germany's biggest conurbation in North Rhine-Westphalia.

The most popular choice is the major German newscast (distributed by public service television), closely followed by a major tabloid, a quality newspaper and the leading newscast on commercial TV. Other quality newspapers, commercial and public service TV newscasts and the major political weekly magazine share fifth place together with a nationwide public service radio broadcaster. The media outlets named here are all known for their provision of political coverage and largely regarded as the most central ones in all theoretical descriptions. At first sight one might wonder about the two regional newspapers (*Rheinische Post* and *Westdeutsche Allgemeine Zeitung*) in the table, yet the fact that their area of distribution is Germany's biggest conurbation and that they enjoy very high circulations may explain this finding.

Again, the table hardly reflects any conceptualisations of a digitised media sphere; arguably the very same findings could have been made before the proliferation of digital technology. But which role does digital media play here? Do political spokespersons and communication managers opt for these outlets when getting into contact with the media? How popular are well known online media outlets as communication partners?

The following table lists those online news outlets that were most popular among German recipients in 2014 and gives their degree value for incoming informational ties:

	million page visits (online and mobile) in 08/2014[84]	**degree centrality value** (incoming informational ties only)
Bild.de	275.41	**0.438**
Spiegel Online	196.02	**0.438**
Focus Online	98.44	0.125
n-tv.de	74.58	0.063
Die Welt (Online)	49.62	0.250
Sueddeutsche.de	48.03	**0.438**
ZEIT Online	35.50	**0.313**
FAZ.net	33.56	0.125
Stern.de	27.66	0.250
Handelsblatt.com	17.79	0.188

Tab. 22: The 10 most popular online media outlets (according to page visits) and their popularity as communication partners among political actors (based on degree based centrality, only incoming ties from interviewed political actors included; degree values over 0.3 are in bold).

There are in fact vast differences in terms of popularity within the media relations network. Some online media outlets that enjoy high numbers of visitors are

84 Source: Informationsgesellschaft zur Feststellung der Verbreitung von Werbeträgern e.V. (IVW), data for August 2014; available online: http://de.statista.com/statistik/daten/studie/154154/umfrage/anzahl-der-visits-von-nachrichtenportalen/ (last access: 23.09.2014).

chosen by between at least a third and almost half of the interviewed spokespersons and communication managers as partners of communicative exchange, others play hardly any role. The ranking according to page visits does not necessarily correspond with the communicative choices made by political actors: *Bild.de* and *Spiegel Online,* the most popular outlets among recipients, are also fairly popular as partners of communicative exchange, while *Focus Online* and *n-tv.de*, which occupy third and fourth places regarding page visitors, are hardly ever named.

There are in fact some popular online media outlets, but the key players still come from the offline sphere. None of the high ranking online media outlets would make it into the top ten of media contacts here. A comparison of centrality values between off- and online media shows that while the offline media outlets occupying the top five places have a mean centrality value of 0.781 (SD= 0.044), online outlets only achieve a mean centrality value of 0.354 (SD= 0.094).[85] A visualisation of the networks surrounding these actors illustrates the difference:

85 Values based on the network of incoming ties described and analysed before; degree-based centrality.

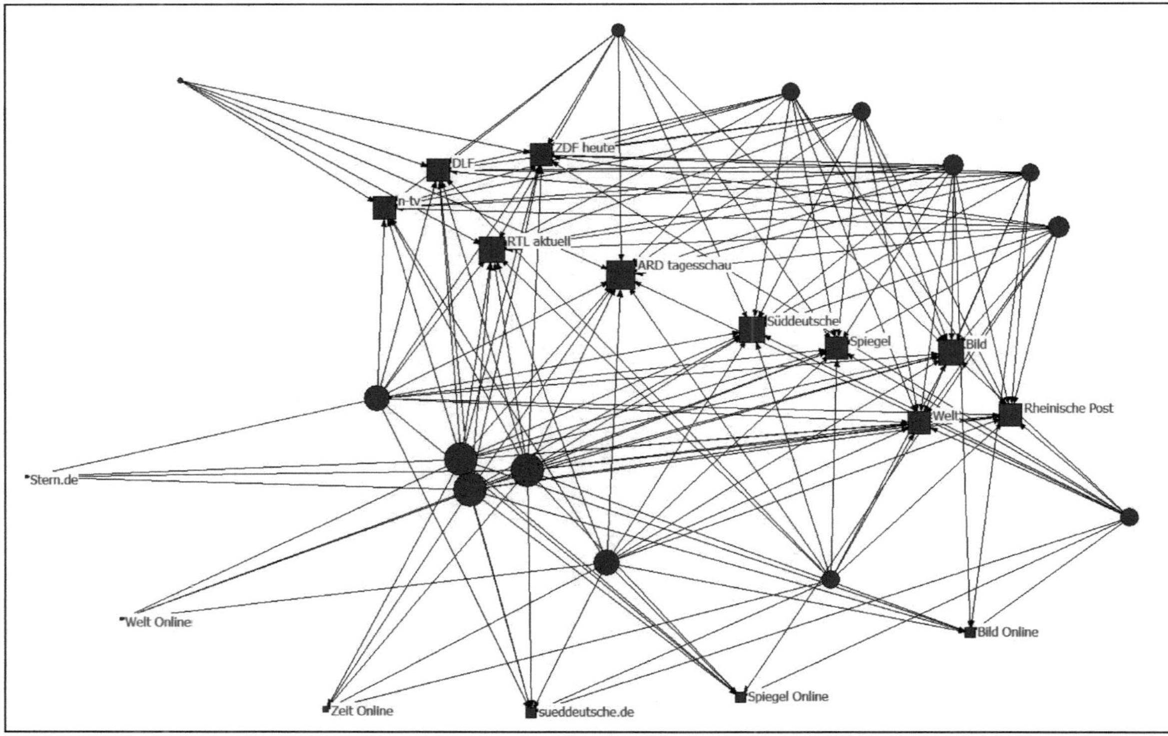

Fig. 26: Information network (incoming ties) surrounding the on- and offline actors occupying the top five ranks of centrality [node size adjusted according to degree-based centrality (n(offline)=10, n(online)=6); circles: political actors, squares: media outlets; visualisation composed according to geodesic distance].

The central positions are occupied by those ten offline actors that share the top five centrality ranks; their six online counterparts occupy comparatively fringe positions despite being the most central online media outlets in the network analysed here. When those accounting for the external communication of political actors engage in informational exchange, they primarily opt for offline media outlets.

The question though is whether or not these findings regarding informational exchanges within the media relations network analysed here reflect other dimensions such as (perceived) influence. Since the interviewed political actors generally opt for established offline media outlets when engaging in informational exchange, one could expect that they generally see these as influential for their specific field. But is this actually the case?

The 16 interviewed spokespersons and communication managers were asked to name up to three media outlets with which they had especially strong contact and with which they engaged in very comprehensive communicative exchange. Four outlets (*Bild*, *Frankfurter Allgemeine Zeitung*, *Süddeutsche Zeitung* and *ARD tagesschau*) were named four times in this regard, a further three outlets (*Handelsblatt*, *Der Spiegel* and *ZDF heute*) at least twice. The only online media outlet present in this classification (named in one case) is *Spiegel Online*, which in terms of page visits is the second most popular outlet in Germany.

Subsequently, interviewed spokespersons and communication managers were asked about media outlets that had recently set actual topics for them, thereby directly influencing their work. The most popular choice (named six times) here was a major tabloid (*Bild*), closely followed by a quality newspaper and a weekly magazine (*Frankfurter Allgemeine Zeitung* and *Der Spiegel*, which were both named five times). The third rank is shared by two quality newspapers (*Die Welt* and *Süddeutsche Zeitung*) and one online media outlet (*Spiegel Online*). In fourth place one finds the major public service TV newscast (*ARD tagesschau*) and a nationwide public service radio station (*DLF*).

Perceiving a contact as strong and attributing the ability to actually set topics to it could be understood as indicators of influence. Integrating this information on patterns of influence into the modelling of the media relations network, the following picture emerges:

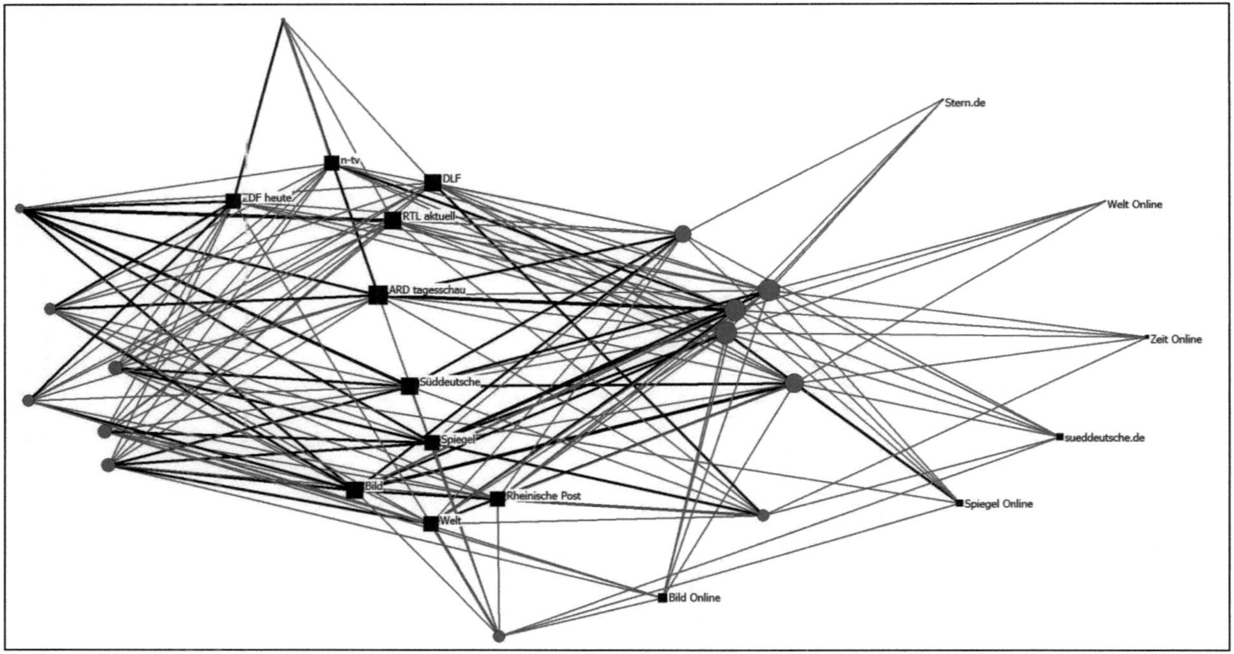

Fig. 27: Information and influence in the media relations network; based on an additive index of informational exchange, the strength of this exchange and topic-setting functions; higher values lead to darker and thicker ties [node size adjusted according to degree-based centrality (n(offline)=10, n(online)=6); circles: political actors, squares: media outlets; visualisation composed according to geodesic distance].

This network combines basic information about informational exchanges, about informational exchanges that are additionally perceived as strong and about the actual setting of topics. The underlying matrix between political actors and media outlets focuses on the information given by representatives of political actors and counts each of the three possible connections.

The close and tight connections between established offline media outlets and important political actors again become apparent while even important online media outlets remain in rather fringe positions. The integration of an influence dimension generally supports this picture, those nodes that occupy central positions are also (perceived as) influential, they are connected to each other by stronger ties than to others. In sum, the finding of a closely knit network-core is reflected in the influence dimension.

In the next analytical step, the similarities and dissimilarities between the contact portfolios of media outlets are taken into account. Which medium is contacted by which political actor and how similar are these contacts between the various outlets? The following table illustrates this for the 15 most central offline media outlets and for the five most central online media outlets; it is employing a Jaccard similarity coefficient.[86]

86 The Jaccard coefficient is to be understood as measuring the degree of similarity, for example between two finite sample sets; mathematically it is the size of the intersection divided by the size of the union.

	Bild	Bild.de	DLF	Focus	FAZ	HB	heute	n-tv	N24	Rh.Post	RTLakt.	Spiegel	SpOn	Stern.de	SZ	sz.de	tagessch	WAZ	Welt	Zeit.de
Bild		0.54(7)	0.79(11)	0.85(11)	0.85(11)	0.85(11)	0.79(11)	0.79(11)	0.71(10)	0.92(12)	0.86(12)	0.92(12)	0.54(7)	0.31(4)	1.00(13)	0.54(7)	0.93(13)	0.85(11)	0.92(12)	0.38(5)
Bild.de	0.54(7)		0.43(6)	0.50(6)	0.55(6)	0.50(6)	0.46(6)	0.46(6)	0.50(6)	0.58(7)	0.43(6)	0.46(6)	0.56(5)	0.38(3)	0.54(7)	0.56(9)	0.50(7)	0.64(7)	0.58(7)	0.50(4)
DLF	0.79(11)	0.43(6)		0.64(9)	0.71(10)	0.64(9)	0.85(11)	0.85(11)	0.77(10)	0.71(10)	0.92(12)	0.71(10)	0.36(5)	0.33(4)	0.79(11)	0.36(5)	0.86(12)	0.64(9)	0.71(10)	0.31(4)
Focus	0.85(11)	0.50(6)	0.64(9)		1.00(11)	1.00(11)	0.64(9)	0.64(9)	0.69(9)	0.92(11)	0.71(10)	0.83(10)	0.64(7)	0.36(4)	0.85(11)	0.64(7)	0.79(11)	0.83(10)	0.92(11)	0.45(5)
FAZ	0.85(11)	0.55(6)	0.71(10)	1.00(11)		1.00(12)	0.64(9)	0.64(9)	0.69(9)	0.92(11)	0.71(10)	0.92(11)	0.73(8)	0.36(4)	0.85(11)	0.64(7)	0.79(11)	0.83(10)	0.92(11)	0.45(5)
HB	0.85(11)	0.50(6)	0.64(9)	1.00(11)	1.00(12)		0.64(9)	0.64(9)	0.69(9)	0.92(11)	0.71(10)	0.92(11)	0.64(7)	0.36(4)	0.85(11)	0.73(8)	0.79(11)	0.83(10)	0.92(11)	0.36(4)
heute	0.79(11)	0.46(6)	0.85(11)	0.64(9)	0.64(9)	0.64(9)		0.85(11)	0.77(10)	0.71(10)	0.85(11)	0.79(11)	0.46(6)	0.33(4)	0.79(11)	0.36(5)	0.86(12)	0.64(9)	0.71(10)	0.21(3)
n-tv	0.79(11)	0.46(6)	0.85(11)	0.64(9)	0.64(9)	0.64(9)	0.85(11)		0.92(11)	0.71(10)	0.92(12)	0.71(10)	0.38(5)	0.33(4)	0.92(12)	0.36(5)	0.86(12)	0.64(9)	0.71(10)	0.31(4)
N24	0.71(10)	0.50(6)	0.77(10)	0.69(9)	0.69(9)	0.69(9)	0.77(10)	0.92(11)		0.77(10)	0.85(11)	0.64(9)	0.50(6)	0.36(4)	0.76(11)	0.38(5)	0.79(11)	0.69(9)	0.77(10)	0.31(4)
Rh.Post	0.92(12)	0.58(7)	0.71(10)	0.92(11)	0.92(11)	0.92(11)	0.71(10)	0.71(10)	0.77(10)		0.79(11)	0.85(11)	0.58(7)	0.33(4)	0.92(12)	0.58(7)	0.86(12)	0.92(11)	1.00(13)	0.42(5)
RTLakt.	0.86(12)	0.43(6)	0.92(12)	0.71(10)	0.71(10)	0.71(10)	0.85(11)	0.92(12)	0.85(11)	0.79(11)		0.79(11)	0.43(6)	0.31(4)	0.86(12)	0.43(6)	0.93(13)	0.71(10)	0.79(11)	0.38(5)
Spiegel	0.92(12)	0.46(6)	0.71(10)	0.83(10)	0.92(11)	0.92(11)	0.79(11)	0.71(10)	0.64(9)	0.85(11)	0.79(11)		0.58(7)	0.33(4)	0.92(12)	0.58(7)	0.86(12)	0.77(10)	0.85(11)	0.42(5)
SpOn	0.54(7)	0.56(5)	0.36(5)	0.64(7)	0.73(8)	0.64(7)	0.46(6)	0.38(5)	0.50(6)	0.58(7)	0.43(6)	0.58(7)		0.57(4)	0.54(7)	0.75(6)	0.50(7)	0.58(7)	0.58(7)	0.50(4)
Stern.de	0.31(4)	0.38(3)	0.33(4)	0.36(4)	0.36(4)	0.36(4)	0.33(4)	0.33(4)	0.36(4)	0.33(4)	0.31(4)	0.33(4)	0.57(4)		0.31(4)	0.57(4)	0.29(4)	0.36(4)	0.33(4)	0.50(3)
SZ	1.00(13)	0.54(7)	0.79(11)	0.85(11)	0.85(11)	0.85(11)	0.79(11)	0.92(12)	0.76(11)	0.92(12)	0.86(12)	0.92(12)	0.54(7)	0.31(4)		0.54(7)	0.79(11)	0.85(11)	0.92(12)	0.38(5)
sz.de	0.54(7)	0.56 (5)	0.36(5)	0.64(7)	0.64(7)	0.73(8)	0.36(5)	0.36(5)	0.38(5)	0.58(7)	0.43(6)	0.58(7)	0.75(6)	0.57(4)	0.54(7)		0.50(7)	0.55(6)	0.58(7)	0.71(5)
tagessch	0.93(13)	0.50(7)	0.86(12)	0.79(11)	0.79(11)	0.79(11)	0.86(12)	0.86(12)	0.79(11)	0.86(12)	0.93(13)	0.86(12)	0.50(7)	0.29(4)	0.79(11)	0.50(7)		0.79(11)	0.86(12)	0.36(5)
WAZ	0.85(11)	0.64(7)	0.64(9)	0.83(10)	0.83(10)	0.83(10)	0.64(9)	0.64(9)	0.69(9)	0.92(11)	0.71(10)	0.77(10)	0.58(7)	0.36(4)	0.85(11)	0.55(6)	0.79(11)		0.92(11)	0.45(5)
Welt	0.92(12)	0.58(7)	0.71(10)	0.92(11)	0.92(11)	0.92(11)	0.71(10)	0.71(10)	0.77(10)	1.00(13)	0.79(11)	0.85(11)	0.58(7)	0.33(4)	0.92(12)	0.58(7)	0.86(12)	0.92(11)		0.42(5)
Zeit.de	0.38(5)	0.50(4)	0.31(4)	0.45(5)	0.45(5)	0.36(4)	0.21(3)	0.31(4)	0.31(4)	0.42(5)	0.38(5)	0.42(5)	0.50(4)	0.50(3)	0.38(5)	0.71(5)	0.36(5)	0.45(5)	0.42(5)	

Tab. 23: Similarities between media outlets in terms of informational exchanges with political actors; based on a Jaccard similarity coefficient [again based on a matrix of incoming informational ties; values in brackets: absolute number of common contacts for each pair; light grey areas represent online media outlets].

Here one finds high degrees of similarities between leading newspapers; the political actors contacting them are in many cases the same. There is no large difference, neither according to their position in the political spectrum nor according to the type of coverage that they provide (i.e. whether they are to be considered tabloid newspapers, illustrated magazines or actual quality newspapers focusing on in-depth political coverage). The analysed broadcasters are also quite similar to each other and – to a slightly smaller degree – also to the analysed newspapers and weekly magazines. When it comes to informational exchanges with governmental bodies and leading political parties there is no large difference between the analysed media outlets; they are all contacted by these political actors and subsequently engage in communicative exchange.

The situation is however slightly different when it comes to online media outlets. Not only does their rather fringe positioning reflect the fact that they share relatively low numbers of common partners of exchange with offline media outlets but that they also do not show greater similarities between each other. Otherwise one could have assumed that a specific set of political actors would principally engage in communicative exchange with online media outlets while others generally would refuse to do so, but this is clearly not the case.

Considering the degree of similarity between media outlets, the preceding reflections on network structures (both in an informational dimension and in one additionally focusing on patterns of influence) are confirmed; the analysed network of political media relations is (on the media side) indeed dominated by established media outlets. Furthermore, these outlets are quite similar when it comes to their profile of communicative exchanges with political actors. Online media outlets are mostly confined to rather fringe positions within the network; they are contacted less often and are not perceived as equally influential. Similarities between them and between them and offline media outlets are smaller; there is no specific set of political actors generally opting for exchange with online media outlets.

So far, the analysed network appears to some extent to be structurally conservative. Central positions are occupied by established actors: large political parties and some ministries that are quite active with in regards of political communication engage in exchange with established offline media outlets. Media outlets regarded as influential by political spokespersons and communication managers also tend to be from the offline sphere; the information network and the one focusing on patterns of influence are in concordance.

Given these findings, the integration of new actors into these patterns of political communication remains to be clarified. In how far do the interviewed journalists, spokespersons and communication managers engage in communicative exchange with actors that would – in a classical understanding – not automatically be considered members of these networks? Which new actors are actually named as members of their personal communication networks by the interviewees? Last but not least: in how far do individual citizens play a role here?

Since weblogs are often described as a contemporary alternative to established media outlets or more generally as new players in the field of (political) communication, the first question concerns their integration in the communication networks surrounding the interviewees from both the political and the journalistic field. In an open network sampling, they were asked to name contacts that have so far not been integrated into the analysis. Do bloggers play any substantial role in this regard?

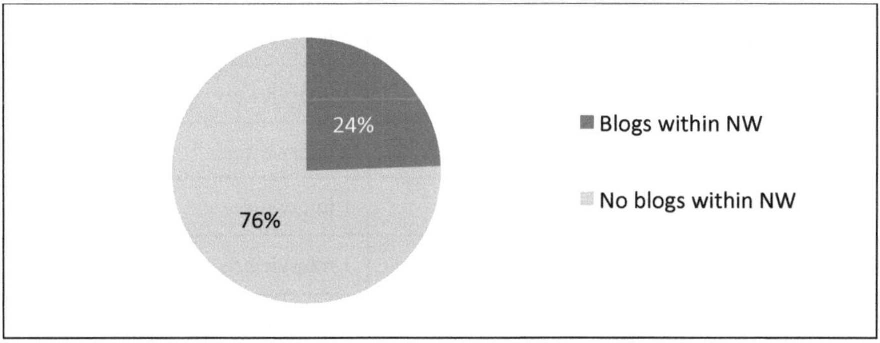

Fig. 28: Blogs as contacts within communication networks [based on network sampling; n(interviewees)=45, 11 of these named bloggers as contacts here].

It emerges that only about a quarter of the interviewees (n=11) consider blogs (or bloggers) to be members of their personal communication network while a large majority does not name any such contacts.

Weblog / Blogger:	Named by:
'Augen Geradeaus' ***(Thomas Wiegold)***	1 interviewee
'heute.de-Blog'	1 interviewee
Christopher Lauer	1 interviewee
'LawBlog' ***(Udo Vetter)***	1 interviewee
'Nachdenkseiten'	1 interviewee
'Netzpolitik.org'	2 interviewees
Stefan Niggemeier	1 interviewee
'Peerblog'	1 interviewee
'Piratenfraktion NRW-Blogs'	1 interviewee
Marina Weisband	1 interviewee
Anne Wizorek	1 interviewee
'Wir in NRW'	2 interviewees
-unspecific- ('French blog about tax evasion scandals')	1 interviewee

Tab. 24: Blogs named as nodes within their communication networks by the interviewees [n(interviewees)=45, n(interviewees naming blogs)=11, n(blogs)=13; multiple answers possible].

Interviewees named 13 different blogs here; only two of these were actually named twice. Among these one finds four that are maintained by political actors (in one case by a leading politician of the *SPD* and in three cases by leading figures or parliamentary fractions from the *Pirate Party*) while five are connected to bloggers that either were or still are active in professional journalism, often with work experience with leading media outlets. One blog is maintained by an online media outlet, one by a renowned lawyer and one by a professional digital media consultant and feminist activist. One does not find any bloggers here that are not somehow involved in politics and political communication in other regards. What is especially noteworthy is the fact that all but one weblog were named here by journalistic interviewees. Only one spokesperson actually named a weblog within the network sampling – and this was the one that is actually maintained by a major online media outlet (*heute.de-Blog*).

Apart from weblogs, there are hardly any other actors named within the network sampling that could actually be considered 'new'. In many cases interviewees working as political spokespersons or communication managers (which hardly ever mentioned weblogs here) made references instead to some regional newspapers of specific importance for them and their organisations while journalists did – as indicated – often opt for weblogs.

Although political media relations as a part of political communication would usually imply exchanges between political organisations and the media, network integration of new actors could principally also regard individual citizens. Their integration into patterns of communication could indicate some form of network opening. In how far are these integrated here, what percentage of actors actually engages in communicative exchanges with them?

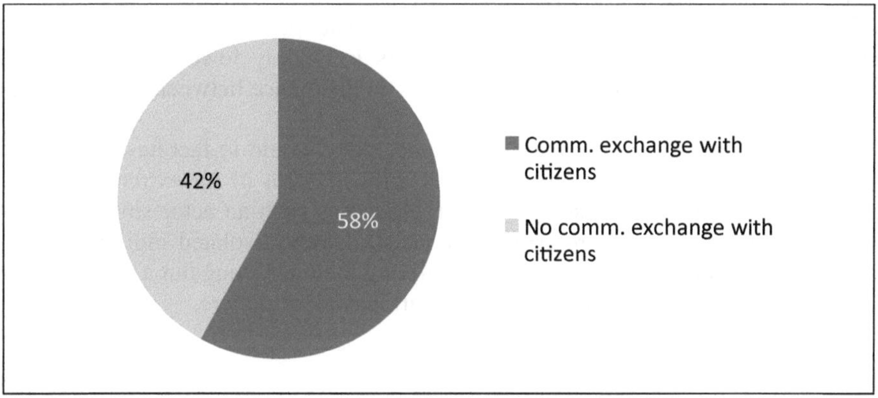

Fig. 29: Communicative exchange with individual citizens
[n(interviewees)=45; 24 of these named citizens as partners of communicative exchange here].

Over 50% of the interviewees here name individual citizens as partners of exchange when recalling recent professional communicative activities, even though these citizens are never named as strong contacts. Closer inspection shows that there are some differences between the two groups of interviewees:

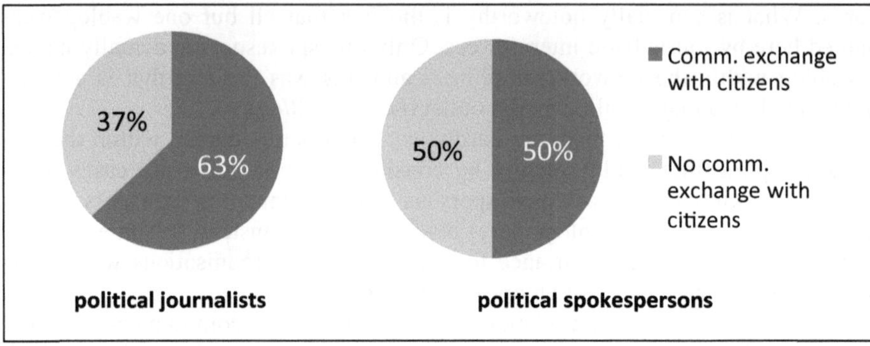

Fig. 30: Communicative exchange with individual citizens by journalists and political spokespersons and communication managers [n(journalists)=29, n(spokespersons and comm. managers)=16].

Around 63% of the interviewed political journalists name individual citizens as recent partners of communicative exchange. The percentage among political spokespersons and communication managers is slightly lower with only 50% referring to such contacts. There is however no difference between governmental and party spokespeople.

If individual citizens were a unitary actor, they would in fact have a place in the informational network but not necessarily in form of an extremely fringe node. Yet they are of course not to be regarded as such an actor since the contacts the interviewees are referring to consist of rather isolated individuals that are not connected to each other at all, rendering them anything but a unitary actor and again excluding them from the informational network here.

Summary

The preceding analyses conceptualise political media relations as a network of information and additionally also as one of influence. They seek to measure informational ties between political actors and media outlets and to thereby identify both well-connected nodes and nodes that are more at the fringe of the larger network of political communication. They then additionally focus on attributions of influence, seeking to identify those actors that are generally regarded as influential by their counterparts.

Findings indicate a network structure that is largely shaped by what might be described as structural conservatism: patterns resemble traditional conceptualisations of political media relations as a form of political communication taking place between established political actors and large offline media outlets.

On the political side, one finds strong network connections for all political parties. The relatively far-left socialist party *Die Linke* and the more regionally orientated conservative *CSU* do however rank slightly lower than the other established parties with parliamentary representation. Larger differences are visible between governmental bodies. Some of these are in fact some very well-connected; this goes especially for the *Federal Ministry of Economic Cooperation and Development* and the *Federal Ministry of Family Affairs, Senior Citizens, Women and Youth*. Others show less informational ties, yet one cannot identify governmental bodies on positions that would have to be considered fringe. In comparison to political parties, governmental bodies show a greater variance of centrality; parties, which have to cover all political fields, maintain a higher number of informational connections.

On the media side, one finds national quality newspapers and major newscasts on central positions; regionally orientated newspapers play also some role if their area of distribution is large enough. Compared to this, most online media outlets remain on rather fringe network positions. Even those leading the German market come nowhere near the leading offline variants in terms of network centrality. This becomes even more apparent when only the choices made by political spokespersons and communication managers are taken into account. The high number of contacts some online journalists name elevates their medium's centrality in the analysis, the (prestige-related) measuring of incoming informational ties renders them even more fringe.

This largely reflects in the influence dimension as well. Usually those media outlets that inhabit central network positions are the ones that are also generally regarded as influential. One leading online media outlet (*Spiegel Online*) ranks slightly better here, but apart from that, the influence network corresponds to its informational counterpart. Established quality newspapers and major newscasts clearly dominate the field.

New actors are hardly integrated into the analysed information networks. In some cases interviewees make reference to weblogs and bloggers they have been in contact with, yet these do not play any substantial role here. Besides, no blogger is in fact named by more than two interviewees at all. Other new actors are not of any importance either.

Findings do however differ when it comes to the integration of individual citizens into the information networks surrounding actors here. More than 50 % of the interviewees point out recent communicative exchanges with these; the numbers are especially high among journalists, where about 63% name individual citizens in this regard. As indicated, if individual citizens were to be regarded as a unitary actor (which of course is not the case) these figures would actually indicate a relatively high centrality.

Focusing on an influence dimension, new actors do not play any substantial role here at all. Neither bloggers nor individual citizens are ever named as strong contacts or attributed with a topic setting function by the interviewees. Citizens are quite often partners of communicative exchange, yet they are not considered especially strong or important contacts here.

In sum, the social network analysis conducted here reveals a picture of a closely knit informational network between actors that have long been established. Governmental bodies, large political parties and leading offline media outlets tend to stick to each other in communicative exchanges – and they only attribute each other with actual importance for their actual work. This renders the media relations network under online conditions very much structurally conservative.

4.4.4 Summary and Interim Conclusion

The preceding analyses seek to enquire into the ways in which elite actors from the field of political communication in Germany and their specific organisations actually adapt to the process of digitisation (RQ2).

This question regards the construction of political online presences, communicative exchanges between journalists and political spokespersons and the construction of networks in the sub-field of political media relations, especially with regard to their in- or exclusiveness

The first research question (RQ2a) focuses on the online presences of political actors, here on those of governmental bodies and political parties: *How do organisational political actors construct their online presences? Which communication options do they maintain and in how far do they integrate reciprocal elements?*

From a theoretical perspective, one would assume an elevated importance of external communication. This holds true for unidirectional communication, seeking to distribute information and to create a public image of the elite actors in question and the superordinate system of elites, and, to a significantly smaller extent, also for some form of bidirectional communication. Maintaining an elite position requires communicating. This communication does not necessarily have to be bidirectional, let alone symmetrical, yet it has to appeal to public demand and hold to the audience's expectations.[87]

Adapted to a context of political media relations in a contemporary democratic society in the online-age, these arguments indicate an elevated importance of online communication for political actors. Political online presences function as means of elite to non-elite communication and additionally offer potential for elite with non-elite communication. From a theoretical perspective it is expectable that political actors will maintain professional online presences and seek to be present on a variety of social media platforms to distribute information and to thereby cope with popular expectations. Dialogic means, feasible in technical terms, might play a role for political parties. Presumably this might, inter alia due to legal reasons, be different among governmental bodies.

As indicated, the empirical state of research in this area generally supports these assumptions. The findings of the precedent enquiry into the perceptions of digitisation also indicate a (perceived) high state of digitisation in the political sphere. Since the interviewed spokespersons and communication managers account for the external communication of their specific organisations, a state of digitisation corresponding to these perceptions is expectable.

But are the empirical findings deriving from the present analyses of political online presences in accordance with theoretical assumptions, the state of research and the findings from precedent analyses of perceptions?

The online presences of political actors appear professional and well maintained. All actors maintain a website; these are regularly updated with new informational content. Websites target both professional journalists and the general public. Their usability is very good. Professional journalists are provided with regular press releases and additional audio-visual material for their coverage. Political actors ensure that their press departments can be reached easily by journalists, often naming a variety of press contacts on their websites.

By integrating such elements aiming at professional journalists, political organisations render their online presences tools of political media relations. Originally, digital media in general and political online presences in particular were not necessarily considered instruments of political media relations. Instead, they were often discussed as effective means to circumvent media gatekeepers, to bypass journalistic thresholds to address relevant audiences directly and unmediated (cf. Hallahan, 1994, pp. 17-19; van de Donk et al., 2004, p. 19).

87 The motives underlying the mandatory external communication of elite actors differ between approaches. Functional approaches would recur to the societal functions of elites and accordingly argue in terms of democratic organisation, leadership and societal cohesion. Critical approaches primarily argue in terms of the self-interests of elites and describe external communication as a means to mask elite dominion and secure advantages for specific elite actors.

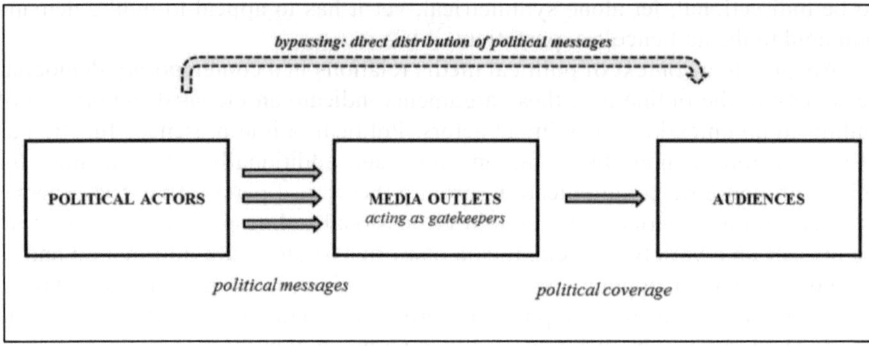

Fig. 31: 'Bypassing', the circumvention of media gatekeepers; based on a conceptualisation by Neuberger (2009).

This is however not confirmed here, findings indicate a dual use of political online presences; they address both professional journalists and general audiences.

As expected, the content distributed on the analysed political websites is predominantly informational; this holds especially true for the websites of governmental bodies. Political parties show slightly stronger mobilising tendencies yet a preference for informational content is ascertainable among them as well. The websites of political parties and especially of governmental bodies only offer a limited amount of bidirectional or dialogic functions. This is in contrast with the large amount of textual and informational content that they otherwise provide.

Social media sites are also employed for predominantly informational purposes, especially by governmental bodies. Both groups of political actors are active here, yet with distinct patterns of usage. Political parties engage in social networks, distribute visual content via *YouTube* and micro-blog on *Twitter*. Governmental are hardly active in social networks, yet very often opt for the distribution of video-material via *YouTube*. *Twitter* has also gained popularity among them between the two waves of analysis.

As expected, dialogic functions are only offered to a very limited extent. Allowing for some form of feedback is hardly common among governmental bodies. Political parties sometimes allow for such forms of communicative interaction, yet also preferably opt for unidirectional communication. Accordingly, governmental online communication appears as distributive communication executed through professional and well maintained digital channels. Political parties' online communication can be described as distributive communication supplemented by some dialogic options and executed through similarly professional and well maintained modern channels.

From a perspective focusing on (theoretical conceptualisations of) elite communications, the communication found here is best described as elite to non-elite communication with only few elements of (generally asymmetrical) elite with non-elite communication. The degree of professionalisation and diversification is explicable given the assumed importance of external communication in general and the need to cope with public demand in particular. Given the overall degree of popularity of online-communication among the general public in Germany (cf. van Eimeren & Frees, 2014), maintaining an online presence can accordingly be considered a necessity for political actors. In sum, the findings here correspond to the analytical heuristic, the existing state of empirical research and the findings from the precedent analyses of perceptions of digitisation.

The second research question (RQ2b) here then concentrates on actual communicative exchanges between individual communicators: *Through which channels do individual actors from the field of political communication (i.e. political spokespersons and journalists) engage in communicative exchange in the online age?*

From a perspective of elite theory, the communicative exchange between political spokespersons, communication managers and journalists has to be understood as elite with elite communication. It is attributed with a high degree of importance since both sides are mutually dependent. Actors are interconnected and seek to maintain such connections, it is therefore in their interest to communicate with each other. Accordingly, one should assume matching communicative preferences.

Given the high level of digitisation in the fields of politics and political communication and with additional regard to the strong perceptions of digitisation that the interviewees generally express, the employment of digital means in communicative exchanges seems expectable.

Yet empirical findings indicate that, apart from ubiquitous e-mails, most means employed by individual communicators are fairly traditional. Spokespersons and communication managers often rely on direct conversations with journalists, either via telephone or face-to-face. Personal encounters between organisational representatives and journalists often take place in established forums such as press conferences or political background circles. Yet at least among party communicators, one also finds social networks regarded as an important channel of external communication.

As indicated, the preferences of political journalists largely correspond to those of their counterparts in political organisations. They conduct large shares of their research via e-mail but also rely on traditional means, namely face-to-face and telephone conversations. *Twitter* is especially popular among online journalists, many also opt for social networks. Apart from relying on direct communicative exchanges, the interviewed journalists also utilise existing coverage for their research or employ information that has already been aggregated by news agencies.

While communicative preferences generally match for the most part, there are some considerable differences regarding new channels such as *Twitter* and social networks. Their popularity among journalists exceeds their proliferation among organisational communicators; especially governmental communicators show a relatively high degree of structural conservatism in their communicative preferences.

Actual communicative exchanges are affected by digitisation, yet the state of digitisation is comparatively lower than in other fields of external communication. While political organisations employ a large variety of new channels in their one-to-many communication, the actual exchanges their representatives undertake are often conducted by fairly traditional means. Here, media relations in the online-age hardly appear as actual media relations online.

The third research question (RQ2c) focuses on media relations networks: *How are communication networks between politics and the media constructed under the conditions of digitisation?* It is directly related to the fourth research question which then specifically concentrates of aspects of in- and exclusion in these networks: *Which role do new or formerly marginal actors play in political media relations under online conditions?*

The former questions primarily concerns elite with elite communication while the latter integrates a dimension of elite with non-elite communication (and subsequent non-elite ascent) by focusing on the potential integration of non-elites into networks of communication.

From a theoretical viewpoint, network ties are to be considered a form of social capital. By connecting to an actor (of individual or, as in this case, organisational nature) other actors potentially gain access to valuable resources, e.g. to further contacts and inside information. Political organisations need their communicators to connect to leading journalists from important media outlets in order to gain coverage and arguably also inside information on other political actors and political processes. Vice versa, media outlets rely on their journalistic employees to connect to important political organisations and their spokespersons to gain information to substantiate their political coverage.

Theoretically, elite with elite communication is considered a central form of communication. It is in the very interest of elite actors to establish and maintain ties to other elite actors, to allow for the accumulation of social capital and, more generally, for inter-elite coordination. This also holds true for the field of political media relations and for the organisations and organisational representatives active in it. Accordingly, strong connections between central elite actors are expectable.

The integration of non-elite actors – which would first constitute a form of elite with non-elite communication before then leading to the ascent of non-elite actors into the elite sphere – is theoretically expectable, yet only on a small scale. Considered a necessity for maintaining established power structures, some degree of non-elite ascent would lie in the very interest of elite actors striving to maintain their elevated standing. In a context of political media relations, this would indicate the small-scale integration of new actors such as political blogs and bloggers or new political and civil society organisations into otherwise elite-dominated communication networks.

The state of research indicates that political media relations would (still) have to be considered primarily as dominated by elite actors from politics and the media. Some studies indicate network integration on a very small scale while emphasising that gaps between political centre and periphery generally tend to widen. The emerging picture is largely coined by the exclusiveness of media relations networks.

Yet the preceding analysis on perceptions of digitisation indicates that especially political spokespersons and communication managers see new and formerly marginal actors as the main beneficiaries of digitisation, describing a (perceived) ascent of these groups into the centre of the field of political communication. Generally, and despite higher levels of scepticism among political journalists, both groups of interviewees indicate a (perceived) inclusion of new actors into the field of political media relations.

The empirical findings concerning actual adaptations of digitisation however indicate a network structure that is largely shaped by structural conservatism. The patterns identified by social network analysis resemble traditional conceptualisations of political media relations.

Political parties are generally well-connected. The relatively far-left socialist party *Die Linke* and the more regionally orientated conservative *CSU* do however rank slightly lower. In comparison to political parties, governmental bodies show a greater variance of centrality; parties, which are active in all political fields, maintain a higher number of informational ties. On the media side, national quality newspapers and major newscasts occupy central positions. Regional newspapers play some role if their area of distribution is large enough. Compared to this, most online media outlets remain in rather fringe network positions. Even those leading the German market are nowhere to be found among the leading offline media outlets in terms of network centrality.

Media outlets that occupy central positions in the information network are also generally regarded as influential by the actors in question; centrality and (perceived) influence mostly correspond. Apart from one online media outlet (*Spiegel Online*), the influence dimension is dominated by established quality newspapers and major newscasts.

As indicated, new actors are hardly integrated into the analysed information networks. Despite being mentioned as contacts by some interviewees, weblogs and bloggers do not play any substantial role here. The same holds true for other new actors. Individual citizens however are named as contacts by political spokespersons and communication managers and, to an even higher degree, by political journalists. This does not render them a central node within the media relations network due to them lacking the quality of a unitary actor. On an influence dimension, neither bloggers and other new actors nor individual citizens occupy any important rank at all.

The networks analysed appear to be closely knit and largely dominated by established actors. Governmental bodies, large political parties and leading offline media outlets maintain close ties and attribute high levels importance to each other. The media relations network under online conditions often appears structurally conservative.

Interim conclusion

Political media relations in the online age are sometimes highly digitised. Political organisations are very active in the online sphere. They maintain a variety of presences and keep them up to date with an abundance of information. These presences are not only conceptualised as channels of bypassing but constitute instruments of political media relations by targeting professional journalists.

At the same time, these presences are mostly a means of unidirectional communication. They do not foster communicative exchange with the recipients but rather seek to distribute information or, to a considerably lesser extent, to mobilise the recipients. Given the fact that especially social media sites were originally conceptualised as a means of bidirectional communication, this clearly indicates a transfer of established patterns of usage into a new sphere of communication. Nevertheless, political organisations have adopted new means of communication to a very large extent in this regard.

Findings are different however on a level of actual communicative exchanges. This part of political media relations is often hardly digitised with individual communicators overwhelmingly opting for established means of exchange. When political spokespersons and journalists engage in communicative exchange, they still talk to each other, either via telephone or in person. Social network sites have not largely altered communicative customs here.

This finding is replicated on a level of network ties. Established political actors primarily connect to established offline media outlets. Despite their wide proliferation and their large numbers of page visits, online media outlets hardly play any substantial role here. As analysis employing an index of similarity indicates, there is no specific set of actors that generally connects to online media; they are generally at rather fringe positions within the media relations network.
In sum, digitisation has affected some areas of political media relations while having a lesser impact in others. Political media relations in the online age are not necessarily political media relations in the online sphere. However, are they to be considered an elite phenomenon?

Findings indicate that this is (still) the case. Positional elites – central organisations and their representatives or the journalists working for them – largely dominate the networks in this field in Germany. The ways in which they communicate and construct their networks often correspond to assumptions derived from sociological elite theory.

Despite being originally fitted to the role of individual actors within societies, this theoretical heuristic is often highly accurate in assuming the ways in which organisational actors from the field of political media relations and the individuals working for them adapt to process of change affecting them. Communicative preferences correspond to assumptions derived from this heuristic and the construction of networks specifically reflects assumptions on inter-elite coordination and the accumulation of social capital.

Political organisations have strived to become fitted to processes of change in the conceptualisation of their external communication through websites and social media presences, yet the ways in which they interact with the media have often remained unaltered. Vice versa, media professionals integrate new means in their research, yet more often they opt for established means. Their networks also reveal a high degree of structural conservatism. Political media relations in the online age are a largely exclusive phenomenon, sometimes more exclusive than one would assume from a viewpoint based on a heuristic of elite theory.

5 Discussion, Conclusion & Outlook

> *"For unto every one that hath shall be given, and he shall have abundance"*
> *– [Matthew 25-29, King James Version]*

Interactions between politics and political journalism – political media relations – have long been regarded as a field of political communication that is largely dominated by few professional communicators. Political spokespersons seek communicative exchange with high ranking journalists working for leading media outlets to generate favourable coverage for their organisations and a general presence in the public debate. Professional journalists on the other hand seek contact with representatives of focal political organisations to provide a basis for the political coverage of their medium. The arrangement is exclusive and it is potentially beneficial to both sides.

Digitisation has been discussed as a process that could potentially alter such established patterns of communication and structures of power, potentially leading to new arrangements in political media relations. Given the almost ubiquitous online media, there are questions concerning the actual implications the process of digitisation has for political media relations.

The present thesis seeks to enquire into perceptions and adaptations of digitisation, into the ways in which focal political communication professionals see digitisation and in which they and their organisations adapt to these processes. Political spokespersons and communication managers and political journalists are considered to be positional elites, as actors shaping political media relations. Their perceptions and adaptations are the centre of interest.

5.1 Perceptions and Adaptations of Digitisation

The analysis of perceptions indicates that interviewees from both politics and the media perceive digitisation as an important process, affecting political communication in general and the specific interactions in this field in particular.

Journalistic interviewees generally tend to perceive stronger effects than their counterparts in political communication. They regard the field as highly affected by technological change and perceive considerable intra-organisational changes and altered patterns of interaction. At the same time, their overall evaluation of future developments tends to be ambiguous. Often they critically reflect on perceived effects and sometimes even describe processes of change primarily benefiting already established actors.

Political spokespersons and communication managers are often less critical here about the potential implications of digitisation, predominantly considering it as a process benefiting new and formerly marginal actors. They perceive comparatively weaker effects in the first place yet consider digitisation from a more cyber-optimistic perspective.

In general, both groups of interviewees see a medium influence of new and formerly marginal actors. They specifically refer to bloggers, civic initiatives and pressure groups and NGOs. Political spokespersons and communication managers often predict further increases in the influence of such actors.

As indicated, these views do not entirely correspond to the existing state of research concerning the implications of digitisation for politics and political communication. While empirical studies often describe political communication in general and political media relations in particular as rather exclusive phenomena, even under the conditions of digitisation, the interviewees tend to see them as becoming more inclusive due to digital media. Additionally, the general debate on digitisation as systematised here also tends to go in a different direction, clearly steering away from the postulation of such cyber-optimistic scenarios and often discussing the process in increasingly sceptical terms.

To clarify this possible contradiction, it is necessary to analyse the professional communicative surroundings of the interviewed spokespersons, communication managers and political journalists, the actual impact of digitisation in their field. In how far do they and their specific organisations actually adapt to digitisation? How does the process affect networks of political communication?

As analyses of actual adaptations show, political media relations are in some regards highly digitised. The analysed political organisations are very active in the online sphere, maintain a variety of presences and keep them up-to-date with large amounts of political information. They target both professional journalists and the general public. Yet simultaneously their presences are often means of unidirectional communication. Actors seek to distribute informational content or, to a considerably lesser extent, to mobilise their audiences. Political organisations have adopted new means of communication, yet they often replicate established patterns of communication.

Actual communicative exchanges on the other hand are often hardly digitised. Individual communicators overwhelmingly opt for established means here. This finding is also replicated on a level of network ties. Established political actors primarily connect to established offline media outlets. Notwithstanding their high degree of proliferation and their large numbers of page visits, online media outlets hardly play any substantial role here.

The same holds true for weblogs. Despite being mentioned as contacts by some interviewees, these do not play any substantial role in the analysed networks. Neither do other new (civil society) actors. Individual citizens are named as contacts, especially by political journalists. However, lacking the quality of a unitary actor, they do not constitute a node within the analysed network of political media relations. On an influence dimension, neither bloggers and other new actors nor individual citizens occupy any important rank at all.

In sum, the analysed perceptions and adaptations of digitisation are in accordance in some regards but also show considerable divergence in many others. Interviewees perceive strong technological effects of digitisation and indeed, analyses indicate that political media relations are highly digitised in some regards. Hardly surprising, the inhabitants of a highly digitised field perceive a strong impact of digitisation. Yet actual communicative exchanges are conducted through fairly traditional means. Even more important, the actual construction of networks in particular is not in accordance with some of the perceptions expressed here. There appears to be an actual perception gap, a divergence between perceived inclusion and actual exclusiveness. This holds especially true for the group of political spokespersons and communication managers.

It is not possible to identify the undoubted cause for this finding, yet there are several potential explanatory factors for the discrepancy between perceptions and actual adaptations. First, there might simply be effects of social desirability affecting expressed perceptions here. Interviewees and their organisations occupy focal positions in a so far largely exclusive and structurally conservative network. Perceived popular demand for modern, digitised and inclusive communication could account for expressed perceptions that overemphasise the role of new and formerly marginal actors in the media relations network.

Then, as a literature review shows, cyber-optimism has always been a practitioners' domain, especially for public relations practitioners. Members of this professional group often tend to emphasise the potential of digitisation and to argumentatively set aside potential perils. Per definition, perceptions are the product of processes of the organisation, identification and interpretation of sensually grasped stimuli. The surroundings of an individual actor directly influence the ways in which these stimuli are elaborated. Inhabiting a field largely coined by cyber-optimism could therefore influence perceptions of digital change. Organisational factors could also contribute here with organisations facing strong normative demands for inclusive communication triggering such perceptions among their representatives.

Differences between journalistic interviewees and their counterparts from the political field can possibly be explained via professional role conceptions. Here journalistic interviewees especially emphasise their function as critical observers – which might also account for their more critical perspective on phenomena of digitisation – and negate role concepts that emphasise an interconnectedness with citizens, that emphasise the need to provide the latter with a chance to be heard. Journalistic role conceptions show a weaker normative dimension in this regard, potentially accounting for a smaller social desirability of network integration.

However the finding remains that there are perception gaps especially in terms of network construction and inclusiveness. This holds at least true for the situation in Germany in 2012/13 analysed here; future (longitudinal) analyses might of course lead to divergent findings. But political media relations as analysed here are an exclusive phenomenon, a field that is (still) largely determined by established elite actors.

5.2 Political Media Relations Online as an Elite Phenomenon

As the analyses conducted here indicate, political media relations in Germany are, at least in their current state, still regarded as a largely exclusive field, as an elite phenomenon. Yet what implications does this finding have?

In accordance with the general direction of the debate on the process of digitisation and its implications and consequences, the findings here again refute overly cyber-optimistic assumptions about the actual impact of technological change. Network structures and general patterns of communication appear as largely unaltered, potentially indicating a state of normalisation in which technological change does not induce communicative, political or societal change.

As social network analysis shows, elite actors from the field of political communication form dense networks in which they closely interact. These networks are largely exclusive and very much structurally conservative. This is in accordance with the state of research concerning political media relations in the online age, which however is relatively small so far. Furthermore, it can also be explained from a viewpoint based on a theoretical heuristic derived from sociological elite theory. Inter elite communication and coordination are regarded as being highly important and since ties with powerful actors allow for the accumulation of social capital, it is only consequent that elite actors striving to maintain their position predominantly opt for such ties.

Political media relations are an elite phenomenon and they are so in accordance with both the state of research and theoretical considerations. But is this actually problematic?

It is true that elite actors from the field of political media relations are closely connected within exclusive elite networks. Yet, as the recent debate surrounding Krüger's (2013) network analysis concerning political media relations in Germany shows, equating closeness to (illegitimate) influencing might be stretching a point (cf. Neuberger, 2014).

Depending on the theoretical perspective, the political and societal role of elites differs. Functional elite theory considers elites a necessity for societal leadership and guidance and, at least in some highly affirmative accounts, actually frames them as groups of actors primarily occupied with the greater good of state and society. Critical elite theory on the other hand predominantly frames elites in terms of collusion and the pursuit of self-interest, in some regards even as a peril to democracy. Both perspectives arguably tend to sometimes mark extreme points in an analytical spectrum.

However, one does not have to adopt the often overly affirmative perspective of some functional accounts to admit to at least two particularities of the elites analysed: On the one hand, the political organisations here are democratically legitimated. Governmental bodies exist due to electoral majorities and, as the federal election conducted shortly after the present analyses illustrates, decreases in voter support directly affect their existence. Major political parties are considered major because of their membership, their share of votes and their parliamentary representation. Again, the overall population has a direct influence on their elevated status and can, as the *FDP*'s elimination from parliament after the 2013 federal elections illustrates, deprive them of parts of their status through democratic means. Professional journalism then has a democratic function – without necessarily constituting a fourth estate – and furthermore it is also dependent on readership to maintain high circulation numbers. Both elite groups considered here are connected to non-elites and often highly dependent on them.

The analysed field of political media relations in Germany is not determined by clandestine elites masking their illegitimate dominion behind propagandistic formulas. Of course, the elite actors analysed here have a high interest in maintaining their elevated status and they arguably also do so by influencing non-elites. Yet there is a clear difference between this form of often exclusive elite interaction and the authoritarian model of elite separation discussed in the elite model of political communication presented at the beginning of this thesis.

A further aspect that has to be taken into consideration in the evaluation of findings here regards the professionalisation of political communication (e.g. Holtz-Bacha, 2007; Raupp, 2009). In a functionally differentiated society, professional roles are highly specified. This holds true in many areas and of course also in the field of political communication. Contemporary society is based on the division of labour and it seems only consequent that large shares of political media relations should be conducted by professionals within a relatively closed network.

Nevertheless, the analysed exclusiveness of political communication networks could also pose problems. From a perspective of elite theory, segregated elites potentially endanger their elite status. If politics and political communication become too remote, this potentially undermines their societal function and thereby endangers the roles of those inhabiting the field. Elite remoteness and an overly high degree of network exclusivity have the potential to foster popular resentment against politics and the established mainstream media. The necessary consensus between the general public and political communication elites is then endangered.

Theoretically, online media have the potential to create echo chambers and counter public spheres, ultimately even triggering some form of communicative and political Balkanisation. There is no substantial evidence for such developments in the current situation (cf. Emmer & Wolling, 2010, pp. 45-50), yet elite remoteness could potentially trigger them.

Political media relations in their current form as an elite phenomenon are not inherently problematic, yet (further) developments towards overly high levels of elite remoteness could potentially induce problems.

5.3 Outlook

The present thesis focuses on one national context and on one timeframe. It analyses political media relations in Germany between 2012 and 2013, focusing on a small set of elite actors from the field of political communication. Findings are therefore to be considered valid in this specific context and not necessarily generalisable.

Given the salience of processes of digitisation and societal and political centrality of the sub-field of political media relations, there is a need for further research. On the one hand, similar analyses would have to be repeated. Only longitudinal empirical research can monitor patterns of change in media, political communication and ultimately also in politics. Whether or not the inclusiveness of communication networks evolves over time continues to be a salient question and answering it requires long term monitoring of such networks.

Additionally, the influence of national communication cultures and national frameworks is largely under-explored. Here, an actual influence of communicative restraints demanded by the German constitutional court has repeatedly been supposed; further established patterns and routines of interaction might also act as intervening or moderating variables. International comparative studies could help to identify such influences by controlling additional context factors.

The role of challenging actors also deserves additional empirical research. Here findings indicate that they do not play any substantial role in the general network of political media relations. Yet since they clearly do communicate, it remains to analyse the networks they inhabit and the potential they have for their messages to spill over into the general network and the wider political debate.

Political communication in the digital age continues to be one of the most central fields for communication research, this also holds true with regard to the specific sub-field of political media relations under the conditions of technological change. Digitisation is not a static event but should rather be regarded as an ever accelerating process. This substantiates a continuous need for empirical research.

For the time being, it only remains to emphasise that political media relations in Germany constitute an elite phenomenon and that they do so to a degree that is often even higher than those actors involved actually perceive. Whether or not this continues to hold true is a matter of future research.

Literature

Abbott, A. D. (2004). *Methods of discovery: heuristics for the social sciences*. New York: Norton.

Albertoni, E. A. (1987). *Mosca and the Theory of Elitism*. Oxford: Basil Blackwell.

Allern, S., & Blach-Ørsten, M. (2011). The news media as a political institution: A Scandinavian perspective. *Journalism Studies, 12*(1), 92–105.

Altmeppen, K.-D. (2006). *Journalismus und Medien als Organisation. Leistungen, Strukturen und Management*. Wiesbaden: VS Verlag.

Anstead, N., & Chadwick, A. (2009). Parties, election campaigning, and the internet: Toward a comparative institutional approach. In A. Chadwick & P. N. Howard (Eds.), *Routledge Handbook of Internet Politics* (pp. 56–71). Abingdon: Routledge.

Auty, C. (2005). UK elected representatives and their weblogs: first impressions. *Aslib Proceedings, 57*(4), 338–355.

Bader, K. (2013). *Medialisierung der Parteien, Politisierung der Medien*. Wiesbaden: VS Verlag.

Bell, D. (1958). The power elite-reconsidered. *American Journal of Sociology, 64*(3), 238–250.

Bennett, W. L. (1990). Toward a Theory of Press-State Relations in the United States. *Journal of Communication, 40*(2), 103–127. doi: 10.1111/j.1460-2466.1990.tb02265.x

Bennett, W. L., Lawrence, R. G., & Livingston, S. (2007). *When the Press Fails: Political Power and the News Media from Iraq to Katrina*. Chicago: University of Chicago Press.

Berkeley, G. (1971). *A treatise concerning the principles of human knowledge*. Menston: Scolar Press.

Bessette, J. (1980). Deliberative Democracy: The Majority Principle in Republican Government. In R. A. Goldwin & W. A. Schramba (Eds.), *How democratic is the constitution?* (AEI studies 294) (pp. 102–116). Washington: American Enterprise Institute for Public Policy Research.

Bimber, B. (1998). The Internet and Political Transformation: Populism, Community, and Accelerated Pluralism. *Polity, 31*(1), 133–160.

Blumler, J. G. (1998). Public Spheres in Contention. In C. Holtz-Bacha, H. Scherer, & N. Waldmann (Eds.), *Wie die Medien die Welt erschaffen und wie die Menschen darin leben* (pp. 83–102). Opladen: Westdeutscher Verlag.

Blumler, J. G., & Gurevitch, M. (2001). The new media and our political communication discontents: Democratizing cyberspace. *Information, Communication & Society, 4*(1), 1–13.

Bonfadelli, H. (2002). Die Wissenskluft-Perspektive: Theoretische Perspektive, methodische Umsetzung, empirischer Ertrag. In M. Schenk (Ed.), *Medienwirkungsforschung* (pp. 568–604). Tübingen: Mohr Siebeck.

Bongiorno, A. (1930). A Study of Pareto's Treatise on General Sociology. *American Journal of Sociology, 36*(3), 349–370. doi: 10.2307/2767275

Borgatti, S. P., Everett, M. G., & Johnson, J. C. (2013). *Analyzing social networks*. London: Sage.

Bourdieu, P. (1982). *Die feinen Unterschiede: Kritik der gesellschaftlichen Urteilskraft*. Frankfurt am Main: Suhrkamp.

Bourdieu, P. (1992). *Die verborgenen Mechanismen der Macht*. Hamburg: VSA.

Bourdieu, P. (1997). *Der Tote packt den Lebenden. Schriften zu Politik & Kultur* (Vol. 2). Hamburg: VSA.

Bourdieu, P. (1998). *Über das Fernsehen*. Frankfurt am Main: Suhrkamp.

Bourdieu, P. (2010). *Politik: Schriften zur Politischen Ökonomie 2* (Vol. 7). Konstanz: UVK.

Brants, K. (2005). Guest Editor's Introduction: The Internet and the Public Sphere. *Political Communication, 22*(2), 143–146. doi: 10.1080/10584600590933133

Brockhaus Enzyklopädie. (2001) *Brockhaus – Die Enzyklopädie (Studienausgabe)* (20th ed., Vol. 1). Leipzig: F.A. Brockhaus.

Brundidge, J., & Rice, R. E. (2009). Political engagement online: Do the information rich get richer and the like-minded more similar? In A. Chadwick & P. N. Howard (Eds.), *Routledge Handbook of Internet Politics* (pp. 144–156). Abingdon: Routledge.

Burgert, D. (2009). *Politisch-mediale Beziehungsgeflechte: Ein Vergleich politikfeld-spezifischer Kommunikationskulturen in Deutschland und Frankreich* (Vol. 3). Münster: LIT Verlag.

Canél, M. J., & Sanders, K. (2012). Government Communication: An emerging field in political communication research. In H. A. Semetko & M. Scammell (Eds.), *The Sage Handbook of Political Communciation* (pp. 85–96). London: Sage.

Carey, J. (1992). *The Intellectuals and the Masses: Pride and Prejudice among the Literary Intelligentsia, 1880–1939*. London: Faber & Faber.

Chadwick, A. (2007). Digital network repertoires and organizational hybridity. *Political Communication, 24*(3), 283–301.

Chadwick, A. (2009). Web 2.0: New Challenges for the Study of E-Democracy in an Era of Informational Exuberance. *I/S: A Journal of Law and Policy for the Information Society, 5*(1), 9–42.

Chadwick, A., & May, C. (2003). Interaction between States and Citizens in the Age of the Internet: 'e-Government' in the United States, Britain, and the European Union. *Governance, 16*(2), 271–300. doi: 10.1111/1468-0491.00216

Chandler, D., & Munday, R. (2011). *A Dictionary of Media and Communication*. Oxford: Oxford University Press.

Chen, P., Gibson, R., Lusoli, W., & Ward, S. (2007). Australian government and online-communication. In S. Young (Ed.), *Government communication in Australia* (pp. 161–180). Cambridge: Cambridge University Press.

Coleman, S., & Blumler, J. G. (2009). *The Internet and democratic citizenship: Theory, practice and policy*. Cambridge: Cambridge University Press.

Coleman, S., & Gøtze, J. (2002). *Bowling together: Online public management in policy deliberation*. London: Hansard Society.

Collins English Dictionary. (2009) (10th ed.). Glasgow: Harper Collins.

Cooper, J. (2006). The digital divide: The special case of gender. *Journal of Computer Assisted Learning, 22*(5), 320–334.

Daloz, J. (2007). Elite distinction: Grand theory and comparative perspectives. *Comparative Sociology, 6*(1), 27–74.

Dasgupta, P. (2000). *Digitalization.* Retrieved from http://cactus.eas.asu.edu/partha/Columns/12-24-digital.htm

Davis, A. (2002). *Public Relations Democracy: Public Relations, Politics and the Mass Media in Britain*. Manchester: Manchester University Press.

Davis, A. (2003). Whither Mass Media and Power? Evidence for a Critical Elite Theory Alternative. *Media, Culture & Society, 25*(5), 669–690.

Davis, A. (2009). Journalist-Source Relations, Mediated Reflexivity and the Politics of Politics. *Journalism Studies, 10*(2), 204–219. doi: 10.1080/14616700802580540

Davis, A. (2010a). New media and fat democracy: the paradox of online participation. *New Media & Society, 12*(5), 745–761.

Davis, A. (2010b). *Political Communication and Social Theory*. London: Routledge.

Davis, R. (2005). *Politics online: Blogs, chatrooms, and discussion groups in American democracy.* New York: Routledge.

Davis, S., Elin, L., & Reeher, G. (2002). *Click on Democracy: The Internet's Power to Turn Political Apathy into Action*. Boulder: Westview Press.

Decker, F. (2013). Parteiendemokratie im Wandel. In F. Decker & V. Neu (Eds.), *Handbuch der deutschen Parteien* (pp. 21–59). Wiesbaden: VS Verlag.

Dellarocas, C. (2003). The Digitization of Word of Mouth: Promise and Challenges of Online Feedback Mechanisms. *Management Science, 49*(10), 1407–1424.
Descartes, R. (1994). *Meditationen über die Grundlagen der Philosophie mit den sämtlichen Einwänden und Erwiderungen.* Hamburg: Felix Meiner Verlag.
Dohle, M., & Bernhard, U. (2013). Presumed Online Media Influence and Support for Censorship: Results from a Survey among German Parliamentarians. *International Journal of Public Opinion Research, 26*(2): 256–268. doi: 10.1093/ijpor/edt027
Dohle, M., Blank, C., & Vowe, G. (2012). Wie sehen Parlamentarier den Einfluss der Medien? Ergebnisse einer Befragung der Bundestagsabgeordneten. *Zeitschrift für Parlamentsfragen, 43*(2), 344–355.
Donges, P. (2006). Mediatisierung. In G. Bentele, H.-B. Brosius, & O. Jarren (Eds.), *Lexikon Kommunikations- und Medienwissenschaft* (pp. 164–165). Wiesbaden: VS Verlag.
Donges, P. (2008). *Medialisierung politischer Organisationen. Parteien in der Mediengesellschaft.* Wiesbaden: VS Verlag.
Downey, J., & Fenton, N. (2003). New media, counter publicity and the public sphere. *New Media & Society, 5*(2), 185–202. doi: 10.1177/1461444803005002003
Dudenhöffer, K., & Meyen, M. (2012). Digitale Spaltung im Zeitalter der Sättigung. Eine Sekundäranalyse der ACTA 2008 zum Zusammenhang von Internet-nutzung und digitaler Spaltung. *Publizistik, 57*(1), 7–26.
Edwards, A. (2008). What e-politicians do with words: Online communication between councillors and citizens. *Information Polity: The International Journal of Government & Democracy in the Information Age, 13*(3/4), 233–248.
Elias, N. (1978). *The Civilizing Process: The History of Manners.* Oxford: Basil Blackwell.
Elter, A. (2013). Interaktion und Dialog? Eine quantitative Inhaltsanalyse der Aktivitäten deutscher Parteien bei Twitter und Facebook während der Landtagswahlkämpfe 2011. *Publizistik, 58*(2), 201–220.
Emmer, M., & Bräuer, M. (2010). Online-Kommunikation politischer Akteure. In W. Schweiger & K. Beck (Eds.), *Handbuch Online-Kommunikation* (pp. 311–337). Wiesbaden: VS Verlag.
Emmer, M., Vowe, G., & Wolling, J. (2011). *Bürger online: Die Entwicklung der politischen Online-Kommunikation in Deutschland.* Konstanz: UVK.
Emmer, M., & Wolling, J. (2010). Online-Kommunikation und politische Öffentlichkeit. In W. Schweiger & K. Beck (Eds.), *Handbuch Online-Kommunikation* (pp. 37–59). Wiesbaden: VS Verlag.
Engesser, S., & Wimmer, J. (2009). Gegenöffentlichkeit(en) und partizipativer Journalismus im Internet. *Publizistik, 54*(1), 43–63. doi: 10.1007/s11616-009-0024-2
Ettrich, F., & Utz, R. (2002). Zwischen „Prominenz" und „Nomenklatura". Überlegungen zu neuerer Eliten-Literatur. *Berliner Journal für Soziologie, 12*(3), 389–403.
Ferguson, R., & Griffiths, B. (2006). Thin Democracy? Parliamentarians, Citizens and the Influence of Blogging on Political Engagement. *Parliamentary Affairs, 59*(2), 366–374. doi: 10.1093/pa/gsl006
Francoli, M., & Ward, S. (2008). 21st century soapboxes? MPs and their blogs. *Information Polity: The International Journal of Government & Democracy in the Information Age, 13*(1/2), 21–39.
Fraser, N. (1990). Rethinking the Public Sphere: A Contribution to the Critique of Actually Existing Democracy. *Social Text* (25/26), 56–80. doi: 10.2307/466240
Gabriel, O. W. (2001). *Parteiendemokratie in Deutschland* (2nd ed.). Bonn: Bundeszentrale für politische Bildung.
Gastil, J. (2008). *Political communication and deliberation.* Thousand Oaks: Sage.

Gerhards, J., & Schäfer, M. (2007). Demokratische Internet-Öffentlichkeit? Ein Vergleich der öffentlichen Kommunikation im Internet und in den Printmedien am Beispiel der Humangenomforschung. *Publizistik, 52*(2), 210–228. doi: 10.1007/s11616-007-0084-0

Gibson, R., Margolis, M., Resnick, D., & Ward, S. J. (2003). Election Campaigning on the WWW in the USA and UK. *Party Politics, 9*(1), 47–75.

Gore, A. (1994). *Remarks prepared for delivery by U.S. Vice-President Al Gore.* Paper presented at the World Telecommunication Development Conference, Buenos Aires.

Grossman, L. K. (1995). *The electronic republic: Reshaping democracy in the information age.* New York: Viking.

Grunig, J. E., & Hunt, T. (1984). *Managing Public Relations.* New York: Holt, Rinehart and Winston.

Gulati, G. J., & Williams, C. B. (2013). Social Media and Campaign 2012: Developments and Trends for Facebook Adoption. *Social Science Computer Review, 31*(5), 577–588.

Habermas, J. (1990). *Strukturwandel der Öffentlichkeit. Untersuchungen zu einer Kategorie der bürgerlichen Gesellschaft.* Frankfurt am Main: Suhrkamp.

Habermas, J. (1997). *Faktizität und Geltung: Beiträge zur Diskurstheorie des Rechts und des demokratischen Rechtsstaats.* Frankfurt am Main: Suhrkamp.

Hallahan, K. (1994). Public Relations and Circumvention of the Press. *Public Relations Quarterly, 39*(2), 17–19.

Hallin, D. C., & Mancini, P. (2008). *Comparing media systems: three models of media and politics.* Cambridge: Cambridge University Press.

Hand, M. (2009). *Making digital cultures: access, interactivity, and authenticity.* Farnham: Ashgate.

Hartmann, M. (2004a). Eliten in Deutschland. *Aus Politik und Zeitgeschichte, B 10*, 17–24.

Hartmann, M. (2004b). *Elitensoziologie: Eine Einführung.* Frankfurt am Main: Campus Verlag.

Hartmann, M. (2007). *The sociology of elites* (Vol. 50). London: Routledge.

Haustein, K. O., Assmann, I., & Fiehring, H. (1980). Problems of Rapid Digitalization in Severe Congestive Heart-Failure. *European Journal of Cardiology, 11*(2), 135–146.

Heinze, J. (2012). *Regierungskommunikation in Deutschland: Eine Analyse von Produktion und Rezeption.* Wiesbaden: VS Verlag.

Held, D. (2006). *Models of democracy* (3rd ed.). Cambridge: Polity Press.

Heller, M. (2008). Global and European Information Society. In P. Ludes (Ed.), *Convergence and Fragmentation: Media Technology and the Information Society* (pp. 29–46). Bristol: Intellect.

Henn, P., Dohle, M., & Vowe, G. (2013). "Politische Kommunikation": Kern und Rand des Begriffsverständnisses in der Fachgemeinschaft. Ein empirischer Ansatz zur Klärung von Grundbegriffen. *Publizistik, 58*(4), 367–388.

Hirzalla, F., Van Zoonen, L., & de Ridder, J. (2010). Internet use and political participation: Reflections on the mobilization/normalization controversy. *The Information Society, 27*(1), 1–15.

Hoffmann, J. (2003). *Inszenierung und Interpenetration: Das Zusammenspiel von Eliten aus Politik und Journalismus.* Wiesbaden: VS Verlag.

Hoffmann-Lange, U. (1992). *Eliten, Macht und Konflikt in der Bundesrepublik.* Opladen: Leske & Budrich.

Hollstein, B. (2011). Qualitative approaches. In J. Scott & P. Carrington (Eds.), *The Sage handbook of social network analysis* (pp. 404–416). London: Sage.

Holtz-Bacha, C. (2007). Professionalisation of Politics in Germany. In R. Negrine, P. Mancini, C. Holtz-Bacha, & S. Papathanassopoulos (Eds.), *The Professionalisation of Political Communication* (pp. 63–80). Bristol: Intellect.

Holtz-Bacha, C. (2013). Government communication in Germany: Maintaining the fine line between information and advertising. In K. Sanders & M. J. Canel (Eds.), *Government Communication: Cases and Challenges*. New York: Bloomsbury Academic.

Hornig, E.-C. (2013). Intention und Effekt direkter Demokratie im deutschen Parteienstaat. In O. Niedermayer, B. Höhne, & U. Jun (Eds.), *Abkehr von den Parteien?* (pp. 125–154). Wiesbaden: VS Verlag.

Howard, P. (2001). Can Technology Enhance Democracy? The Doubters' Answer. *Journal of Politics, 63*(3), 949–955. doi: 10.1111/0022-3816.00096

Håkansson, N., & Mayerhöffer, E. (2010). *Great expectations: Elites' democratic demands on the media*. Paper presented at the Annual Conference of the International Communication Association (ICA), Singapore.

Håkansson, N., & Mayerhöffer, E. (2014). Democratic Demands on the Media. In B. Pfetsch (Ed.), *Political Communication Cultures in Europe: Attitudes of Political Actors and Journalists in Nine Countries* (pp. 126–147). London: Palgrave Macmillan.

Irvine, A., Drew, P., & Sainsbury, R. (2013). 'Am I not answering your questions properly?' Clarification, adequacy and responsiveness in semi-structured telephone and face-to-face interviews. *Qualitative Research, 13*(1), 87–106.

Iske, S. (2005). Differences in Internet Usage-Social Inequality and Informal Education. *Social Work & Society, 3*(2), 215–223.

Jackson, N. A. (2006). Dipping their big toe in the blogosphere: The use of weblogs by the political parties in the 2005 general election. *Aslib Proceedings, 58*(4), 292–303.

Jackson, N. A., & Lilleker, D. G. (2004). Just Public Relations or an Attempt at Interaction? *European Journal of Communication, 19*(4), 507–533.

Jackson, N. A., & Lilleker, D. G. (2009). Building an Architecture of Participation? Political Parties and Web 2.0 in Britain. *Journal of Information Technology & Politics, 6*(3/4), 232–250. doi: 10.1080/19331680903028438

Jansen, D., & Diaz-Bone, R. (2011). Netzwerkstrukturen als soziales Kapital. In J. Weyer (Ed.), *Soziale Netzwerke: Konzepte und Methoden der sozialwissenschaftlichen Netzwerkforschung* (pp. 71–108). München: Oldenbourg.

Jarren, O., & Donges, P. (2006). *Politische Kommunikation in der Mediengesellschaft: Eine Einführung* (2nd ed.). Wiesbaden: VS Verlag.

Jarren, O., & Röttger, U. (1999). Politiker, politische Öffentlichkeitsarbeiter und Journalisten als Handlungssystem. Ein Ansatz zum Verständnis politischer Public Relations. In L. Rolke & V. Wolff (Eds.), *Wie die Medien die Wirklichkeit steuern und selbst gesteuert werden* (pp. 199–221). Opladen: Westdeutscher Verlag.

Jensen, M. A. (2006). *Rechtsprobleme regierungsamtlicher Öffentlichkeitsarbeit im Internet-Zeitalter*. Hamburg: Verlag Dr. Kovac.

Johnson, T. J., & Kaye, B. K. (1998). A vehicle for engagement or a haven for the disaffected? Internet use, political alienation, and voter participation. In T. J. Johnson, C. E. Hays, & S. P. Hays (Eds.), *Engaging the public: How government and the media can reinvigorate American democracy* (pp. 123–135). Lanham: Rowman & Littlefield.

Jones, N. (1995). *Soundbites and Spin Doctors: How politicians manipulate the media and vice versa*. London: Cassell.

Kalnes, Ø. (2009). Norwegian Parties and Web 2.0. *Journal of Information Technology & Politics, 6*(3/4), 251–266. doi: 10.1080/19331680903041845

Kamps, K. (2007). *Politisches Kommunikationsmanagement. Grundlagen und Professionalisierung moderner Politikvermittlung*. Wiesbaden: VS Verlag.

Keen, A. (2007). *The cult of the amateur: how today's internet is killing our culture*. New York: Doubleday.

Keller, S. (1963). *Beyond the ruling class: strategic elites in modern society*. New York: Random House.

Keller, S. (1983). Celebrities as a National Elite. In M. Czudnowski (Ed.), *Political Elites and Social Change: Studies of Elite Roles And Attitudes* (pp. 3–14). Illinois: Illinois University Press.

Kepplinger, H. M. (2002). Mediatization of Politics: Theory and Data. *Journal of Communication, 52*(4), 972–986.

Kies, R. (2010). *Promises and Limits of Web-deliberation*. New York: Palgrave Macmillan.

Kloepfer, M. (2012). *Staatsrecht kompakt: Staatsorganisationsrecht – Grundrechte – Bezüge zum Völker- und Europarecht*. Baden-Baden: Nomos.

Kochiadakis, G. E., Kanoupakis, E. M., Igoumenidis, N. E., Mavrakis, H. E., Kafarakis, P. K., & Vardas, P. E. (2005). Efficacy and safety of oral amiodarone in controlling heart rate in patients with persistent atrial fibrillation who have undergone digitalisation. *Hellenic journal of cardiology: HJC = Hellenike kardiologike epitheorese, 46*(5), 336–340.

Kocks, J. N., & Raupp, J. (2014a). *Open like Obama? Possibilities and limitations of governmental online-communication in Germany*. Paper presented at the 23rd World Congress of the International Political Science Association, Montreal.

Kocks, J. N., & Raupp, J. (2014b). Rechtlich-normative Rahmenbedingungen der Regierungskommunikation – ein Thema für die Publizistik- und Kommunikationswissenschaft. *Publizistik, 59*(3), 269–284.

Kocks, J. N., & Raupp, J. (2014c). *Socialist Public Relations: A contradictio in adiecto?* Paper presented at the International History of Public Relations Conference, Bournemouth.

Kocks, J. N., & Raupp, J. (2015). Media Relations Online – Zur Interaktion von politischer PR und Journalismus im digitalen Zeitalter. *prmagazin, 2,* 42–46.

Kocks, J. N., & Raupp, J. (2016). Flesh and Bone or the Integration of Perspectives in Social Network Analysis. In G. Vowe & P. Henn (Eds.), *Political Communication in the Online World: Theoretical Approaches and Research Designs* (pp. 248–261). New York: Routledge.

Kocks, J. N., Raupp, J., & Schink, C. (2014). Staatliche Öffentlichkeitsarbeit zwischen Distribution und Dialog: Interaktive Potentiale digitaler Medien und ihre Nutzung im Rahmen der Außenkommunikation politischer Institutionen. In R. Fröhlich & T. Koch (Eds.), *Politik – PR – Persuasion*. Wiesbaden: VS Verlag.

Kornhauser, W. (1968). 'Power Elite' or 'Veto Groups'? In G. W. Domhoff & H. B. Ballard (Eds.), *C. Wright Mills and The Power Elite* (pp. 37–59). Boston: Beacon Press.

Krotz, F. (1998). Gegenöffentlichkeit. In O. Jarren, U. Sarcinelli, & U. Saxer (Eds.), *Politische Kommunikation in der demokratischen Gesellschaft. Ein Handbuch mit Lexikonteil* (pp. 653). Opladen: Westdeutscher Verlag.

Krotz, F. (2009). Mediatization: A concept with which to grasp media and societal change. In K. Lundby (Ed.), *mediatization: concept, changes, consequences* (pp. 21–40). New York: Peter Lang.

Krysmanski, H. J. (2004). *Hirten & Wölfe*. Münster: Westfälisches Dampfboot.

Krüger, U. (2013). *Meinungsmacht: Der Einfluss von Eliten auf Leitmedien und Alpha-Journalisten: Eine kritische Netzwerkanalyse*. Köln: Halem.

Lanier, J. (2006). *Digital Maoism: The Hazards of the New Online Collectivism*. Retrieved from http://www.edge.org/3rd_culture/lanier06/lanier06_index.html

Lasswell, H. D. (1948). The Structure and Function of Communication in Society. In L. Bryson (Ed.), *The Communication of Ideas* (pp. 37–52). New York: Harper & Brothers.

Lasswell, H. D. (1951). *Politics: Who Gets What, When, How – The Political Writings of Harold D. Lasswell*. Glencoe: Free Press.

Lasswell, H. D. (1966). *World revolutionary elites: studies in coercive ideological movements*. Cambridge: M.I.T. Press.

Lasswell, H. D., Lerner, D., & Rothwell, C. E. (1952). *The comparative study of elites: An introduction and bibliography*. Stanford: Stanford University Press.
Latimer, C. P. (2007). Utilizing the Internet as a Campaign Tool: The Relationship Between Incumbency, Political Party Affiliation, Election Outcomes, and the Quality of Campaign Web sites in the United States. *Journal of Information Technology & Politics, 4*(3), 81–95.
Le Bon, G. (1960). *The Crowd: A study of the poplular mind*. New York: Viking.
Leibniz, G. W., Remnant, P., & Bennett, J. (1996). *New essays on human understanding*. Cambridge: Cambridge University Press.
Lesmeister, C. (2008). *Informelle politische Kommunikationskultur: Hinter den Kulissen politisch-medialer Kommunikation*. Wiesbaden: VS Verlag.
Lewis, J., Williams, A., & Franklin, B. (2008). A compromised fourth estate? UK news journalism, public relations and news sources. *Journalism Studies, 9*(1), 1–20.
Liff, S., Shepherd, A., Wajcman, J., Rice, R., & Hargittai, E. (2004). An evolving gender digital divide? *OII Internet Issue Brief* (2).
Locke, J. (1970). *An essay concerning human understanding*. Menston: Scolar Press.
Ludes, P. (2008). *Convergence and fragmentation: media technology and the information society*. Bristol: Intellect.
Luhmann, N. (1995). *Soziologische Aufklärung 6. Die Soziologie und der Mensch*. Opladen: Westdeutscher Verlag.
Machatzke, J. (1997). Die Potsdamer Elitenstudie – Positionsauswahl und Ausschöpfung. In W. Bürklin & H. Rebenstorf (Eds.), *Eliten in Deutschland* (pp. 35–68). Opladen: Leske & Budrich.
Mannheim, K. (1951). *Freedom, Power and Democratic Planning*. London: Routledge & Kegan Paul.
Mannheim, K. (1954). *Man and society in an age of reconstruction*. London: Routledge & Kegan Paul.
Margolis, M., & Resnick, D. (2000). *Politics as usual: The cyberspace 'revolution'*. Thousand Oaks: Sage.
Mathes, R., & Pfetsch, B. (1991). The Role of the Alternative Press in the Agenda-Building Process: Spill-over Effects and Media Opinion Leadership. *European Journal of Communication, 6*(1), 33–62. doi: 10.1177/0267323191006001003
Maurer, P. (2011). Explaining perceived media influence in politics. *Publizistik, 56*(1), 27–50. doi: 10.1007/s11616-010-0104-3
Maurer, P., & Vähämaa, M. (2014). Methods and Challenges of Comparative Surveys of Political Communication Elites. In B. Pfetsch (Ed.), *Political Communication Cultures in Europe: Attitudes of Political Actors and Journalists in Nine Countries* (pp. 57–75). London: Palgrave Macmillan.
Mausfeld, W. (2005). Wahrnehmungspsychologie: Geschichte und Ansätze. In J. Funke & P. Fresch (Eds.), *Handwörterbuch Allgemeine Psychologie: Kognition*. Göttingen: Hogrefe.
Mayer, H. O. (2004). *Interview und schriftliche Befragung* (Vol. 3). München: Oldenbourg.
Mayer, K. U. (2006). Abschied von den Eliten. In H. Münkler, G. Straßenberger, & M. Bohlender (Eds.), *Deutschlands Eliten im Wandel* (pp. 455–479). Frankfurt am Main: Campus Verlag.
Mazzoleni, G., & Schulz, W. (1999). 'Mediatization' of politics: A challenge for democracy? *Political Communication, 16*(3), 247–261. doi: 10.1080/105846099198613
Michels, R. (1949). *Political parties: a sociological study of the oligarchical tendencies of modern democracy*. Glencoe: Free Press.
Mills, C. W. (1956). *The Power Elite*. New York: Oxford University Press.

Mills, C. W. (1958). The Structure of Power in American Society. *British Journal of Sociology, 9*(1), 29–41.
Mills, C. W. (1963). Mass Society and Liberal Education. In C. W. Mills (Ed.), *Power, Politics and People* (pp. 353–373). New York: Oxford University Press.
Mills, C. W. (1968). Comment on Criticism. In G. W. Domhoff & H. B. Ballard (Eds.), *C. Wright Mills and The Power Elite* (pp. 229–250). Boston: Beacon Press.
Misnikov, Y. (2010). Discursive qualities of public discussion on the Russian Internet: Testing the Habermasian communicative action empirically. In F. d. Cindio, A. Machintosh, & C. Peraboni (Eds.), *From e-Participation to Online Deliberation, Proceedings of the Fourth International Conference on Online Deliberation, OD2010.* (pp. 60–74).
Morris, D. (2001). Direct Democracy and the Internet. *Loyola of Los Angeles Law Review, 34*(3), 1033–1054.
Mosca, G. (1953). *Elementi di scienza politica*. Bari: Laterza.
Mosca, G. (1962). Endgültige Fassung der Theorie der herrschenden Klasse. In J. Meisel (Ed.), *Der Mythus der herrschenden Klasse: Gaetano Mosca und die "Elite"* (pp. 385–394). Düsseldorf: Econ.
Mosse, W. E. (1987). *Jews in the German Economy: the German-Jewish Economic Elite 1820 – 1935*. Oxford: Clarendon Press.
Möhring, W., & Schlütz, D. (2010). *Die Befragung in der Medien- und Kommunikationswissenschaft: Eine praxisorientierte Einführung*. Wiesbaden: VS Verlag.
Möhring, W., & Schlütz, D. (2013). Standardisierte Befragung: Grundprinzipien, Einsatz und Anwendung. In W. Möhring & D. Schlütz (Eds.), *Handbuch standardisierte Erhebungsverfahren in der Kommunikationswissenschaft* (pp. 183–200). Wiesbaden: VS Verlag.
Negroponte, N. (1998). Beyond digital. *Wired, 6*(12), 288.
Neuberger, C. (2009). Internet, Journalismus und Öffentlichkeit: Analyse des Medienumbruchs. In C. Neuberger, C. Nuernbergk, & M. Rischke (Eds.), *Journalismus im Internet: Profession – Partizipation – Technisierung* (pp. 19–105). Wiesbaden: VS Verlag.
Neuberger, C. (2014). Meinungsmache statt Macht. *medium magazin, 11*, 24–25.
Nitschke, P., Donges, P., & Schade, H. (2014). Political organizations' use of websites and Facebook. *New Media & Society*, 1-21. doi: 10.1177/1461444814546451
Noam, E. M. (2005). Why the Internet Is Bad for Democracy. *Communications of the ACM, 48*(10), 57–58.
Nye, R. A. (1977). *The Anti-Democratic Sources of Elite Theory: Pareto, Mosca, Michels*. London: Sage.
Oeckl, A. (2011). *Taschenbuch des öffentlichen Lebens – Deutschland*. Bonn: Festland Verlag.
Page, B. I. (1996). *Who deliberates?: Mass media in modern democracy*. Chicago: University of Chicago Press.
Palfrey, J., & Gasser, U. (2013). *Born digital: Understanding the first generation of digital natives*. New York: Basic Books.
Papacharissi, Z. (2009). The virtual sphere 2.0: The internet, the public sphere, and beyond. In A. Chadwick & P. N. Howard (Eds.), *Routledge Handbook of Internet Politics* (pp. 230–245). Abingdon: Routledge.
Pareto, V. (1964a). *Trattato di sociologia generale* (Vol. 2). Milano: Edizioni di Comunitá.
Pareto, V. (1964b). *Trattato di sociologia generale* (Vol. 1). Milano: Edizioni di Comunitá.
Paris, R. (2003). Autorität – Führung – Elite: Eine Abgrenzung. In S. Hradil & P. Imbusch (Eds.), *Oberschichten – Eliten – Herrschende Klassen* (pp. 55–72). Opladen: Leske & Budrich.
Parsons, T. (1952). *The social system* (2nd ed.). Glencoe: Free Press.
Parsons, T. (1963). On the Concept of Political Power. *Proceedings of the American Philosophical Society, 107*(3), 232–262.

Pfetsch, B. (2003). *Politische Kommunikationskultur: Politische Sprecher und Journalisten in der Bundesrepublik und den USA im Vergleich*. Wiesbaden: VS Verlag.

Pfetsch, B., & Mayerhöffer, E. (2011). Vordergründige Nähe: Zur Kommunikationskultur von Politik- und Medieneliten in Deutschland. *Medien- & Kommunikationswissenschaft, 59*(1), 40–59.

Pfetsch, F. R. (2012). *Theoretiker der Politik: Von Platon bis Habermas*. Baden-Baden: Nomos.

Piaget, J. (1926). *La représentation du monde chez l'enfant*. Paris: Alcan.

Pough, G. D. (2004). *Check it while I wreck it: Black womanhood, hip-hop culture, and the public sphere*. Boston: Northeastern University Press.

Pöttker, H. (2013). Journalismus in der Krise. In K. Imhof, R. Blum, H. Bonfadelli, & O. Jarren (Eds.), *Stratifizierte und segmentierte Öffentlichkeit* (pp. 29–45). Wiesbaden: VS Verlag.

Quandt, T., & Scheufele, B. (2011). Die Herausforderung einer Modellierung von Mikro-Meso-Makro-Links in der Kommunikationswissenschaft. In T. Quandt & B. Scheufele (Eds.), *Ebenen der Kommunikation* (pp. 9–22). Wiesbaden: VS Verlag.

Raupp, J. (2009). Wie professionell ist die PR-Beratung?: Ein Beitrag zu Stand und Perspektiven der Professionalisierungsdebatte in der PR-Forschung. In U. Röttger & S. Zielmann (Eds.), *PR-Beratung. Theoretische Konzepte und empirische Befunde* (pp. 173–186). Wiesbaden: VS Verlag.

Raupp, J. (2010). *Politische Kommunikation in der Online-Welt: Voraussetzungen und Folgen des strukturellen Wandels der politischen Kommunikation.* Antrag auf Finanzierung einer Forschergruppe durch die Deutsche Forschungsgemeinschaft (DFG).

Raupp, J. (2011). Organizational Communication in a Networked Public Sphere: Strategische Organisationskommunikation in einer Netzwerköffentlichkeit. *Studies in Communication/Media, 1*(1), 71–93.

Rauschenbach, R. (2010). *Mit direktdemokratischen Verfahren zu postkonventionellen politischen Kulturen: theoretische Überlegungen anhand von Jürgen Habermas und Lawrence Kohlberg*. Berlin: Duncker & Humblot.

Rebenstorf, H. (2009). Wieder gelesen: Zur ungebrochenen Aktualität Paretos und Moscas in der Elite-Diskussion. *Beiträge zur Sozialinnovation Nr. 6.* Berlin: Institut für Sozialinnovation.

Reed, M. I. (2012). Masters of the universe: Power and elites in organization studies. *Organization Studies, 33*(2), 203–221.

Reich, Z. (2009). *Sourcing the news: key issues in journalism – an innovative study of the Israeli press*. Cresskill: Hampton Press.

Reitmayer, M. (2010). *Eliten, Machteliten, Funktionseliten, Elitenwechsel*. Retrieved from http://docupedia.de/zg/Eliten

Resnick, D. (1998). The normalization of cyberspace. In C. Toulouse & T. W. Luke (Eds.), *The politics of cyberspace* (pp. 48–68). New York: Routledge.

Rheingold, H. (1993). *Virtual Community: Homesteading on the Electronic Frontier*. Retrieved from http://www.rheingold.com/vc/book/

Rinke, E. M., Schlachter, M., & Agel, F. (2006). *Netzwerk Berlin: Informelle Interpenetration von Politik und Journalismus* (Vol. 7). München: Martin Meidenbauer Verlag.

Ross, K. (2010). Danse macabre: Politicians, journalists, and the complicated rumba of relationships. *The International Journal of Press/Politics, 15*(3), 272–294.

Ross, K., Fountaine, S., & Comrie, M. (2014). Facing up to Facebook: politicians, publics and the social media(ted) turn in New Zealand. *Media, Culture & Society*. doi: 0163443714557983

Rudzio, W. (2011). *Das politische System der Bundesrepublik Deutschland*. Wiesbaden: VS Verlag.

Ruzé, F. (1997). *Délibération et pouvoir dans la cité grecque: de Nestor à Socrate* (Vol. 43). Paris: Publications de la Sorbonne.

Ryfe, D. M. (2005). Does deliberative democracy work? *Annual Review of Political Science, 8*, 49–71. doi: 10.1146/annurev.polisci.8.032904.154633
Sahlins, M. D., Harding, T. G., Kaplan, D., & Service, E. R. (1960). *Evolution and culture*. Ann Arbor: University of Michigan Press.
Salazar, J. F. (2003). Articulating an Activist Imaginary: Internet as Counter Public Sphere in the Mapuche Movement 1997/2002. *Media International Australia, Incorporating Culture & Policy, 107*, 19–30.
Sanders, K., Canél, M. J., & Holtz-Bacha, C. (2011). Communicating governments. A three country comparison of how governments communicate with citizens. *International Journal of Press and Politics, 16*(4), 523–547.
Savage, M., & Williams, K. (2008). Elites: remembered in capitalism and forgotten by social sciences. *The Sociological Review, 56*(Supplement s1), 1–24.
Scheyli, M. (2000). *Politische Öffentlichkeit und deliberative Demokratie nach Habermas: Institutionelle Gestaltung durch direktdemokratische Beteiligungsformen?* Baden Baden: Nomos.
Schink, C., Raupp, J., & Kocks, J. N. (2013). *Der neue Draht zu den Mitgliedern? Eine organisationstheoretisch begründete Systematisierung von Onlinekommunikation*. Paper presented at the Jahrestagung der Deutschen Gesellschaft für Publizistik- und Kommunikationswissenschaft (DGPuK), Mainz.
Schnell, R., Hill, P. B., & Esser, E. (2008). *Methoden der empirischen Sozial-forschung*. München: Oldenbourg.
Schulz, W. (2004). Reconstructing mediatization as an analytical concept. *European Journal of Communication, 19*, 87–101.
Schwab Cammarano, S. (2013). *Rollen in der Politikvermittlung: Die Interaktion zwischen Politik und Journalismus in der Schweiz*. Baden-Baden: Nomos.
Schwab Cammarano, S., Donges, P., & Jarren, O. (2010). Politische Kommunikationskultur im Wandel. *Studies in Communication Science, 10*(1), 7–21.
Schweitzer, E. J. (2008). Innovation or Normalization in E-Campaigning?: A Longitudinal Content and Structural Analysis of German Party Websites in the 2002 and 2005 National Elections. *European Journal of Communication, 23*(4), 449–470.
Schweitzer, E. J. (2011). Normalization 2.0: A longitudinal analysis of German online campaigns in the national elections 2002–9. *European Journal of Communication, 26*(4), 310–327.
Schweitzer, E. J. (2012). The mediatization of E-campaigning: Evidence from German party websites in state, national, and European parliamentary elections 2002–2009. *Journal of Computer-Mediated Communication, 17*(3), 283–302. doi: 10.1111/j.1083-6101.2012.01577.x
Schürmann, F. (1992). *Öffentlichkeitsarbeit der Bundesregierung: Strukturen, Medien, Auftrag und Grenzen eines informalen Instruments der Staatsleitung*. Berlin: Duncker & Humblot.
Scott, J. (2001). *Power*. Cambridge: Polity Press.
Scott, J. (2008). Modes of power and the re-conceptualization of elites. *The Sociological Review, 56*(Supplement s1), 25–43.
Shuy, R. W. (2003). In-person versus telephone interviewing. In J. A. Holstein & J. F. Gubrium (Eds.), *Inside Interviewing: New Lenses, New Concerns* (pp. 175–193). Thousand Oaks: Sage.
Small, T. A. (2008). Equal Access, Unequal Success – Major and Minor Canadian Parties On the Net. *Party Politics, 14*(1), 51–70.
Stammer, O. (1965). Das Elitenproblem in der Demokratie. In O. Stammer (Ed.), *Politische Soziologie und Demokratieforschung* (pp. 63–90). Berlin: Duncker & Humblot.
Stegbauer, C. (2001). Von den Online-Communities zu den computervermittelten sozialen Netzwerken: eine reinterpretation klassischer Studien. *Zeitschrift für qualitative Bildungs-, Beratungs- und Sozialforschung, 2*, 151–173.

Strobel, R. (1991). Vor vierzig Jahren: Raumschiff Bonn. *Die Zeit*. Retrieved from http://www.zeit.de/1991/11/raumschiff-bonn

Strömbäck, J., & Nord, L. W. (2006). Do politicians lead the tango? A study of the relationship between Swedish journalists and their political sources in the context of election campaigns. *European Journal of Communication, 21*(2), 147–164.

Sunstein, C. R. (2001). *republic.com*. Princeton: Princeton University Press.

Swanson, D. L. (1992). The political-media complex. *Communications Monographs, 59*(4), 397–400.

Sweeney, A. D. P. (2007). Electronic government-citizen relationships: Exploring citizen perspectives. *Journal of Information Technology & Politics, 4*(2), 101–116. doi: 10.1080/19331680802076165

Ter Wal, A. L. J., & Boschma, R. A. (2009). Applying social network analysis in economic geography: framing some key analytic issues. *The Annals of Regional Science, 43*(3), 739–756.

The New Encyclopaedia Britannica. (2003a) *The New Encyclopaedia Britannica – Micropaedia* (15th ed., Vol. 1). Chicago: Encyclopaedia Britannica Inc.

The New Encyclopaedia Britannica. (2003b) *The New Encyclopaedia Britannica – Micropaedia* (15th ed., Vol. 9). Chicago: Encyclopaedia Britannica Inc.

The Oxford American Dictionary of Current English. (2002). Abate, F. (Ed.). Oxford: Oxford University Press.

The Oxford Dictionary of English. (2010) (3rd ed.). Stevenson, A. (Ed.). Oxford: Oxford University Press.

Thimm, C., Einspänner, J., & Dang-Anh, M. (2012). Politische Deliberation online – Twitter als Element des politischen Diskurses. In F. Krotz & A. Hepp (Eds.), *Mediatisierte Welten* (pp. 283–305). Wiesbaden: VS Verlag.

Tichenor, P. J., Donohue, G. A., & Olien, C. N. (1970). Mass media flow and differential growth in knowledge. *Public Opinion Quarterly, 34*(2), 159–170.

Tomasi di Lampedusa, G. (1957). *Il Gattopardo*. Milano: Feltrinelli.

Trammell, K. D., Williams, A. P., Postelnicu, M., & Landreville, K. D. (2006). Evolution of Online Campaigning: Increasing Interactivity in Candidate Web Sites and Blogs Through Text and Technical Features. *Mass Communication & Society, 9*(1), 21–44. doi: 10.1207/s15327825mcs0901_2

Trankovits, L. (2011). *Weniger Demokratie wagen: Wie Politik und Wirtschaft wieder handlungsfähig werden*. Frankfurt: Frankfurter Allgemeine Buch.

Trankovits, L. (2012). Eine Verteidigung der Demokratie – gegen den maßlosen Bürger. *Aus Politik und Zeitgeschichte, 38/39*, 3–6.

Trippi, J. (2004). *The Revolution Will Not Be Televised: Democracy, the Internet and the Overthrow of Everything*. New York: Regan Books.

van Aelst, P., Sehata, A., & Dalen, A. V. (2010). Members of Parliament: Equal Competitors for Media Attention? An Analysis of Personal Contacts Between MPs and Political Journalists in Five European Countries. *Political Communication, 27*(3), 310–325. doi: 10.1080/10584609.2010.496711

Van Aelst, P., & Vliegenthart, R. (2014). Studying the tango: An analysis of parliamentary questions and press coverage in the Netherlands. *Journalism Studies, 15*(4), 392–410.

van de Donk, W., Loader, B. D., Nixon, P. G., & Rucht, D. (2004). Introduction: Social movements and ICTs. In W. van de Donk, B. D. Loader, P. G. Nixon, & D. Rucht (Eds.), *Cyberprotest: New media, citizens and social movements* (pp. 1–25). London: Routledge.

van Dijk, J. A. G. M. (2005). *The deepening divide: Inequality in the information society*. Thousand Oaks: Sage.

van Dijk, J. A. G. M. (2009). One Europe, digitally divided. In A. Chadwick & P. N. Howard (Eds.), *Routledge Handbook of Internet Politics* (pp. 288–304). Abingdon: Routledge.

van Eimeren, B., & Frees, B. (2014). 79 Prozent der Deutschen online – Zuwachs bei mobiler Internetnutzung und Bewegtbild: Ergebnisse der ARD/ZDF-Onlinestudie 2014. *Media Perspektiven,* 7/8, 378–396.

Vogel, M. (2010). *Regierungskommunikation im 21. Jahrhundert: ein Vergleich zwischen Großbritannien, Deutschland und der Schweiz.* Baden-Baden: Nomos.

Voss, K. (2010). Grassrootscampaigning und Chancen durch Neue Medien. *Aus Politik und Zeitgeschichte, 19,* 28–33.

Ward, S., & Gibson, R. (2009). European political organizations and the internet: Mobilization, participation, and change. In A. Chadwick & P. N. Howard (Eds.), *Routledge Handbook of Internet Politics* (pp. 25–39). Abingdon: Routledge.

Ward, S., & Lusoli, W. (2005). 'From weird to wired': MPs, the internet and representative politics in the UK. *Journal of Legislative Studies, 11*(1), 57–81. doi: 10.1080/13572330500158276

Wasner, B. (2004). *Eliten in Europa: Einführung in Theorien, Konzepte und Befunde.* Wiesbaden: VS Verlag.

Waters, R. D., Tindall, N. T. J., & Morton, T. S. (2010). Media Catching and the Journalist-Public Relations Practitioner Relationship: How Social Media are Changing the Practice of Media Relations. *Journal of Public Relations Research, 22*(3), 241–264.

Watson, J., & Hill, A. (Eds.). (2006) *Dictionary of Media and Communication Studies* (7th ed.). London: Hodder Education.

Weiner, P., Bassan, M. M., Jarchovsky, J., Iusim, S., & Plavnick, L. (1983). Clinical Course of Acute Atrial-Fibrillation Treated with Rapid Digitalization. *American Heart Journal, 105*(2), 223–227. doi: 10.1016/0002-8703(83)90517-3

Wells, H. G. (1945). *Mind at the end of its tether.* London: W. Heinemann Limited.

Wenzler, M. (2008). *Journalisten und Eliten: das Entstehen journalistischer Nachrichten über Energie-und Kulturpolitik.* Konstanz: UVK.

Westerbarkey, J. (2004). Illusionsexperten: Die gesellschaftlichen Eliten und die Verschleierung der Macht. In J. Raupp & J. Klewes (Eds.), *Quo vadis Public Relations?* (pp. 30–41). Wiesbaden: VS Verlag.

Wigand, F. D. L. (2010). Adoption of Web 2.0 by Canadian and US Governments. In C. G. Reddick (Ed.), *Comparative E-Government* (pp. 161–181). New York: Springer.

Wimmer, J. (2007). *(Gegen-)Öffentlichkeit in der Mediengesellschaft: Analyse eines medialen Spannungsverhältnisses / Öffentlichkeit in der Mediengesellschaft / Mythos Gegenöffentlichkeit.* Wiesbaden: VS Verlag.

Wong, W., & Welch, E. (2004). Does E-Government Promote Accountability? A Comparative Analysis of Website Openness and Government Accountability. *Governance, 17*(2), 275–297. doi: 10.1111/j.1468-0491.2004.00246.x

Wright, S. (2012). Politics as usual? Revolution, normalization and a new agenda for online deliberation. *New Media & Society, 14*(2). doi: 10.1177/1461444811410679

Xenos, M. (2008). New Mediated Deliberation: Blog and Press Coverage of the Alito Nomination. *Journal of Computer-Mediated Communication, 13*(2), 485–503. doi: 10.1111/j.1083-6101.2008.00406.x

Young, I. M. (2004). *Inclusion and democracy.* Oxford: Oxford University Press.

Zald, M. N., & Lounsbury, M. (2010). The wizards of Oz: Towards an institutional approach to elites, expertise and command posts. *Organization Studies, 31*(7), 963–996.

Zauels, G. (1968). *Paretos Theorie der sozialen Heterogenität und Zirkulation der Eliten.* Stuttgart: F. Enke Verlag.

Zielmann, S., & Röttger, U. (2009). Characteristics and Developments of Political Party Web Campaigns in Germany, France, the United Kingdom, and the United States between

1997 and 2007. In S. Baringhorst, V. Kneip, & J. Niesyto (Eds.), *Political Campaigning on the Web* (pp. 69–92). Bielefeld: transcript Verlag.

Zimbardo, P. G., Gerrig, R. J., & Graf, R. (2004). *Psychologie* (16th ed.). München: Pearson Studium.

Zittel, T. (2009). Lost in Technology? Political Parties and the Online Campaigns of Constituency Candidates in Germany's Mixed Member Electoral System. *Journal of Information Technology & Politics, 6*(3/4), 298–311. doi: 10.1080/19331680903048832

Appendix

List of Interviewees

Code Number	Type of Interviewee	Background *(anonymised for published version)*
J01	Offline Journalist	*newspaper (tabloid)*
J02	Offline Journalist	*weekly political magazine*
J03*	Offline Journalist	*weekly political magazine*
J04	Offline Journalist	*radio newscast (public service)*
J05	Offline Journalist	*newspaper*
J06	Offline Journalist	*newspaper*
J07*	Offline Journalist	*weekly newspaper*
J08	Offline Journalist	*press agency*
J09	Offline Journalist	*weekly political magazine*
J10	Offline Journalist	*newspaper*
J11	Offline Journalist	*newspaper*
J12	Offline Journalist	*newspaper*
J13	Offline Journalist	*newspaper*
J14	Offline Journalist	*newspaper*
J15	Offline Journalist	*newspaper*
J16	Offline Journalist	*television newscast (commercial)*
J17	Offline Journalist	*newspaper*
J18	Offline Journalist	*newspaper*
J19**	Offline Journalist	*television newscast (public service)*
J20**	Offline Journalist	*television newscast (public service)*

J21	Online Journalist	*online newspaper*
J22	Online Journalist	*online newspaper*
J23	Online Journalist	*online newscast (commercial)*
J24	Online Journalist	*online newspaper*
J25	Online Journalist	*online newspaper*
J26	Online Journalist	*online newscast (public service)*
J27	Online Journalist	*online newspaper*
J28**	Online Journalist	*online newscast (public service)*
J29**	Online Journalist	*online newscast (public service)*
S01	Party Spokesperson	*political party (governing)*
S02	Party Spokesperson	*political party (governing)*
S03	Party Spokesperson	*political party (oppositional)*
S04	Party Spokesperson	*political party (governing)*
S05	Party Spokesperson	*political party (oppositional)*
S06	Party Spokesperson	*political party (oppositional)*
S07	Governmental Spokesperson	*governmental body (federal ministry)*
S08	Governmental Spokesperson	*governmental body*
S09	Governmental Spokesperson	*governmental body*
S10	Governmental Spokesperson	*governmental body (federal ministry)*
S11	Governmental Spokesperson	*governmental body (federal ministry)*
S12	Governmental Spokesperson	*governmental body (federal ministry)*
S13	Governmental Spokesperson	*governmental body (federal ministry)*
S14	Governmental Spokesperson	*governmental body (federal ministry)*

S15	Governmental Spokesperson	*governmental body (federal ministry)*
S16	Governmental Spokesperson	*governmental body (federal ministry)*

* The interviews with J03 and J07 were not audio-recorded and transcribed.

** J19 and J28 were interviewed together, the same goes for J20 and J29; the transcripts allow the individual interviewees to be identified.

Empirical Fact Sheet

Analysis	Context	Overview
Content Analysis, 2011	DFG project "Media Relations Online"	content analysis of political websites and social media presences; three coders (incl. 40% codings by the author); threshold for intercoder-reliability set at: r(Holsti) >.80
Content Analysis, 2013	DFG project "Media Relations Online"	content analysis of political websites and social media presences; two coders (incl. 10% codings by the author); threshold for intercoder-reliability set at: r(Holsti) >.80
Add. Content Analysis, 2013	MA Seminar "Online in die Illegalität" *(Freie Universität Berlin, winter term 13/14)*	content analysis of governmental social media presences; 17 coders (excl. author); threshold for intercoder-reliability set at: r(Holsti) >.80
Semi-structured Interviews, 2012-13	DFG project "Media Relations Online"	semi-structured personal interviews with political spokespersons (n=50) and political journalists (n=29); interviews with political journalists (n=29) conducted by the author; here only governmental (n=10) and party spokespersons (n=6) are taken into consideration;

MIX
Papier aus verantwortungsvollen Quellen
Paper from responsible sources
FSC® C105338
FSC
www.fsc.org

If you have any concerns about our products,
you can contact us on
ProductSafety@springernature.com

In case Publisher is established outside the EU,
the EU authorized representative is:
Springer Nature Customer Service Center GmbH
Europaplatz 3, 69115 Heidelberg, Germany

Printed by Libri Plureos GmbH
in Hamburg, Germany